Bryn Thomas was born in 1959 on a farm in Southern Rhodesia (now Zimbabwe) where his wanderlust began early with camping holidays by the Indian Ocean in Mozambique and journeys to game parks in other parts of Africa.

From Charterhouse he went to Durham University graduating with a degree in Anthropology in 1981. After a trip to the Sahara in a kit-car he built himself, he spent the next four years working and travelling abroad. He taught in Cairo, then spent some time in India and South East Asia before starting work for a Singapore publisher. After writing his first two books (English courses for foreign students), he moved to Tokyo and taught English to Ginza businessmen. An Andean cycling trip (from Quito to Lima) followed before he returned to the East via the USSR.

The first edition of this book, shortlisted for the Thomas Cook Travel and Guide Book Awards, was the result of several trips on the Trans-Siberian Railway and six months in the Reading Room of the British Library. For this revised second edition the author travelled 20,000 kilometres on the Trans-Siberian, Trans-Mongolian and Trans-Manchurian routes and visited the newly opened towns in Siberia.

Trans-Siberian Handbook
First edition Aug 1988
This second revised edition Aug 1991

Publisher: Trailblazer Publications
The Old Manse, Tower Road, Hindhead, Surrey, GU26 6SU

British Library Cataloguing in Publication Data
Thomas, Bryn, *1959-*
Trans-Siberian Handbook - 2nd ed.
1. Title
914.704854

ISBN 1-873756-00-3

Cover photograph by Ron Ziel (USA)
Other photographs by the author unless otherwise indicated
Engravings from *Siberia and the Exile System* by Kennan, G (London, 1891)
Cover design by Vanessa Charles
Maps and index by Jane Thomas

Distribution: Through Roger Lascelles (47 York Rd, Brentford, Middx, TW8
OQP. Tel 081-847 0935. Fax 081-568 3886) to the following countries:
Belgium (Brussels: Peuples et Continents); Germany (through major
booksellers); Italy (Milan: Libreria dell' Automobile); Netherlands (Weesp:
Nilsson & Lamm); Denmark (Cophenhagen: Arnold Busck, Boghallen); Finland
(Helsinki: Akateeminen Kirjakauppa); Norway (Oslo: Arne Gimnes, Tanum);
Sweden (Stockholm: Esselte, Akademi Bokhandel, Fritzes, Hedengrens;
Gothenburg: Gumperts, Esselte; Lund: Gleerupska); Switzerland (Basel: Bider;
Berne: Atlas; Geneva/Lausanne: Artou; Zurich: Travel Bookshop; UK/Ireland
(through all booksellers with good travel sections); South Africa (Hillbrow:
Faradawn); Canada (Vancouver: International Travel Maps & Books)

Set in Times and Univers by Trailblazer Publications
Printed and bound by Stamford Press Pte Ltd, 48 Lorong 21, Singapore 1438

TRANS-SIBERIAN HANDBOOK

BRYN THOMAS

TRAILBLAZER PUBLICATIONS

For Tanya

Acknowledgements

It takes more than one person to compile a comprehensive and accurate guide-book. I am greatly indebted to the numerous people who have helped me with the research and execution of this project. First, I should like to thank my sister, Jane Thomas, for her extensive work in drawing the two-language strip-maps and town-plans (without which this guide would be incomplete) and also for compiling the index. I should also like to thank Patricia Thomas for her thorough editing of the text.

The previous edition generated a considerable amount of feedback from readers. Thanks to the following who wrote in and provided information: Chris Gammell; John Stratton; Ian Button; Colin Baker (for information on the Beijing to Hong Kong route); Jim Deneulain for the loan of *The Imperial Japanese Government Railways Guide to East Asia 1913*; Michèle Burlington-Green (for considerable help in getting information from Intourist); Jane Bull; Heather and Steve Oxley; André de Smet of Monkey Business (Hong Kong); Kirsty Burnett (for information on tickets from Beijing); Sophie Mackenzie-Ross; Christopher Knowles; Bob and Hilda Helling; Kathy and Stephen Olley; Pam Buttrey; Andrew and Val White; Colin Belcher; Christopher Turner; Keith Fothergill (Guernsey); Keith Watson; Jeffrey de Forrestier (Canada); Daniel Ludszuweit (Thailand); Nigel and Fiona of Lily's Tea Shoppe (Eire); Jack Carter (USA); Anna Udagawa; Joan Eriksson (Finland); Nicola Wong for her help in unscrambling Cyrillic texts and timetables; Simon Vail; Bill Edwards (NZ); Robert Bray; Kevin Lee; Joan Nicholls; John King (Hong Kong); John Webb; Philip Robinson; Andrew Brannan; Fiona Graham (for information on Kate Marsden and other travellers). In the USSR, thanks to André Lvov (Yakutsk) and Svetlana Rabdanova and Tatiana (Ulan Ude). Thanks also to Bernard Taylor for the photograph opposite page 112, Jim Malcomson for the photograph opposite page 160, and Ron Ziel (USA) for cover photograph.

Finally I should like to thank Roger Lascelles for his help in this project over the last five years and for kindly permitting the publication of this new edition under the Trailblazer imprint.

Quotations used in the Route Guide (Part 5) are from the original *Guide to the Great Siberian Railway 1900*, published by the Tsarist Government in St Petersburg at the turn of the century.

A Request

The author and publisher have tried to ensure that this guide is as accurate and up-to-date as possible. However things are now changing fast in the USSR after years of stagnation. Railway timetables are adjusted, towns are added or taken off the list of places open to tourists, hotels and restaurants open and close and prices go up and down. If you notice any changes that should be included in the next edition of this book, please write to Bryn Thomas, c/o the publisher (address on page 2). A free copy of the new edition will be sent to persons making a significant contribution.

Front cover: A rare picture, taken in the early 1970s, of the Trans-Siberian being hauled by a steam engine. Wherever electric locomotives are not used today in the USSR, diesel power has now replaced steam. (Ron Ziel, USA)

CONTENTS

PART 4: CITY GUIDES AND PLANS

Leningrad

Moscow

Novosibirsk

Irkutsk

Ulan Ude

INTRODUCTION

There can be few people who have not, at some time in their lives, wondered what it must be like to travel on the Trans-Siberian Railway - to cross Russia and the wild forests and steppes of Siberia on the world's longest railway journey. The distances spanned by this famous line are immense: almost six thousand miles (a seven-day journey) between Moscow and the Pacific port of Nakhodka (for boat connections to Japan) and just under five thousand miles (five days) between Moscow and Beijing.

Ever since a rail service linking Europe with the Far East was established at the turn of the century, foreign travellers and adventurers have been attracted to this great rail trip. Most of the early travellers crossed Siberia in the comfort of the carriages of the Belgian Wagon Lits company, which were as luxurious as those of the Venice-Simplon Orient Express of today. Things changed somewhat after the Russian Revolution in 1917 and it became increasingly difficult for foreigners to obtain travel permits for Siberia. It was not until the 1960s that the situation improved and Westerners began to use the railway again, for trips to Japan, taking the boat from Nakhodka for the last part of the journey. In the early 1980s, travel restrictions for foreigners visiting China were eased and since then many people have found the Trans-Siberian a cheap and interesting way to get to or from the Middle Kingdom.

The Soviet Union has a surprising amount to offer the traveller, even though it may not be the first place one thinks of for a holiday. It is very much a country of extremes. Within its far-flung borders there are boiling-hot deserts (in Soviet Central Asia) as well as places in the far north so cold that your breath turns to ice-dust and exposed skin peels on contact with the air. As you travel round this vast country, the sights you may be shown range from gargantuan hydro-electric power stations to treasure houses such as the Hermitage in Leningrad (crammed so full of famous works of art that to spend three minutes looking at each you would have to stay a whole year in the gallery). You may experience extremes of cuisine too, from stodgy 'school' dinners to mouth-watering blinis and caviare. As with travelling in any other country, you will come into contact with a wide range of people. Some of the officials and people in the street in the USSR may appear to react to you in a rather abrupt and distant fashion, but you also meet Russians who overwhelm you with their Slavonic warmth and friendliness. The relaxed atmosphere on the train makes it a good place to meet the people on their own ground and you will soon realise that the popular image of the Russian as a dour, humourless and unhappy individual is simply not true.

As readers will be well aware from the amount of press coverage now devoted to the USSR, the country is undergoing phenomenal changes after years of stagnation. *Glasnost* has brought about the opening up of many hitherto 'closed' areas (the most interesting on the railway being Ulan Ude where you can now stop off to see the Buddhist monastery).

Although travel in Siberia today presents few of the dangers and difficulties that it did earlier this century, a journey on the Trans-Siberian still demands a considerable amount of planning and preparation. The aim of this guide is to help you cut through the red tape when arranging the trip, to provide background information on the USSR and Siberia with a kilometre-by-kilometre guide to the route of the last great rail adventure - the Trans-Siberian.

PART 1: PLANNING YOUR TRIP

Routes, costs and making a booking

ROUTE OPTIONS

Travellers crossing Siberia have a choice of three trains. Since the early 1980s, when China opened its doors to the independent traveller the first two routes (to Beijing via Mongolia and Manchuria respectively) have rapidly increased in popularity. A journey on the Trans-Siberian Railway makes an interesting start or end to a visit to China. The third route follows a line due east to Nakhodka on the Pacific coast where passengers can board the ship to Japan. It's possible to add side trips to these main routes: from Beijing to Shanghai or Hong Kong, or the interesting newly-opened route between Khabarovsk and Beijing via Pyongyang (North Korea).

COSTS

Depending on the level of comfort you demand and the amount of time you are prepared to devote to getting hold of a budget ticket, the cost of a trip on the world's longest railway line can be as little as £120-150 (from Beijing to Moscow). If a luxurious forty-three day guided tour from London to Hong Kong via Siberia on the 'Central Kingdom Express' is more your idea of travelling, then be prepared to part with more than £3000.

With the cheapest hotel rooms starting at £50 for a double (minimal reduction for a single), the USSR is not a cheap place to visit and there is a very good reason for this: the country is desperately short of hard currency, and tourism is an important source. There are far too few hotels and far too many foreigners wanting to visit the country so the authorities can charge almost whatever they like. In the summer in Moscow or Leningrad you may have to pay up to £80 or more for a room if you book through Intourist. There are ways, however, around these ridiculously high charges. Several travel agents have formed links with youth groups and 'homestay' associations in the USSR enabling travellers to stay in hostels for around £20/US$35 for a double, or with a family for about the same amount. For details see page 18. Alternatively you could get yourself invited to stay with a Russian friend or family and you will qualify for a tourist visa.

Any public service that your average Russian would need to use (the railway system being the best example) is, in fact, remarkably good value for the tourist too. However, services which cater primarily for the foreign tourist (international flights, ships and hotel rooms) represent some of the worst value for money you will ever encounter.

Budget USSR

The story on cheap (or Black Market) tickets on the Trans-Siberian gets ever more complex. The £30/US$50 tickets available in Budapest became difficult to get in the late 1980s but in 1990 some determined travellers managed to get hold of confirmed tickets in Hungary for this price (see page 23). This incredible travel bargain is highly unlikely to continue since Hungary is no longer part of the Communist Bloc. In early 1991 it was rather easier and quicker to obtain tickets in Hong Kong for £190/US$330 (see page 28) for the trip from Beijing to Berlin or Budapest, or for £130/US$225 for Beijing to Moscow.

When considering which ticket to go for, bear in mind two things: first, hidden costs involved in the 'cheap' tickets, such as getting to the country to buy the ticket and spending time there while your visas are being processed; secondly, the cheap ticket scene is constantly changing so you should contact the agencies listed in 'Making a booking' to check prices and availability. If your schedule does not allow for changes of plan it might be better to pay more and book through Intourist or CITS.

If you want to arrange the trip in Europe or North America and visit the USSR for the lowest capital outlay then you must arrange an itinerary that excludes flights and boat trips and includes as few nights spent in hotels as possible. The price of a ticket (bought in London, Paris or any other West European country) from Moscow to Beijing, with one night in a Moscow hotel, is £250-350/US$450-600. The two-day train journey from London to Moscow will add another £150/US$250 to this sum.

Accommodation on the train

Foreigners are offered three levels of accommodation:
● **First/Soft Class two berth** The compartment comprises a washbasin and two bunk beds. Prices (booked in the West) are £800-900 for the **Moscow-Japan** route (including a two berth cabin on the ship). If you fly part of the route, the cost goes down to £750, or

£600 for a four berth cabin on the boat. If you're travelling on the **Moscow-Beijing** route and wish to go first class the Trans-Mongolian train (run by the Chinese) is better because their first class compartments also include a **shower-room** shared between the next compartment. These are the only showers on the whole railway system! Fares (booked in the West) are £350-450.

• **First/Soft Class four berth** For the Moscow-Beijing journey (booked in the West) it is £320-400.

• **Second/Hard Class** The cheapest rail accommodation is clean and adequately comfortable for the seven-day journey across Siberia, but with four berths in the small compartment, life can be a bit cramped. Prices are £250-350 for the Moscow-Beijing route; £450-500 for the Moscow-Japan trip.

Most travellers opt for second class tickets since accommodation in first class is essentially the same (unless you're in First Class, with showers, on the Chinese train) - there is just a little more space. Foreigners, even those travelling on individual itineraries, usually find themselves sharing with other Westerners, at least for part of the trip. When it comes to sharing compartments, I'm not sure which is worse - the elderly German who complains non-stop about the food or the female tractor-driver from the Ukraine who snores like a Massey-Ferguson. For other prices see the sections on booking tickets in Hong Kong, Tokyo and Beijing.

Hotel accommodation

In the USSR these are classed as deluxe, first and tourist class and now star-rated. Note that hotels in Moscow and Leningrad are considerably more expensive than hotels in Siberia. Note also that you will not always be allotted the hotel you request. If no more rooms are available in the class of hotel you asked for you may be placed in another class of hotel and expected to pay the difference. Prices and type of accommodation are as follows:

• **Deluxe Accommodation** for one or two people comprising a suite of up to four rooms including a private bathroom. Prices in Moscow and Leningrad range from £100-200; and in other cities from £60-150.

• **First Class** Usually the cheapest accommodation available. All rooms have private bathrooms and breakfast is included. Prices for single accommodation range from £70-100 in Moscow and Leningrad. Prices in other cities range from £40-80. Since two people sharing a room are charged only a few roubles more, it pays to have a travelling companion.

• **Tourist Class** Accommodation of this type is usually available only to student tour groups but since this cheaper accommodation may be made available to independent travellers in the future it's worth asking about. Intourist, the USSR's state tourist organisation, no longer has the monopoly on hotel accommodation and travel facilities although it does own most of the hotels.

BREAKING YOUR JOURNEY

If you can afford to break your journey and spend a few nights in the USSR this is well worth doing for two reasons. First, because the train passes through some interesting places worth at least a day's exploring and secondly, since washing facilities on the train are limited, you may enjoy the journey more if you do it in stages. However, everything must be planned, arranged and paid for in advance and before you can get your visa.

A day in **Moscow** will give you time to visit Lenin in Red Square and see the Kremlin. A detour or side-trip to **Leningrad** is highly recommended if only for a visit to the Hermitage Museum. If your starting (or ending) point is Helsinki, you could arrange a stop in Leningrad.

In Siberia, many more places are being opened up to foreign tourism and it's worth checking with Intourist to see what's new on the list. However, just because a place has been declared 'open' doesn't mean you'll be able to visit it - you may be told that the hotel is full. Travellers are now permitted to stay in **Sverdlovsk** (in the Urals, opened in late 1990); **Abakan** (south of Krasnoyarsk and pleasantly situated in the foothills of the Sayan Mountains); **Omsk** (on the Trans-Siberian line, opened 1991); **Tomsk** (north of Omsk); **Novosibirsk**, the capital of West Siberia; **Bratsk** (beside the dam); **Irkutsk**, the Eastern capital on the shores of Lake Baikal (the world's deepest freshwater lake); **Yakutsk** (in the far north permafrost region, 600km south of the Arctic Circle and worth visiting for the river trip to the Lena Pillars); **Ulan Ude** (the most interesting and accessible newly-opened city, near the Buddhist Monastery) and **Khabarovsk**, capital of the Far Eastern Territories. Until recently a stop in Khabarovsk was obligatory in order to connect with the train to the Pacific port of **Nakhodka** (open to tourists) and **Vladivostok** (opened in 1990). Other Siberian cities now open include **Ust-Kamenogorsk** (south of Novosibirsk); **Petropavlovsk-Kamchatskii** (Far Eastern Territories) and **Yuzhno-Sakhalinsk** (Sakhalin Island, Far Eastern Territories).

If you plan to travel via Mongolia you may wish to stay a night in **Ulan Bator** on the way. For further information see Parts 4 and 5.

WHEN TO GO

For most people the mention of Siberia evokes a picture of snowy scenes from the film *Doctor Zhivago* and if they are not to be disappointed, then winter is probably the best time to go. It is, after all, the most Russian of seasons, a time of fur-coats, sleigh-rides and vodka. In temperatures as low as minus thirty centigrade, with the bare birch trees and firs encased in ice, Siberia looks as one imagines it ought to - a bare desolate waste-land. The train, however, is kept well heated. Russian cities, too, look best and feel most 'Russian' under a layer of snow. Leningrad with its brightly painted Classical architecture is far more attractive in the winter months, when the weather is crisp and skies clear. If you want to visit some of the Siberian cities, (Irkutsk and Lake Baikal with their unique flora and fauna are especially interesting) you will probably find it more enjoyable to go in the spring, summer or autumn, when there is more to do.

In Siberia, the heaviest snowfalls and coldest temperatures (as low as minus 40°C in some of the towns the train passes through), occur in November and December. Between January and early April the weather is generally cold and clear. Spring comes late and then the warmest months are July and August, when it is warm enough for an invigorating dip in Lake Baikal. The birch and aspen provide a beautiful autumnal display in September and October. The weather in summer and autumn is particularly unpredictable.

In Moscow the average temperature is 17°C in summer, minus 9°C in winter. There are occasional heavy showers in summer. Leningrad's climate is marginally milder with average temperatures 16°C in summer, minus 8°C in winter.

The tourist season reaches its peak between mid July and early September. In the low season, between October and April discounts of up to 25 per cent are offered on tours. You will also find it much easier to get a booking for the train at short notice at this time. During the summer it is virtually impossible to get a place on the popular Moscow - Beijing route without giving notice of at least a few months.

MAKING A BOOKING

Organised tours or individual itineraries?

To a certain extent, all travel within the Soviet Union is 'organised' since every night you spend there must be accounted for as an hotel booking (unless you have a visa allowing you to stay with a Russian friend) or train reservation before you go. Most people visit the country in a tour group, and this is how the USSR would prefer you to travel. Groups are far easier to keep track of, whereas lone travellers have the annoying habit of wandering off where they're not supposed to. As a result Intourist tends to discriminate against 'individual' travellers by making them pay for certain services that package tourists get in the price paid for their tour. It will cost you more to travel on an individual itinerary but the freedom that this gives you is worth the extra cost. There are, however, several good organised tours where Intourist guides travel with the group on the Trans-Siberian, ensuring that all the minor frustrations that beset the individual traveller do not happen to the group.

In 1990 Intourist, the USSR's national tourist organisation, lost its monopoly of the hotel and tourist facilities market. In theory, your friendly local travel agent should be able to book you into the Siberian hotel of your choice without going through Intourist in Moscow or its branches in the UK. In practice it does not seem as if much has changed yet, since Intourist is still by far the largest tourist organisation in the country, owning the majority of the hotels. In Europe and North America travel agents are recognising the strength of interest in Siberia and the rail journey and there are a number of companies now competing with the local branch of Intourist, often with much keener prices.

(See Appendix B for a list of Intourist offices worldwide).

Independent travel - booking procedure

Wherever you buy your ticket, the same procedure must be followed. Before a visa can be issued you must be in possession of train tickets and hotel vouchers for every night you will be spending in the USSR and, of course, a valid passport. Before the tickets can be issued, confirmation must be received from Mother Russia that the hotel beds in question will be available and that there will be a place on the train for you.

First you must decide on the train you wish to take. This can be more complicated than it sounds since the journey has to be planned in reverse. If you are travelling from Europe to Japan you must begin by deciding on the date of your sailing between the USSR and Japan. There are four sailings a month in both directions and the service runs only between mid-April and mid-October. If you are stopping off anywhere on your journey across the USSR, the hotel confirmations will have to be received before the intermediate rail journeys can be booked. This complication will be dealt with by the travel agent or Intourist office you are dealing with. All this takes

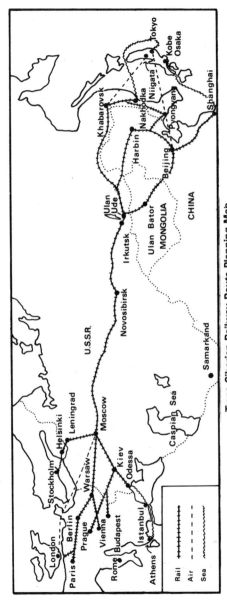

Trans-Siberian Railway Route Planning Map
(10mm = 1000km approx)

Rail ++++++++++
Air – – – – – –
Sea ∿∿∿∿∿∿∿

time and Intourist confidently suggest you allow them four weeks to deal with your booking. This is an absolute minimum and, unless you don't mind waiting until almost the day you leave before being told whether your booking has got through and your visa issued, a couple of months would be much safer.

If you're travelling on the train to or from Beijing, or from Japan, then a visa for the USSR will not be issued unless you already have (or are of a nationality that does not need) a visa for the country you will enter from the Soviet Union. If you're travelling from Beijing or Japan, this will be Poland (although German nationals do not need a visa for Poland) and if you're going the other way it will be China. The idea behind this rule is that the Soviets want to be sure that you won't be refused entry to one of their bordering countries when you arrive at the border.

Thus the procedure for getting tickets (described more fully below) is first make a booking and then, once the booking is confirmed, get your visas in reverse order - the last country you'll be travelling through, first. Then get your Russian visa and pay for and collect your ticket.

Itineraries to China

Summer is the most difficult time to get bookings for these two routes so make arrangements several months in advance. The Trans-Mongolian train, operated by the Chinese, leaves Moscow every Wednesday at 00.20 (ie Tuesday night), arriving in Beijing the following Monday at 15.33. The Trans-Manchurian train is run by the Russians and leaves Moscow every Saturday at 01.20 (ie Friday night) reaching Beijing the following Friday at 06.32. There's an additional service from June to September leaving Moscow at the same time on Sunday (ie Saturday night) and arriving the following Saturday. It's a longer journey as the train travels round Mongolia, passing through the Chinese province of Manchuria. This means that you don't need the Mongolian transit visa. Nevertheless the Chinese train is more popular with Westerners since it takes six rather than seven days to reach Beijing and there are showers (first class, 2 berth only). Contrary to rumours the food is not better in the 'Chinese' train, only in the Chinese dining-car, which is attached to both trains only as far as the border.

If all the through trains (Nos 4 & 20) are booked up, it's worth considering a stopover in Mongolia, since the direct Moscow-Ulan Bator train (No 6) is far less popular (see below).

The Beijing-Moscow route booked in the West is often cheaper to arrange than the Moscow-Beijing route. You will be given a voucher to be exchanged with the CITS office in Beijing. Train No 3 ('Chinese' train via Ulan Bator) departs Beijing every Wednesday at 07.40, arriving in Moscow the following Monday. Train No 19 ('Russian' train via Manchuria) departs Saturday at 20.32, arriving Moscow the following Friday at 11.35. From late May to September there is a second service at the same time on Sunday, arriving in Moscow the following Saturday.

Stopping off in Mongolia

If you're taking the Trans-Mongolian route to Beijing and want to spend a night or two in Ulan Bator (interesting but expensive) all arrangements should be made before you leave through **Zhuulchin** (the Mongolian Tourist Organisation). Tourism in Mongolia is even more strictly organised than in the USSR but there are rumours that things may become more relaxed. At present individual travellers are offered either accommodation only (US$100 (per night!) late September to May; US$160 June to early September) or accommodation, full-board, guide, driver and car (US$160 per day early September to May; US$200 June to late September). Payment is made when you arrive in Ulan Bator.

Making a booking Before beginning your dealings with the Mongolians you must have confirmed reservations as far as Ulan Bator. Train No. 4 leaves Moscow on Wednesday 00.20hrs, ie Tuesday night, arriving the following Sunday 09.30hrs; train No. 6 leaves Moscow daily (except Wednesday) at 20.15hrs (June to mid-September) and only on Friday and Saturday at the same time (mid-September to May). From Irkutsk there is a daily, year-round service at 14.13 (No.264). Trains out of Ulan Bator leave on Sunday (No. 4) and also Tuesday and Friday to Beijing; Thursday to Moscow direct (No. 3); daily to Irkutsk (Train No. 263). First telephone the embassy (in London on 071-937 0150) to find out if bookings must still be made by telex or whether Zhuulchin in Mongolia has got around to buying a fax yet. If not then you must telex Zhuulchin on Mongolia 232 (answerback code is *Zhuln MH*) state arrival date, type of package (accommodation only or with meals and tours) and request onward travel arrangements to Beijing (train/flight number hard/soft class) and ask them to telex confirmation as soon as possible. This confirmation telex is most important as you need to take it to the embassy in order to get a visa.

Side trip to North Korea

It is now possible to arrange tickets from Moscow to Pyongyang (via Ussuriyisk, near Khabarovsk), and also from Beijing to Khabarovsk.

via Pyongyang. Regent Holidays in the UK (see below) sell the
Moscow to Pyongyang ticket and can help with individual itineraries.

MAKING A BOOKING IN EUROPE

From Britain

● **Regent Holidays** 13 Small Street, Bristol BS1 1DE. Tel 0272
211711. Specialises in individual travel to the USSR, China, Mongolia and North Korea. Offers tickets for Moscow-Beijing (from £280),
Beijing-Moscow (from £250), Moscow-Pyongyang (from £150).
Recommended by several readers for their efficient and helpful
service.

● **Intourist Travel Ltd London**: Intourist House, 219 Marsh Wall,
Isle of Dogs, London E14 9FJ. Tel 0800-181361 (freephone for
brochures), 071-538 3202 (tours), 071-538 5965 (independent
travel). **Manchester**: Suite 2F, Central Buildings, 211 Deansgate,
Manchester M3 3NW. Tel 061-834 0230. **Glasgow**: 29 St Vincent
Place, Glasgow G1 2DT. Tel 041-204 1402. **Tours:** Intourist's two-
week tour from Britain includes two nights on the Trans-Siberian
between Khabarovsk and Irkutsk, which is the most scenic part of
the whole line; visits to Irkutsk and Lake Baikal and Bratsk, and
costs £700-839. They also do a 'Siberian Adventure' for £595 (8
nights) or £809 (14 nights) but the train is not used.
Independent travel: Prices for the Moscow-Beijing trip start at £285
(Oct-May) to £365 (June-Sept) and they do cheaper tickets for the
trip in the other direction (Beijing-Moscow) from £205. They have a
range of packages for this route including stops from £330-580 (per
person based on two people sharing). For the route to Japan, there's
a range of packages ranging from £455 for the cheapest rail ticket
from Moscow to Nakhodka and including the boat to Yokohama. No
hotels or meals are included except on the boat. Other packages
include a flight for part of the trip. Prices are from Moscow so you
will need to add about £150-200 for train or flight. Note that hotels
booked through Intourist are expensive (from £50) but cheaper
accommodation may become available in the future.

● **Progressive Tours** 12 Porchester Place, Connaught Square,
London W2 2BS. Tel: 071-262 1676. Specialists in budget and youth
travel to the USSR, this helpful company offers tickets on the
Moscow-Beijing run for £275-340. They are able to organise individual itineraries as well and run a 'homestay' programme where
you can stay with a Russian family for £13 per night (min. one
week).

● **Room with the Russians** Lynton Cooper Travel, Station Chambers, High Street North, London E6 1JE. Tel 081-471 2328. This organisation can help with cheap accommodation in the USSR.

● **China Travel and Information Centre** 3-5 Charlton Street, London NW1 1JD. Tel 071-388 8838. The friendly and efficient staff in this office can help with tickets from Beijing to Moscow, as well as with tickets and tours in all parts of China. For the Trans-Siberian you will be given a voucher which you exchange for a confirmed ticket in Beijing. Prices from £170, which makes this the cheapest ticket available in Britain.

● **One Europe Travel Ltd** Research House, Fraser Rd, Perivale, Middlesex UB6 7AQ. Tel 081-566 9424. Able to arrange budget accommodation in the USSR from £20/US$35 in a hostel and from £40/US$75 in a hotel. Also able to tailor Trans-Siberian trips to travellers' requirements.

● **China Travel Service UK Ltd** 24 Cambridge Circus, London WC2H 8HD. Tel 071-836 3366. Offers a 17 day all-inclusive tour ('All Aboard') from London to Hong Kong and back, using the Trans-Siberian from Moscow to Hong Kong (£1090-1290). Also able to book individuals on the train both from and to Beijing (£280-420). Some trips include a night in a hotel in Moscow.

The following companies offer organised tours only:

● **Page & Moy Ltd** 136-40 London Road, Leicester LE2 1EN. Tel: 0533-524463. This company continues to get good reports from readers for its Trans-Siberian packages. There's an 11 day trip (from £599-779) including return flight from London to Moscow, rail journey from Moscow to Khabarovsk (including stopover in Irkutsk) and a flight back to Moscow.

● **Thomson Tours** Greater London House, Hampstead Road, London NW1 7SD. Tel: 071-387 1900. For between £695 and £875 (depending on the season) this company offers 14 day tours to Russia and Siberia with two days spent on the Trans-Siberian, flights being used between most cities visited.

● **Bales Tours** Bales House, Junction Road, Dorking, Surrey, RH4 3HB. Tel: 0306-885991. This company offers an 18-day escorted tour from London to Beijing via the Trans-Siberian Express and a flight back to London for £1699 with all transport, accommodation and meals included.

• **Explore Worldwide Ltd** 1 Frederick Street, Aldershot, Hants GU11 1LQ. Tel: 0252-319448. Specialising in adventure holidays for small groups, this company offers a 16-day 'Siberian Lake Baikal' trip including several days on the train, from £1290.

• **Sundowners** 267 Old Brompton Road, London SW5 9JA. Tel: 071-370 1482. Offers a range of comprehensive tours: 'The Complete Trans-Siberian Railway' includes a week in Japan, boat to Nakhodka and the train to Moscow and Leningrad, plus return flights from London (29 days for £3100, £2225 if joining in Tokyo); 'Trans-Siberian with China & Mongolia' (33 days for £3420, £2510 if joining in Beijing); 'Trans-Siberian with Nepal, Tibet, China and Mongolia' (40 days for £4140, £3495 if joining in Kathmandu).

• **Voyages Jules Verne** Travel Promotions Ltd, 10 Glentworth St, London NW1 5PG. Tel: 071-486 8080. The most luxurious Trans-Siberian Railway tours, including a 21-day tour from London to Hong Kong via Siberia, Mongolia and Beijing for £1720 and a 43-day grand tour for £3300, beginning with a champagne breakfast before leaving Victoria station. Every other luxury included.

Rail Enthusiasts' Tours
Operators of special interest tours include:
• **Enthusiasts' Holidays** 146 Forest Hill Road, London SE23 3QR. Tel: 081-699 3654.
• **Dorridge Travel Service** 7, Station Approach, Dorridge, Solihull, B93 8JA. Tel 0564-776252.
• **Railway Travel and Photography** Daton House, Stafford ST17 4AL. Tel 0785-57740.

Getting to Moscow from the UK
By air Flights start at around £180 one-way, £240 return and demand exceeds supply. **By rail** This is not much cheaper than flying because a sleeper is compulsory and no youth discounts are applicable, although the situation may change. The services from London link to two trains one via Hoek van Holland (from Liverpool Street Station, £170 second class inc sleeper, £254.40 first class) the other via Ostend for similar prices. You can book by credit card on 071-828 0892. Take lots of food as only snacks are available and you'll need dollar bills or DM for the Polish hard-currency bar (which is expensive). The Russian carriages have 3 bunks (only 2 used in first class) and a basin. The journey takes 24hrs from Hoek van Holland or Ostend to Warsaw. Crossing the Soviet border on the 2nd evening you arrive in Moscow around mid-day on the 3rd day.

Foreign Embassies in London

- **USSR Embassy** 5 Kensington Palace Gardens, London W8 4QS. Tel: 071-229 3215. Open 10.00-12.30, not Wed or Sat. The queues here are enormous and since most travel agents have a visa-service it is well worth paying for in this case. Note that the visa is a separate document and your passport will not be stamped. Your application should include photocopies of the first five pages of your passport (plus the back pages if you have one of the new-style GB passports), three photos and the application form.

- **Embassy of the People's Republic of China** 31 Portland Place, London W1. Tel: 071-636 1835/5726. Open 09.00-12.00 (Mon to Fri). This is quite easy to do yourself. British passport-holders are charged a high price (£20).

- **Polish Embassy (Visa Section)** 73 New Cavendish Street, London W1N 7RB. Tel: 071-636 4533. Conveniently located near the Chinese Embassy, but phone before you go in case visas become no longer necessary. Open 10.00-14.00, not Wed or Sat.

- **Mongolian Embassy** 7 Kensington Court, London W8 5DL. Tel: 071-937 0150. Open 10.30-12.00 on Mon & Tue, 14.30-16.30 on Thur & Fri. Transit visas cost £10 and rail confirmation is required. If you are stopping in Mongolia a tourist visa is required. Proof of hotel booking in Ulan Bator and onward travel must be shown (telex from Zhuulchin, see page 17). While you are waiting in the embassy, reading matter for your perusal includes old copies of the self-congratulatory *Mongolia* magazine and a list of Mongolian proverbs and sayings. One reads " 'In the land of great expectations, Nine nights on an empty stomach'. The message of this expression is that unrealistically high expectations lead to correspondingly great disappointments". Don't let this put you off - the food isn't great in Mongolia but there's enough to go round! (Note that Mongolia has embassies in Moscow (page 138), Irkutsk (page 161) and Beijing (page 28), along the route of the Trans-Siberian. It's better to get your visa before you go though).

From Denmark

- **The Scandinavian Student Travel Service**, based in Copenhagen specialises in travel to the Soviet Union offering competitively-priced tours, including a 20 day Trans-Siberian trip. The address is: **SSTS**, Hauchsvej 17, DK-1825 Copenhagen V. Tel: 01-21 85 00. It's well worth writing to them for information.

- **Intourist** Vester Farimagsgade 6, Copenhagen V Tel 01-11 25 27.

From Finland

It's possible to book a ticket in Helsinki for the rail journey to Japan and a minimum of five weeks is necessary. There are direct rail services from Helsinki to Leningrad and Helsinki to Moscow. If you're coming from Britain and want to start your journey in Helsinki it's possible (and advisable) to make reservations before you arrive (Intourist in London may oblige) for the rail journey from Helsinki to Leningrad or Moscow.

● **Finnsov Tours Oy** Eerikinkatu 3, 00100 Helsinki. Tel: 694-1422
● **Intourist** Etela Esplanadi 14, 00130 Helsinki 13. Tel: 631-875
● **Finnish Student Travel Service** (Travela FSTS), Mannerheimintie 5C, 00100 Helsinki. Tel 624-101.

From France

Bookings may be made through Intourist in Paris who have also recommended several other travel companies offering individual itineraries across Siberia. The addresses are given below. Note that Intourist prices are about the same for similar itineraries and holidays bought in West European countries.

● **Intourist** 7 Boulevard des Capucines, 75002 Paris. Tel: 742-47-40
● **Association France-URSS**, Bureau de Voyages, 61 rue Boissière, 75016 Paris. Tel: 45-01-59-00
● **Wagon-lits Tourisme** 126 rue de Provence, 75008 Paris. Tel: 42-68-25-83

From Germany

● **Travel Service Asia** (TSA) Kirchberg 15, 7948 Dürmentingen. Tel 07371-4963, fax 07371-4769. This company offers budget tickets on the Trans-Siberian, both to and from Beijing. Their prices are among the best available in Europe and tickets can be arranged from outside Germany, by post or fax. The routes include: Budapest or Berlin to Beijing via Moscow (Train No 20) for DM450-550; Moscow to Beijing DM380-430; Beijing to Budapest or Berlin via Moscow for DM490-590. Return trip from Berlin by train (all the way and back) DM1111. Allow 2 months for bookings in summer or phone them for last-minute cancellations.
● **Intourist-Reisen GmbH** Kurfurstendamm 63, 1000 Berlin. Tel: (030) 88-00-77
● **Intourist-Reisen GmbH** 1 Stephanstrasse, 6000 Frankfurt. Tel: 28-57-79. Offers 8, 13 and 15 day trips on the Trans-Siberian for DM2092-2555.

See page 275 for visitor information for Berlin.

From Hungary

It is unlikely that the rail-bargain of a lifetime (£30/US$50 for Moscow-Beijing tickets bought here) will ever be repeated, since Budapest is no longer part of the Communist Bloc. However, in September 1990 travellers were reporting that tickets were available for less than £120/US$200 from **M.A.V.** at 35 Nep Koztarsasag Utca in Budapest. Check prices before making a special trip out to Hungary as things are changing fast and tickets are likely to be considerably more expensive now. To book a ticket with M.A.V. go to the counter on the right near reception. If they tell you to book your onward seat in Moscow then ask them to send a telex for you. It is necessary to spend approximately two weeks in Hungary just to make the reservation and get the Soviet, Mongolian and Chinese visas. You will then have to come back (or wait) for your departure date. **Star Tours** (Pannonia-Intourist), Jozsef Krt 45 H-1085 (Tel 1137-062, telex 22 3573) are another company that can sometimes sell budget tickets. Alternatively they do a package on the Trans-Siberian for around £300.

Embassies in Budapest

• **Soviet Embassy** VI. Bajzo 35. Tel: 320-911

Open Mon to Fri 10.00 to 13.00. A transit visa costs nothing but takes two weeks to process. Remember to bring three identical photos and confirmation details for your rail ticket.

Star Tours charge $30 to get this visa.

• **Chinese Embassy** VI. Benczier 17. Tel: 224-872

Visas can be issued on the spot for US$35, may be cheaper if you're not in a hurry. Check that the visa starts from the time you enter China, not from the time you leave Budapest. One photo is needed. Situated near the Soviet Embassy.

• **Mongolian Embassy** XII. Istenhegui 59/65. Tel: 556-219

Open Mon, Wed, Fri, 09.00-11.30 and 13.00-15.30. A transit visa costs US$26 and is issued on the spot.

Cheap charter flights are sometimes available from London to Budapest for as little as £70. If you can't afford the fare to Budapest you could always hitch-hike. Buy one of the cheap overnight bus tickets from London to Amsterdam and hitch from there through Germany and Austria.

See page 277 for further information about Budapest.

From the Netherlands

- **China Winkel** Haarlemmerstraat 32, Amsterdam
- **Intourist** Honthorststraat 42, 1071 Amsterdam. Tel 020-798964

MAKING A BOOKING IN NORTH AMERICA

From USA

- **Intourist** 630 Fifth Avenue, Suite 868, New York NY 10111. Tel 212-757 3884. Contact them for a full list of travel agents in North America offering tours/individual travel to the USSR.
- **General Tours** 770 Broadway, New York NY 10003. Tel (800) 221 2216. Recommended by several readers.
- **Russia Tours** 27 Occident Ave, Staten Island, NY 10304. Tel 718-816 6828
- **Russian Travel Bureau Inc** 225 East 44 Street, New York, NY 10017. tel (800) 847 1800
- **Troika Inc** 192 Nickerson Street, Suite 312, Seattle, Washington, 98109. Tel (800) 367 9928
- **Adventure Center** 1311 63rd Street, Suite 200, Emeryville, California 94608. Tel 415-654 1879
- **Baylis International Journeys** 2392 Telegraph Avenue, Berkeley, California 94704. Recently organised a Siberian tour including a visit to Vladivostok and several days on the BAM line.
- **Trains Unlimited Tours** 235 West Pueblo St, Reno, Nevada 89509, USA. Tel 702-329 5590. Fax 702-329 6578.

From Canada

- **Westcan Treks (Vancouver)** 1965 West 4th Avenue, Vancouver BC V6J 1M8. Tel 604-734 1066
- **Westcan Treks (Edmonton)** 8412 109th Street, Edmonton, Alberta T6G 1E2. Tel 403-439 9118
- **Westcan Treks (Calgary)** 336 14th Street NW, Calgary, Alberta T2N 1Z7. Tel 403-283 6115
- **The Adventure Centre** 17 Hayden Street, Toronto, Ontario, M4Y 2P2. Tel 416-922 7584
- **Intours Corporation** 1013 Bloor Street West, Toronto, Ontario M6H 1M1. Tel 416-537 2165, fax 416-537 1627. Offer 29 day trips on the Trans-Siberian including Soviet Central Asia, with flights via Helsinki for Can$5399.
- **Exotik Tours** Suite 905, 1117 Ste-Catherine West, Montreal, Quebec H3B 1H9. Tel 514-284 3324
- **Intourist** 1801 McGill College Avenue, Montreal, Quebec H3A 2N4. Tel 514-849 6394

MAKING A BOOKING IN AUSTRALIA

● **Intourist** Underwood House, 34-49 Pitt Street, Sydney, NSW 2000. Tel 02-277 652
● **Sundowners Travel Centre (Sydney)** 108 Albion Street, Surrey Hills 2010. Tel 02-281 4066
● **Sundowners Travel Centre (Melbourne)** 151 Dorcas Street, South Melbourne 3205. Tel 03-690 2499
● **Sundowners Travel Centre (Perth)** 1167 Hay Street, West Perth 6005. Tel 09-321 2335

MAKING A BOOKING IN NEW ZEALAND

● **Suntravel** PO Box 12 424, 407 Great South Road, Penrose, Auckland. Tel 09-525 3074

MAKING A BOOKING IN ASIA

From Japan

The friendly and efficient Japan Soviet Travel Bureau (JSTB) will handle bookings for rail journeys to Europe. The address is:
● **JSTB** Kamiyacho Building, (3rd Floor), 12-12, Toranomon 5-chome, Minato-ku, Tokyo 105. Tel: 3432-6161. Nearest subway station is Kamiya-cho (Hibiya line). They can offer a series of individual itineraries from about Y218,000/£850 for the voyage to Nakhodka from Yokohama, the rail journey to Moscow and a night in a Moscow hotel. This price is based on double-occupancy of the hotel room. JSTB have a series of other itineraries which are combinations of flights and train journeys and it's possible to fly from Japan (Niigata) to Khabarovsk. In the winter this is necessary since the boat to Nakhodka does not operate. JSTB can also organise your journey via Shanghai, Beijing and Ulan Bator (Y185,000-244,000/£740-976 each for two people travelling together). However, with the Japanese Yen riding high on foreign exchange markets, it would probably be cheaper to buy tickets outside Japan. Write to them for full details and prices.

Alternatively, you could take the boat from Kobe to Shanghai, make your own way to Beijing and organise your ticket there. The journey takes two days and although the boat is Chinese-run, the chef is Japanese, there are *futons* (mattresses) in the cabins and Japanese-style baths. Details of the weekly service and tickets (from a very reasonable Y20,000 or £80 for '*tatami*' class) from:
● **Tokyo Tourist Information Center**   10-1, Yurakucho 2-chome, Chiyoda-ku, Tokyo. Tel 3502-1461 (Subway: Ginza/Yurakucho).

The **Soviet Embassy** is at Roppongi Heights 1-16, 4-chome Roppongi, Minato-ku, Tokyo. Tel 3584-6617.

See page 266 for further information about Japan.

From China

● **CITS Head Office**, Beijing International Hotel, 9 Jianguomenwei Avenue, Beijing. Tel 5120510. Open Mon-Sat, 8.30-11.30 & 13.30-16.30. Check for Sunday opening. This is a ten-minute walk from Beijing Main Railway Station. Walk one block north up Chaoyangmenxiao Street to the junction with the wide Jianguomenwai Ave. Turn right and the hotel is one block on the left-hand side. The old office in the Chongwenmen Hotel will be closing soon. Approximate prices range from US$220-340 to Moscow, US$63-100 to Ulan Bator, US$110-195 to Irkutsk, US$250-410 to Warsaw, US$275-450 to Bucharest and US$300-500 to Sophia. Since Berlin and Budapest are no longer in the Communist Bloc, CITS has discontinued selling tickets to these destinations. In the summer it's often very difficult to get tickets from CITS.

● **Monkey Business Infocenter** Room 716, (New Building), Qiao Yuan Hotel, Dong Binhe Road, Youanmenwai 100054, Beijing. Tel 301-2244 ext 716, fax ext 444. Conveniently located in the popular Qiao Yuan Hotel, these people are very helpful and definitely worth a visit to pick up the latest information on prices. May be able to help with accommodation in Moscow.

● **TSA Information** A similar kind of organisation to the above, in Room 711 at the same address.

Trains

● **Chinese train (No. 3)** via Mongolia. Leaves Beijing every Wednesday at 07.40 arriving in Moscow at 11.45 the following Monday. The visas you will need are Polish, Soviet and Mongolian.

● **Russian train (No. 19)** via Manchuria. Leaves Beijing every Saturday at 20.32, arriving in Moscow the following Friday at 11.35, with a second service (June-September) leaving at the same time on Sunday evening, arriving in Moscow the following Saturday. The visas you will need are for Poland and the USSR.

● **Trains to Pyongyang** It may be possible to travel from Beijing to Pyongyang (North Korea) and then up to the USSR to join the Trans-Siberian at Ussuriyisk near Khabarovsk. Try Monkey Business (above) for information.

Procedure

In the summer trains fill up quickly so if you plan to spend some time travelling round China, make Beijing your first stop and get your reservations. It may also be possible to reserve a place on the train in Shanghai. Ask at the travel bureau in the Peace Hotel. Coming in from Hong Kong it's cheap and convenient to arrange a ticket there (see below).

Once you've made your reservation, and paid a deposit, do the rounds of the embassies and collect your visas. Start with the furthest country you will need a visa for and work backwards. You'll need US$ in cash and a stock of passport photos. You can get these done quickly in the International Club (next door to the Friendship Store).

You pay for your ticket (less the deposit already paid) once you've got your visas. You'll have a reserved berth only as far as Moscow. Reservations for the second stage of the journey are made at Byeloruski station in Moscow, or the Intourist Travel Office (page 269).

Embassies in Beijing
● **Polish Embassy** 1 Ritan Lu, Jianguomenwei Compound. Tel: 532-12-35. Open Mon, Wed and Fri from 08.30 to 14.00. Visa costs FEC50 (+FEC48 express), two photos are needed and it takes about two hours (ready by 13.00, if you apply before 11.00). Transit visa prices FEC41 (32 with student card). Not necessary for Germans.
● **Soviet Embassy** 4 Dongzhimenwei, Beizhongjie. Tel: 532-12-67 Open Mon, Wed and Fri from 09.00 to 13.00. Three photos are needed, your rail booking slip (check to see if this is still required) and either your passport or a photocopy of the first five pages. Anyone can apply on your behalf. Visa costs depend on urgency: FEC90 for same-day; FEC65 for 3 days; FEC35 for 7 days. There are additional fees (FEC39-142 depending on your nationality) to be paid on collection. Note that the queue outside is often very long so get there early (07.00hrs as it can take up to 5hrs to get in!).

Buying a ticket in Beijing
Nineteen days to Christmas and the only response I could get from the booking clerk for trains to Europe was: 'Wo mei yo'. He said there were no places. The last train which would get us home for Christmas was leaving in eight days time. We had to get a place somehow. I tried offering a bribe: 'Wo mei yo'. The prospect of spending Christmas in cold, drab Beijing was not a merry one. We might enjoy the British Embassy's traditional, though rather eccentric, drinks party on New Year's Day. Bemused locals watch in fascination as the expatriates, assembled on the frozen lake below the Summer Palace, sip sherry in temperatures 20 degrees below freezing. I asked the clerk to check his reservations list again. We'd been in that dingy office under the faded posters of the Great Wall and the Forbidden City for over an hour by then. The clerk was thoroughly bored with us. He threw down the comic he'd been trying to read and, thrusting a form at me said 'Okay'. Not really believing him I asked 'Number 19 train okay?'. 'Okay, okay,' he replied. We'd got our tickets. Given enough time, determination and patience, almost anything is possible in China.

● **Mongolian Embassy** 2 Xiushui Beijie. Tel: 532-12-03
Open on Mon, Tue and Fri from 08.30 to 10.30. No photo is needed
and it takes 24 hours to process (US$20, US$28 for UK nationals).
Same-day visas for US$24/36. Near the Polish Embassy.

From Hong Kong
Hong Kong is now a very good place to arrange a ticket or tour on
the Trans-Siberian and there are numerous agencies offering a range
of services.

Trans-Siberian tours & individual itineraries
If you want to book a tour or individual itinerary with stops in the
USSR this will take several weeks to arrange. Although it's easy to
get a visa for China here, there is no Soviet embassy so your passport will have to be sent to Japan or Thailand.
● **Wallem Travel** Hopewell Centre, 46th floor, 183 Queen's Rd
East, Central. Tel 865 1777, fax 865 2652. Best to use them for
tours although they will organise individual travel as they are agents
for Intourist and are expanding their USSR department. Tours include 12 days Beijing-Irkutsk-Moscow-Leningrad with connections
to Warsaw or Helsinki for HK$9200; trips to Mongolia or North
Korea before continuing on the Trans-Siberian and various individual
itineraries, 7-14 days, HK$4620-9770.

Trans-Siberian 'tickets only'
Many of the travel agencies in the Nathan Road area can arrange
tickets for transit travel from Beijing to Europe via the Trans-
Siberian at short notice (under 2 weeks). However, the situation
regarding both price and availability of these tickets is subject to
change so it's worth contacting one of the offices below (most have
faxes) to check before you arrive. Some will sell you a voucher to
exchange at their branch in Beijing for a ticket with reservation.
Others will sell you an open ticket with a reservation voucher and
you must get the ticket endorsed by CITS in Beijing. Getting the
reservation is the difficult bit so don't accept an open ticket without a
reservation voucher. It may sound risky but it seems to work. You
get your Mongolian and Soviet visas in Beijing. Once you've bought
a ticket some of the agents below will give you useful factsheets for
the journey. Tickets for Beijing to Moscow were available from
US$225 in April 1991 but prices are expected to rise.
● **Monkey Business Inc. (Moonsky Star Ltd)** Block E, 4th floor,
Flat 6, Chungking Mansions, Kowloon. Tel 723 1376, fax 723 6653.
Now in new premises, these guys are the experts in Trans-Siberian
discount tickets with routes to many European cities including Berlin

and Budapest. They have an **infocenter in Beijing** (Qiao Yuan Hotel, Room 716, New Building, Dong Binhe Rd, Youanmenwai, 100054 Beijing. Tel 301 2244 ext. 716; fax ext. 444) to help you out when you arrive. There is also a good new and secondhand bookshop here.

● **Time Travel Services** Block A, 16th floor, Chungking Mansions, 40 Nathan Rd, Kowloon. Tel 723 9993, fax 852-739 5413. Conveniently located beside the Travellers' Hostel.

● **Phoenix Services Agency** Room B, 6th floor, Milton Mansion, 96 Nathan Rd, Kowloon. Tel 722 7378, fax 852-369 8884.

● **Hong Kong Student Travel Bureau** Room 1021, 10 floor, Star House, Salisbury Rd, Kowloon. Tel 730 3269. Agents for Scandinavian Student Travel Service (SSTS) they offer tickets and tours on the Trans-Siberian.

● **China Travel Service (HK) Ltd** 1st floor, Alpha House, 27-33 Nathan Road, Kowloon. Tel 721 1331. Fax 721 7757. The Hong Kong branch of this international company can arrange both individual travel and 'tickets only' on the Trans-Siberian. There are other branches at 2nd floor, China Travel Building, 77 Queen's Road, Central (tel 525 2284) and 4th floor, CTS House, 78-83 Connaught Road, Central (tel 853 3533).

See p271 for further information about Hong Kong.

Before you leave

WHAT TO TAKE

Travel as light as possible. Some people advise that you put out everything you think you'll need and then pack only half of it. Remember that unless you're going on an up-market tour, you'll be carrying your luggage yourself.

Clothes

For summer in Moscow and Siberia pack as for an English summer: thin clothes, a sweater and a raincoat. Clothes washing facilities in the USSR are limited so it's easier to take shirts and blouses of a quick-drying cotton/polyester mixture and wash them yourself, although signs in the bathroom will inform you that this contravenes the house rules. Summer in China and Japan is very hot - uncomfortably humid in Tokyo. Winter in the USSR and Northern China is extremely cold, although the trains and buildings are well-heated. In the Trans-Siberian you can be quite warm enough in a thin shirt as you watch Arctic scenes pass by your window. A thick winter overcoat is an absolute necessity, as well as gloves and a warm hat. If you're coming from Beijing you can buy one of the heavy green military jackets that everyone seems to wear in winter, for about £10. Fur hats are expensive in the USSR and in China, cheaper if you buy with local currency in the shops down Wangfujing Dajie beside the Beijing Hotel. Thermal underwear is a good idea but make sure it's not made of nylon as this can freeze to you in very low temperatures! Cheap woollen underwear is available in China and Hong Kong. Shoes should be strong, light and comfortable, as tours usually require a lot of walking. Most travellers take sturdy running shoes of the Adidas or Nike variety. For wearing on the train some

---

Western v Eastern fashions
A friend of mine bought some long, beige thermal underwear in Hong Kong. As it was a size too large and didn't really look like Western underwear, she wore it over her other clothes. We travelled round China for a while and I didn't think we were attracting more than the usual curious stares the Chinese subject foreigners to. This was until someone asked me why my friend wore her underwear **over** her clothes. We looked at the labels and realised it had been made in China, exported to Hong Kong and these were the standard issue garments that everyone else in the country was hiding under their clothes! A good way to attract the waiter's attention and get served quickly in restaurants, though.

people recommend slip-on kung-fu slippers available cheaply from sports shops in the West, Hong Kong or China. Russians wear track-suits or even pyjamas throughout the journey. Dress casually - jeans are quite acceptable even for a visit to the Bolshoi. If you forget anything, clothes are expensive in Japan, over-priced and shoddy in the USSR, cheap and fashionable in Hong Kong, very cheap and curiously dated in China.

Luggage

If you're going on one of the more expensive tours which include baggage handling, take a suitcase. Those on individual itineraries have the choice of rucksack (which is comfortable to carry for long distances but bulky for getting into taxis and buses) or shoulder-bag (not so good for longer walks but more compact than the rucksack). As you are unlikely to be going trekking in the USSR or China, a zip-up hold-all with a shoulder-strap or a frameless backpack are probably the best bet. It's also useful to take along a small day-pack for camera, books and documents. Since bedding on the train and in hotels is supplied you don't need to take a sleeping-bag, even when travelling in winter. However, recently travellers have reported that the sheets they've been given on the train were still damp from the laundry. Sheets or a sheet sleeping-bag might be worth taking along.

A lesson in travelling light

On my first Trans-Siberian trip from Beijing we had so much luggage that sever-al taxi-drivers refused to take us to the station. Unfortunately all thirteen bags were necessary as we were moving back from Japan. We'd managed to get some of them stowed away in the compartments above the door and under the seats when we were joined by a German girl travelling home after three years in China. Her equally voluminous baggage included two full-size theatrical lanterns which were very fragile. Then the man from Yaraslavl arrived with three trunks. We solved the storage situation by covering the floor between the bottom bunks with luggage and spreading the bedding over it, making a sort of triple bed on which we all lounged comfortably - eating, drinking, reading, playing cards and sleeping for the next six days. Dragging our bags around Moscow, Berlin and Paris was no fun, however. On subsequent journeys I didn't even take a ruck-sack, only a light 'sausage' bag with a shoulder strap and a small day-pack. Never travel with an ounce more than you absolutely need.

Medical supplies

Take along aspirin or paracetamol; lipsalve; multi-vitamin tablets (there is very little fresh fruit available in the USSR or China); suntan lotion; lavatory paper; insect repellent (if you're travelling in summer). Note that Western brands of tampons and condoms are not easily available in the USSR and China. Take something for an upset stomach: 'Arrêt', for example. Use it only in an emergency. A change in diet often causes slight diarrhoea which soon stops of its own accord. Avoid rich food, alcohol and strong coffee to give your stomach time to adjust. **Nomad Travel Pharmacy** (3-4 Wellington Terrace, Turnpike Lane, London N8 0PX, tel 081-889 7014) offers travel medical advice and supplies. For vaccination requirements see page 35.

General items

A good pair of **sun-glasses** is necessary in summer as well as in winter when the sun on the snow is particularly bright. The following items are also useful: **soap** and a **universal bathplug** (Soviet basins and baths don't always have both); **penknife** with corkscrew and can-opener (Swiss Army knife is best); **ball-point pens**; **adhesive tape**; **string** (to use as a washing-line); **washing powder** (liquid 'Travel Soap' is good); a few **clothes pegs**; **tissues** (including the wet variety) and **lavatory paper**; **sewing-kit**; folding **umbrella**; **handwarmers** (available from camping shops); pocket **calculator**; **flashlight**; **games** (cards, chess - the Russians are very keen chess players, Scrabble etc); **notebook** or **diary** and some reading matter; **camera** and adequate supplies of film (see below). You may also want to take your Walkman and some cassettes. Note that alkaline batteries are difficult to find, so take spares. Don't forget to take some reading matter (see page 36).

Gifts

Since so many of the things we take for granted in the West are unavailable in the USSR and China, you may wish to take along a few items to use in lieu of tips. The female carriage attendants (*provodnitsi*) greatly appreciate cosmetics and scented soaps, especially if they are made by one of the 'big names'. Tights (pantyhose) are also popular, as are chocolate biscuits and fresh fruit. Postcards of the Royal family and copies of fashion magazines also go down well. Bring things to share with Russians on trains - oranges (not apples), exotic fruit such as peaches & bananas would be great but difficult to transport, chocolate digestive biscuits, slabs of chocolate (for the Russian sweet tooth) as chocolate is often in short supply. Businessmen appreciate sellotape, Tippex, highlighters and other things taken for granted in the modern Western office.

What to bring for the Black Market

On my first Trans-Siberian journey several years ago, there was only one exchange rate for the rouble - a horrendously bad one for one against the pound. This made dabbling on the Black Market very attractive and a pair of Levis could cover all your spending money for a trip. In 1989 a second exchange rate of ten roubles to the pound was introduced, making the Black Market less attractive for the traveller. By 1991 it was almost fifty roubles to the pound. You will still be approached by Russians wanting to buy anything Western and it's worth bringing a few T-shirts with Western logos or writing on them, jars of Nescafé, cigarettes (in 1989-90 Marlboro cigarettes were almost a second currency after the US$ but by early 1991 these were not so sought-after). It's worth talking to people who've recently returned from the USSR to find out what the latest shortage is.

Provisions

Stock up with edibles before you leave the West or Hong Kong. The food in the dining car in the Russian trains is cheap but monotonous and as opening times are erratic it's useful to have something for when you miss a meal. Unlike rail journeys in India or South America, there's not much to buy at stations along the way; although you do find good snacks on some platforms, stops are infrequent. Some travellers bring vast sacks of food, others just some biscuits, tea-bags or coffee powder (hot water is always available from the samovar in each carriage), fresh fruit and perhaps something to drink (alcoholic drinks are no longer available on the train, thanks to the government's anti-alcoholism policy). Some of the things you might consider bringing along are Pot-noodles, dried soups, tins of sardines, muesli, milk powder, fruit-drink powder, cheese and biscuits or crackers (although you can buy bread from the dining-car). In case you miss a hotel meal it's worth having a stock of emergency rations. You may even consider some of the dried meals used by campers and hikers.

TRAILBLAZER feedback 'The Russians don't seem to comprehend what a vegetarian is. They would just take the meat off a plate or out of a meat-based soup and call it 'vegetarian'. We found a packet of Complan very useful'. Hilda Helling (UK).

Money

Since your hotels and travel will already have been paid for, you need to bring only enough money to cover meals, sightseeing and anything you might want to buy to take back with you. If you're on a tour with meals and sightseeing included, you'll need money only for shopping and incidental expenses. Bring your money in travellers' cheques, in your country's currency as long as it's not Peruvian Intis or something similarly obscure. Bring travellers' cheques only from one of the well-known companies like Thomas Cook or American Express. You should also carry some cash (US$ are best) if you're going to be using the hard-currency bars and restaurants. Change may be given in foreign currency here but it will be in whatever foreign currency they happen to have. US$ are also necessary for the Mongolian dining-car.

If you're on a budget you will probably be making use of the Black Market for currency exchange in which case you'll also need US$ in cash. Larger bills are preferred but don't change too much as there's not much to spend your roubles on.

Photographic equipment

Most travellers will want to bring a camera with them. Bring more film than you think you'll need as you'll find there's much to photograph, and the heavy rules and regulations that used to be in force have now been relaxed. Don't forget to bring some faster film for shots from the train (400ASA). If you're flying in, try to avoid letting your film go through the X-ray machines even if the notices tell you it's perfectly safe. Kodak, Fuji, Agfa and Polaroid film is available in some Beriozka shops in the USSR and easily available in Beijing. Have film developed when you return home or in Hong Kong. Developing is naturally of a high standard in Japan but, unless you request otherwise, prints will be small. If you plan to have developing done in the USSR, use Agfa film. Intourist gives the following advice: 'Soviet light sensitive stuff (!) is adapted to the Agfa developing system and not Kodakcolor or Kodakchrome'.

Photography from the train

Used to be forbidden but now you can photograph stations and trains but not bridges and military installations. There are problems with telephone lines getting in the way of pictures, dirty windows and slow film. You won't be allowed to open the windows in summer because this will affect the air-conditioning. Try opening doors and hanging out although this will upset the carriage attendants if they catch you. The door by the kitchen is always left open which you may find useful. It would be worth ingratiating yourself with the kitchen staff first, though.

TRAILBLAZER feedback 'A squeegie, an instrument used by window-cleaners to remove water, can be easily obtained in a small size for car windows. This tool is an invaluable aid for cleaning the train's windows for photography, or for that matter just for passengers' viewing. To apply water an atomiser/plant spray may be used but, unlike the squeegie, there's a space penalty'.Robert Bray (UK)

Vaccinations and health safeguards

No vaccinations are listed as official requirements for Western tourists visiting the USSR, China, Mongolia and Japan. Some vaccinations may, however, be advisable for certain areas (see below). Up-to-date health information and an on-the-spot vaccination service is available in London at Trailfinders (194 Kensington High Street, tel 071-938 3999) and at Thomas Cook, 45 Berkeley St (nearest tube Green Park). You should have **health insurance**, available from any travel agent, wherever you are travelling but especially if you are visiting Japan and Hong Kong where medical costs are astronomical. A useful reference book to take along is *The Traveller's Health Guide* by Dr A C Turner (Lascelles).

● **Tetanus** A tetanus vaccination is advisable if you've not had one in the last ten years. If you then cut yourself badly while travelling you won't need to have another. If you're travelling in the USSR and Japan only, this is the only vaccination you need to have (although it is not a legal requirement for entry).

● **Infectious hepatitis** For those travelling on a tight budget who will be eating in the cheaper type of restaurants in China there is the danger of catching infectious hepatitis, a disease of the liver that drains you of energy and can last from three weeks to a couple of months. It's spread by drinking infected water, and by using utensils or eating food that has been handled by an infected person. Gamma globulin injections give a certain amount of protection against hepatitis and are effective for six months.

● **Malaria** If you plan to go further south than Beijing you may need to take anti-malarial tablets. In certain parts of China, the parasite (carried by the *Anopheles* mosquito) that causes malaria is resistant to chloroquine, so you may need to take two kinds of tablet. Start taking the tablets one week before you go and continue for six weeks after you leave the malarial zone. If you are going to be in a malarial area (even for a few hours) you would be stupid not to take anti-malarials with you as the disease is dangerous, occasionally fatal and on the increase.

● **Others** If you plan to travel on to South East Asia and India you will need typhoid and polio vaccinations and should consider having a cholera shot if you're travelling to or through an epidemic area.

Medical services

Provided free of charge for tourists in the USSR and Mongolia. The receptionist at your hotel will call a doctor for you if necessary. A charge is made if you need to stay in hospital. In Moscow there's a hard-currency pharmacy at the Mezhdunarodnaya Hotel. In Japan and Hong Kong medical services are good but costly. If you need a doctor in China, the bigger hotels often have a doctor in residence. In the days when China was open only to tour-groups, largely composed of rich elderly Americans, it was important to have an English-speaking doctor near at hand. In the 1970s the American Embassy was dealing with between 20 and 30 tourist-deaths a year, usually heart-attacks. In Beijing, Shanghai and Canton there are special hospitals for foreigners. You may be given a choice of Western or Chinese medicine. Take supplies of any prescription medicine you will need. Dentists in the USSR and China are not recommended. Visit yours before you leave.

Drinking water

Do not drink tap-water in Leningrad since it can cause a nasty form of diarrhoea (Giardiasis), especially in summer. Although the water is probably all right in other cities it's better to stick to mineral water. In Irkutsk and Listvyanka you can drink the tap-water and it is especially good since it comes directly from Lake Baikal. Drink only boiled or bottled water in Mongolia and China, where boiled water (in a thermos) is provided on trains and in hotels. Tap water is perfectly safe in Japan and Hong Kong.

BACKGROUND READING

There are a number of excellent books that have been written about the Trans-Siberian, several of which are unfortunately out of print. If they're not in your library they should be available through the inter-library loans system. The following are well worth reading before you go:

• *Journey Into the Mind's Eye* by Lesley Blanch, is a fascinating book, the witty semi-autobiographical story of the author's romantic obsession with Russia and the Trans-Siberian Railway.

• *To the Great Ocean* by Harmon Tupper (Secker and Warburg, 1965 and out of print) gives an entertaining account of Siberia and the building of the railway.

• *Guide to the Great Siberian Railway 1900* by A.I. Dmitriev-Mamanov, a reprint (David and Charles 1971 and also out of print) of the guide originally published by the Tsar's government to publicise their new railway system. Highly detailed but interesting to look at.

• *Peking to Paris: A Journey across two Continents* by Luigi Barzini tells the story of the Peking to Paris Rally in 1907. The author accompanied the Italian Prince Borghese and his chauffeur in the winning car, a 40 horse-power Itala. Their route took them across Mongolia and Siberia and for some of the journey they actually drove along the railway tracks.

- *The Big Red Train Ride* by Eric Newby. A perceptive account of the journey, written in Newby's characteristically humorous style.
- *The Trans-Siberian Railway: A Traveller's Anthology*, edited by Deborah Manley is well worth taking on the trip for a greater insight into the railway and the trip, as seen through the eyes of travellers from Annette Meakin to Bob Geldof.
- *The Princess of Siberia* is Christine Sutherland's biography of Princess Maria Volkonsky who followed her husband to Siberia after he'd been exiled for his part in the Decembrists' Uprising. Her house in Irkutsk is now a museum.
- *Martin Walker's Russia* is a recent account of Soviet life-styles and what it's like to live there.
- *Journey into Russia* by Laurens van der Post is an astute but now slightly dated introduction to the people and the country.

However well written and accurate, these books are only the impressions of foreign travellers. You will get more of an idea of the Russian mind and soul from their own literature, even from the pre-Revolution classics, which tend to be more readable than modern Socialist works. If you haven't already read them you might try some of the following:

- Dostoyevsky's *Crime and Punishment* (set in the Haymarket in Leningrad).
- Tolstoy's *War and Peace*.
- The weird but fascinating *Master and Margarita* by Mikhail Bulgakov
- *Dr Zhivago* by Boris Pasternak (whose grave you can visit in Moscow).
- *The Gulag Archipelago* by Alexander Solzhenitsyn.
- *House of the Dead* is a semi-autobiographical account of Dostoyevsky's life as a convict in Omsk.
- *A Day in the Life of Ivan Denisovitch* by Alexander Solzhenitsyn details 24hrs in the life of a Siberian convict.

The following **guide-books** are recommended:
- *Collins Independent Guide - Soviet Union* (Martin Walker is good on Moscow and Leningrad but not a fan of either Siberia or the Railway)
- *Lascelles City Guides - Moscow & Leningrad* by Christopher Knowles, which contains good, detailed coverage of these cities.

- *USSR - a travel survival kit* new guide from Lonely Planet due Jan 1992.
- *Holy Russia* by Fitzroy Maclean is probably the best historical summary (with walking tours) for the traveller.

If you're going on to China or Japan, the *travel survival kit* series of guide books from Lonely Planet is highly recommended.

TRAILBLAZER feedback 'It's no good going to the Soviet Union expecting things to run like clockwork. You are quite likely to encounter all sorts of administrative mess-ups, altered itineraries, airport delays etc. Take them all in the spirit of adventure and pack, along with the food supplements, a plentiful supply of good humour and lashings of stamina'. Hilda Helling (UK)

PART 2: THE USSR

Facts about the country

GEOGRAPHICAL BACKGROUND

With a total area of 8,647,500 square miles (22,402,200 square km), the Soviet Union is the world's largest country, accounting for 15 per cent of the total land area of the earth. The country measures over 6,000 miles from west to east and more than 2,500 miles from north to south. Among the many other records the USSR can lay claim to is of having the greatest number of frontiers - thirteen, with countries in both Europe and Asia (North Korea, China, Mongolia, Afghanistan, Iran, Turkey, Romania, Hungary, Czechoslovakia, Poland, Finland, Pakistan and Norway). It also has the longest coastline of any country (27,000 miles). The UK could be fitted into the Soviet Union ninety times, the USA twice.

Climate

Much of the country is situated in far northern latitudes. Moscow is in the same latitude as Edinburgh, Leningrad almost as far north as Anchorage in Alaska. Winters are extremely cold and temperatures as low as -68°C (-90°F) have been recorded in Oymyakon in Siberia. It is not only the extremes of latitude which cause the severe winters; the physical make-up of the country is as much to blame. Most of the land is a wide open plain stretching up across Siberia to the Arctic. To the west are the Urals, the low range which divides Europe and Asia. There is higher ground in the south but no mountains in the north to shield it from the cold Arctic air which blows down to fill this plain. The Himalayan and Pamir ranges beyond the southern borders stop warm tropical air from reaching the Siberian and Russian plains. Thus blocked off, the plains warm rapidly in summer and become very cold in winter. Olekminsk, in north-eastern Siberia, holds the record for the place with the greatest temperature range in the world: from -60°C (-87°F) in winter to a record summer high of 45°C (113°F). Along the route of the Trans-Siberian, however, summers are rather more mild.

Transport and communications

The railways remain the principal transport system for both passengers and goods. The network is highly developed and rail traffic is, in some areas including parts of the Trans-Siberian, heavier than anywhere else in the world, with trains passing every few minutes. The importance of railways over road transport is reflected by the ambitious railway building projects that are still in progress (BAM line, see page 111). The road across Siberia is still no more (in parts) than the rough track it was in the days before the Age of the Train.

The rivers of the Soviet Union have always been of vital importance as a communication network across the country. Some of these rivers are huge - navigable by ocean-going ships for considerable distances. The lower parts of the Ob are wider than the English Channel and the Volga is 30 miles wide in the far south and over 2,300 miles long.

The economy
The industrial growth that has taken place in the USSR since the Revolution could not have come about without the enormous natural resources that are to be found here, mainly in Siberia. The USSR has the third largest oil reserves and the largest reserves of natural gas in the world as well as deposits of coal, iron ore, manganese, asbestos, lead, gold, silver and copper that will continue to be mined long after most other countries have exhausted their supplies. The USSR is the second largest producer of electricity in the world (after the USA).

The economy is steered by a series of five-year plans which lay down production targets. The majority of the working population is employed in heavy industry, the fruits of their labour mainly comprising steel, machinery, chemicals and textiles. Agriculture employs only about 15% of the people. It is highly mechanised and the main crops are wheat, barley, rye, oats and potatoes. Recent crop failures have meant that the USSR has had to import large quantities of foodstuffs from the West. As you will notice when you visit GUM (see page 139) - or any other shop - consumer goods are not high on the list of manufacturing priorities.

After years of centralised mismanagement the economy is now in an extremely bad state. Although the country is able to grow enough food to feed its people the distribution system is so disorganised that in 1990 (in spite of record harvests) food shortages in Moscow and Leningrad were so severe in the winter that foreign aid was required, with airlifts from the West.

In March 1991 prices of basic foodstuffs that had been unchanged for decades went up by 300-400%. Prices of clothes rose fourfold.

Landscape zones: flora and fauna (see also Appendix C)
The Soviet Union comprises every extreme of climatic region - Arctic wastelands to the north, fertile plains in European Russia and

southern Siberia and deserts in Soviet Central Asia. The main land-scape zones that are of interest to the Trans-Siberian traveller are as follows:

● **European Russia** West of the Urals the flora and fauna is similar to that found in the rest of northern Europe. Trees include oak, elm, hazel, ash, apple, aspen, spruce, lime and maple.

● **North Siberia and the Arctic regions** The *tundra* zone (short grass, mosses and lichens) covers the tree-less area in the far north. The soil is poor and much of it permanently frozen. In fact *permafrost*, as it is called, affects over 40 per cent of the USSR and extends down into southern Siberia, where it causes building problems for architects and engineers. In this desolate northern zone the wild-life includes reindeer, arctic fox, wolf, lemming and vole. Birdlife is more numerous: ptarmigan, snow-bunting, Iceland falcon and snow-owl as well as many kinds of migratory water and marsh fowl.

● **The Siberian plain** Much of this area is covered with *taiga* (pronounced 'tiger') - thick forest. To the north the trees are stunted and windblown; in the south they grow into dark impenetrable for-ests. More than 30 per cent of all the world's trees grow in this *taiga* zone. The trees include larch, pine and silver fir, intermingled with birch, aspen and maple. Willow and poplar line the rivers and streams. Much of the *taiga* forests along the route of the Trans-Siberian has been cleared and replaced with fields of wheat or sun-flowers. Parts of this region are affected by permafrost and in places rails and roads sink, and houses, trees and telegraph poles keel over at odd angles. Fauna in this region includes many species once common in Europe: bear, badger, wolverine, polecat, ermine, sable, squirrel, weasel, otter, wolf, fox, lynx, beaver, several types of rodent, musk deer, roebuck, reindeer and elk.

● **East Siberia and Trans-Baikalia** Much of the flora and fauna of this region is unique (see page 162) including (in Lake Baikal) such rarities as the world's only fresh-water seals. Amongst the ubiquitous larch and pine there grows a type of birch with dark bark, *betula daurica*. Towards the south and into China and Mongolia, the forests give way to open grassy areas known as the *steppe*. The black earth (*chernozem*) of the northern *steppes* is quite fertile and some areas are under cultivation.

● **The Far Eastern territories: the Amur region** Along the Amur River the flora and fauna are similar to that found in northern China and it is here that the rare Amur tiger (see page 240) is found. European flora makes a reappearance in the Far Eastern region including such trees as cork, walnut and acacia.

HISTORICAL OUTLINE

The first Russians

The earliest evidence of man within the borders of the USSR was recently found at the archaeological site of Dering Yuryakh, north of Lake Baikal, on the Lena River. The evidence suggests that human history may stretch back very much further than had previously been believed, perhaps between one and two million years. Around the thirteenth millennium BC there were Stone Age nomads living beside Lake Baikal. By the second millennium BC when fairly advanced civilisations had emerged here (see page 69), European Russia was inhabited by Ural-Altaic and Indo-European peoples. In the sixth century BC the Scythians (whose magnificent goldwork may be seen in the Hermitage) settled in southern Russia, near the Black Sea. Through the early centuries of the first millennium AD a trade route developed between Scandinavia, Russia and Byzantium, following the Dnieper River. Centres of trade grew up along the route (Novgorod, Kiev, Smolensk, Chernigov) and by the sixth century AD the towns were populated by Slavic tribes known as the Rus (hence the word Russian). The year 830 saw the first of the Varangian (Viking) invasions and in 862 Novgorod fell to the Varangian chief, Rurik, Russia's first sovereign.

Vladimir and Christian Russia

The great Tsar Vladimir (978-1015) ruled Russia from Kiev and was responsible for the conversion of the country to Christianity. At the time the Slavs worshipped a range of pagan gods and it is said that in his search for a new religion Vladimir invited bids from the Muslims, the Jews and the Christians. Since Islam and the consumption of vodka were not compatible and Judaism did not make for a unified nation, he chose Christianity as the state religion and had himself baptised at Constantinople in 988 AD. At his order the mass conversion of the Russian people began, with whole towns being baptised simultaneously. The eleventh century was marked by continual feuding between the heirs of Vladimir. It was at this time that the northern principalities of Vladimir and Suzdal were founded.

The Mongol invasion and the rise of Muscovy

Between 1220 and 1230 the Golden Horde brought a sudden halt to economic progress in Russia, burning towns and putting the local population to the sword. By 1249 Kiev was under their control and the Russians moved north establishing a new political centre at Muscovy (Moscow). All Russian principalities were obliged to pay tribute to the Mongol khans but Muscovy was the first to challenge their authority. Over the next three centuries Moscow gained control of the other Russian principalities and shook off the Mongol yoke.

Ivan the Terrible (1533-84)

When Ivan the Terrible came to the throne he declared himself Tsar of All the Russias and by his military campaigns extended the borders of the young country. He was as wild and blood-thirsty as his name suggests and in a fit of anger in 1582 he struck his favourite son with a metal staff, fatally injuring him (a scene used by Ilya Repin as the subject of one of his greatest paintings). Ivan was succeeded by his mentally-retarded son, Fyodor (the last of the descendants of Rurik), with Boris Godunov ruling first as regent and later as Tsar (1584-98). The early part of the seventeenth century was marked by dynastic feuding which ended with the election of Michael Romanov (1613-45), the first of the long line that lasted until the Revolution in 1917.

Peter the Great and the westernisation of Russia

Peter (1682-1725) well deserved his soubriquet 'the Great' for it was due to his policy of westernisation that Russia emerged from centuries of isolation and backwardness into the eighteenth century. He founded Leningrad in 1703 as a 'window open on the west' and made it his capital in 1712. During his reign there were wars with Sweden and Turkey. Territorial gains included the Baltic provinces and the southern and western shores of the Caspian. The extravagant building programme in St Petersburg continued under Catherine the Great (1762-96). While her generals were taking the Black Sea steppes, the Ukraine and parts of Poland for Russia, Catherine conducted extensive campaigns of a more romantic nature with a series of favourites in her elegant capital.

Alexander I and the Napoleonic Wars

In Russia during the nineteenth century, the political pendulum swung back and forth between conservatism and enlightenment. The mad Tsar Paul I came to the throne in 1796 but was murdered five years later. He was succeeded by his son Alexander I (1801-25) who was said to have had a hand in the sudden demise of his father. In the course of his reign he abolished the secret police, lifted the laws of censorship and would have freed the serfs had the aristocracy not objected so strongly to the idea. In 1812 Napoleon invaded Russia and Moscow was burnt to the ground (by the inhabitants, not by the French) before he was pushed back over the border.

Growing unrest among the peasants

Nicholas I's reign began with the first Russian Revolution, the Decembrists' uprising (see page 123), and ended, after Nicholas had reversed most of his father's enlightened policies, with the Crimean War against the English and the French in 1854-6. Alexander II (1855-81) was known as the Tsar Liberator, for he it was who freed the serfs. His reward was his assassination by a student in St Peters burg in 1881. He was succeeded by the strong Tsar Alexander III, during whose reign work began on the Trans-Siberian Railway.

Nicholas II: last of the Tsars

The dice were heavily loaded against this unfortunate Tsar. Nicholas inherited a vast empire and a restless population that was beginning to discover its own power. In 1905 his army and navy suffered a most humiliating defeat at the hands of the Japanese. Just when his country needed him most, as strikes and riots swept through the cities in the first few years of this century, Nicholas's attention was drawn into his own family crisis. It was discovered that the heir to the throne, Alexis, was suffering from the incurable disease, haemophilia. The Siberian monk Rasputin ingratiated himself into the court circle by his ability to exert a calming influence over the Tsarevich. His influence over other members of the royal family, including the Tsar, was not so beneficial.

October 1917: the Russian Revolution

After the riots in 1905, Nicholas had agreed to allow the formation of a national parliament (Duma) but its elected members had no real power. Reforms came too slowly for the people and morale fell further when, during the First World War, Russia suffered heavy losses. By March 1917 the Tsar had lost all control and was forced to abdicate in favour of a provisional government led by Alexander Kerensky. The Revolution that abruptly changed the course of Russian history took place in October 1917, when the reins of government were seized by Lenin and his Bolshevik Party. Nicholas and all his family were taken to Siberia where they were murdered (see page 203). Civil war raged across the country and it was not until 1920 that the Bolsheviks brought the lands of Russia under their control, forming the Union of Soviet Socialist Republics.

The Stalin era

After the death of Lenin in 1924, control of the country passed to Stalin and it was under his leadership that the USSR was transformed from a backward agricultural country into an industrial world power. The cost to the people was tremendous and most of those who were unwilling to swim with the current were jailed for their 'political' crimes. During the Great Terror in the 1930s, millions were sentenced to the work-camps which provided much of the labour for the ambitious building projects. During the Second World War the USSR played an important part in the defeat of the Nazis and extended its influence to the East European countries that took on Communist governments after the war.

Khrushchev, Brezhnev, Andropov and Chernenko

After Stalin's death in 1953, Khrushchev became Party Secretary and attempted to ease the strict regulations which governed Soviet society when Stalin was in power. In 1962 the Soviet installation of missiles in Cuba almost led to war with the USA. Khrushchev was forced to resign in 1964, blamed for the failure of the country's economy and for his clumsy foreign policy. He was replaced by Brezhnev who continued the USSR's policy of fostering friendly 'buffer' states along the Iron Curtain by ordering the invasion of Afghanistan in 1979 ('at the invitation of the leaders of the country'). When Brezhnev died in 1982, he was replaced by the former head of the KGB, Yuri Andropov. He died in 1984, succeeded by the elderly Chernenko who managed a mere thirteen months in office before becoming the chief participant in yet another State funeral.

Gorbachev, glasnost and perestroika

The present leader, Mikhail Gorbachev, is well-known in the West for his dynamic approach to the USSR's internal problems, for his success in foreign policy and for his catch-phrases *glasnost* (openness) and *perestroika* (restructuring).

● **Foreign policy** In 1990 Gorbachev was awarded the Nobel Peace Prize for his part in ending the Cold War. His signature on the treaty for the restoration of German sovereignty allowed the unification of the country to go ahead. His willingness to discuss disarmament proposals has led to the elimination of medium-range missiles in Europe and the withdrawal of tens of thousands of Soviet troops first from Afghanistan and now from Eastern Europe and Mongolia.

● *Glasnost* and *perestroika* **at home** Success in foreign policy has not (yet) been mirrored by success at home. There is indeed evidence of *glasnost* in many areas, greater freedom of the press, the easing of travel restrictions on Soviet citizens (200,000 Soviet Jews have now emigrated, most of them to Israel), the freeing of many political prisoners (including Andrei Sakharov in 1986) and greater freedom for people to practise their religion. *Perestroika* may have led to a considerable restructuring of society but as far as the average Soviet is concerned there is less in the shops than there was before Gorbachev came to power. A chain reaction of change has been set in motion that has threatened the cohesion of the whole of the USSR. Some of Gorbachev's solutions represent a return to the kind of communism advocated by Lenin himself who, in the early 1920s tried to cut red tape and allow a certain amount of private enterprise. It is, however, doubtful that he will be able to achieve the market economy he desires by attempting to achieve capitalism with a centrally controlled economy based on communist guidelines.

Gorbachev's resilience is unquestionable. He has survived numerous contretemps with Boris Yeltsin, the President of the Russian Republic, and accusations of dictatorship when he became the

USSR's first President in 1990, promising a gradual transition to a multi-party system. It is the resilience of the Soviet people that is less assured for before things get better and the shelves fill with the attractive products of a successful market economy, things may have to get worse.

Russia's new logo
A Russian Federation commission is considering restoring the old double-headed eagle as an emblem but stripped of the orb, crown and sceptre that symbolised the Tsar's authority. Other proposals to replace the hammer and sickle include a Russian warrior striking a snake or a bear, Tass said. (Reuter) The *Times* 14 Feb 1991.

THE PEOPLE

The Soviet Union is the third most populous country in the world (after China and India) with a population of about 286 million, comprising more than 100 ethno-linguistic groups. The country is divided into fifteen **Soviet Socialist Republics**, and Russia, or rather the Russian Soviet Federated Socialist Republic, is only one of them. People from other republics will be insulted if you refer to them as Russians and to the country as Russia. Nevertheless, the Russian Republic is by far the largest and contains half the country's population and three quarters of the entire area of the Soviet Union.

The fifteen Republics are further divided into *oblasts* (the basic administrative unit for economic development programmes), *krays* (smaller territories) and *Autonomous Republics* (containing ethnic minority groups such as the Buryats in Siberia). Siberia forms part of the Russian Republic and now exists only in name as a geographical, not a political unit.

Government

Russia moved briskly down the political path from autocracy to 'socialist' state, with a period of a few months in 1917 when it was a republic. Since November 1917 control of the country has been in the hands of the Communist Party. At the top of the complex hierarchy sits the General Secretary and President (Mikhail Gorbachev) presiding over the Politburo (the policy-making bureau). Once policy has been decided upon it is put into practice by the Central Committee. Although real power lies in the Central Committee and the Politburo, the Supreme Soviet is theoretically the most important organisation in the party. It consists of two 'houses': the Soviet of the Union and the Soviet of Nationalities, each having 750 members. Since Gorbachev became the USSR's first President, in 1990, he has been accused of being granted too much power.

In February 1990 revolutionary changes were heralded by the Soviet Communist Party leadership agreeing to end the party's exclusive right to rule with a gradual transition to the multi-party system.

Education and social welfare

Education and health care are provided free of charge for the entire population. Between the ages of seven and seventeen, education is compulsory and as a result the population has a literacy rate of almost 100 per cent. At schools, extra attention is paid to children who display an aptitude for sciences and the brightest pupils may be sent to special schools (see Akademgorodok, page 151). University places are determined by entrance examination. In the field of health care, the USSR boasts over one million doctors, 75 per cent of them women. Although the standard of health care is similar to those in other industrialised countries, the overall standard of living in the USSR is considerably lower.

Religion

Officially the USSR is an atheist state yet it is estimated that there may be as many as 98 million Christians (85 million Russian Orthodox believers, 8 million Protestants, 5 million Catholics), about 35 million Moslems, 2 million Jews and a few hundred thousand Buddhists. Policies of liberalisation that began when Gorbachev came to power culminated in the Soviet parliament voting overwhelmingly (in October 1990) to back a law that guarantees absolute freedom of conscience.

Russia was a pagan nation until 988 when Vladimir ordered the mass conversion of the country to Christianity. The state religion adopted was that of the Greek Orthodox Eastern Church (Russian Orthodox) rather than Roman Catholicism. After the Revolution religion was suppressed until the late 1930s when Stalin, recognising the importance of the Church's patriotism in time of war, restored Orthodoxy to respectability. In the 1960s Khrushchev reversed this policy, closing half the country's churches, synagogues and mosques and filling labour camps with religious dissidents.

The attitude of the Gorbachev regime towards religion has been one of toleration that has developed into quiet approval. The Russian Orthodox Church in particular has been quick to point out the social importance of the church in areas like education and the care of the sick and elderly, and also in helping the numerous alcoholics and drug addicts. Thousands of churches and cathedrals (including St Basil's in Moscow and Kazan Cathedral in Leningrad) have been given back to the Church and are being restored. Although Gorbachev has declared himself an atheist, his mother is a practising Christian who had her son baptised.

Soviet Jews, historically subjected to the most cruel discrimination in the USSR, have been less trusting of the greater religious freedoms. In 1990 more than 200,000 Soviet Jews moved to Israel, pouring in at the rate of up to 3000 immigrants a day, and the flow is continuing.

In Buryatia, the centre of Soviet Buddhism, many of the monasteries are reopening. Since all were a long way off the tourist beat they have not been kept up in good repair as museums (unlike churches in European Russia like St Basil's, for example).

As you visit religious centres in the USSR, bear in mind the tremendous expense of restoring places of worship that have been closed for decades and give generously, preferably in hard currency.

(Opposite) The Bell Tower of Ivan the Great. Built in 1600 this 81m stone tower withstood Napoleon's attempts to blow it up in 1812.

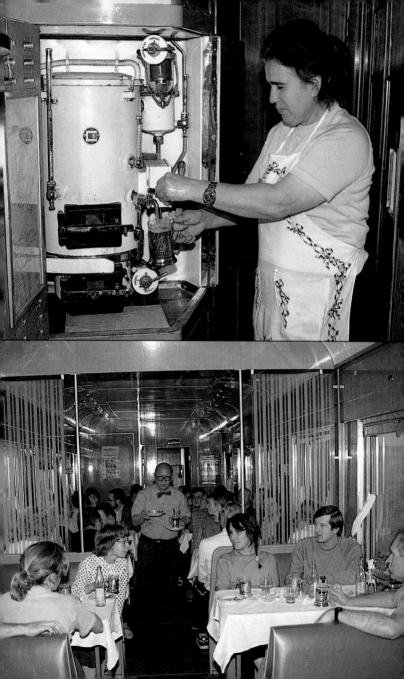

Practical information for the visitor

DOCUMENTS, TICKETS AND VOUCHERS

(Also see Part 1: Planning Your Trip.) I read somewhere of one Englishman who left his passport and tickets behind in London and yet still managed to travel across Russia on the Trans-Siberian using no other document than a six-monthly ticket to the Reading Room at the British Museum. Entry requirements are somewhat stricter these days. The essential documents are your **passport**, Russian visa (which is thoughtfully supplied as a separate document so no-one need ever know that you've been there) and a **visa** for the first country you will be entering after the USSR. If you are travelling independently, don't forget the rail and hotel **vouchers** with which Intourist should have supplied you, and if you've arranged a Beijing-Moscow ticket from the UK don't forget your voucher to exchange for a ticket at CITS in Beijing. It's worth bringing some additional document of identification (e.g. **driving licence**) as your passport will be confiscated by the hotel when you check in. It is now possible to rent self-drive cars in Moscow and Leningrad in which case you will need an International Driving Licence (available from the AA).

An **International Student Card** is useful for buying rail tickets in Hungary but since museums and art galleries are not expensive in the USSR it's not much use there. Part of the IS Card is written in Russian, which might impress someone. Note that if you're arriving from Africa or South America you may be required to show a yellow fever vaccination certificate. Travellers arriving from Asian countries where there have been recent outbreaks of cholera (Bangladesh, for example) may be asked to show cholera vaccination certificates. Check with Intourist before you leave as regulations change.

CROSSING THE BORDER

Baedeker gave the following warning to travellers in his 1914 guidebook (*Russia with Teheran, Port Arthur and Pekin*): 'Whether at the railway frontier station or at a sea-port the customs examination of passengers' luggage is generally thorough.' Things have changed

---

(Opposite) Top: A constant supply of hot water is provided in each compartment by the coal-fired stove-samovar (*batchok*). **Bottom:** Travellers await lunch in the Soviet Railways dining car. Note that no alcohol is sold on the train.

now and Western travellers get off lightly but until the late 1980s Baedeker's advice would have been accurate. A band of over-zealous officials used to rummage through your dirty socks, subject the contents of your wash-bag to their scrutiny and remove any articles of literature to another compartment, where the official censor tried to find magazines and books to add to his collection. The changes show *glasnost* in action.

Customs declaration form

At the border you will be given a customs declaration form on which you must declare the number of pieces of luggage you have, all money (travellers' cheques and cash) and valuables (camera, radio, jewellery etc.). You must keep this form with you until you leave, when it may be checked. You must be sure to get it stamped each time you exchange money. It is now harder for customs officials to determine whether you have or have not been exchanging money on the Black Market since with all the new hard-currency restaurants and shops, it could just as easily have been spent legally. Don't sell anything you've declared on the form (Walkman or camera, for example) or if you're going to don't declare it.

Customs allowances: entering the country

Each person (over 16 years of age) may bring into the USSR one litre of wine, half a litre of spirits and 250 cigarettes or 250g of tobacco without paying duty. You may also bring in a video tape-recorder, camera and up to five blank cassettes, radio, cassette-recorder or typewriter but they must be portable. Reasonable amounts of food are allowed but you may get your fruit confiscated as the USSR is taking no chances with the Californian fruit fly. You are also forbidden to bring into the country any Soviet roubles (these may be obtained at the border), weapons and narcotics.

Customs allowances: leaving the country

Foreigners are allowed to take out two litres of wine, one litre of spirits and 250 cigarettes (although I can hardly imagine anyone wanting to take home that many Cosmos cigarettes), and gifts (not including foodstuffs and tobacco) up to a total value of 30 roubles (approx £30). Antiques may not be exported unless a special permit is obtained. A reasonable number of souvenirs may be taken out of the country.

HOTELS

The two things that immediately strike one about modern Soviet hotels are that they are usually of gargantuan proportions and about as interesting, from the architectural point of view, as the average multi-storey car-park in the West. This having been said, some of the old hotels in Moscow and Leningrad are being restored to a very high standard in joint ventures with foreign companies. Many of the 'Soviet modern' hotels can accommodate over 2000 people and The Rossiya in Moscow holds the record as the world's largest hotel. In its 3200 rooms the hotel has beds for a total of 6000 guests.

Checking in

This is not always the swift procedure it should be. After the receptionist has kept you waiting for a while, she will relieve you of your passport and hand you a small pass-card without which you will be unable to get into your room. (In some of the more expensive hotels you may actually be given your key by the receptionist). The keys to the rooms are usually kept by the *Dezhurnaya* (floor attendant), very often an elderly female busy-body who passes the time drinking tea in her little den, and keeping her eagle eye on all that goes on on her floor. You may be able to get hot water or a kettle off her for drinks.

Bedrooms

Unless you are staying in the most expensive deluxe accommodation, you will be surprised by the shoddiness of your new home, considering the fact that you probably had to fork out a small fortune for it. In some of the older hotels the rooms are vast and comfortable but they're rather smaller in more modern places. They are generally furnished with heavy wooden cabinets and decked out in the worst possible taste. In one room I stayed in, one wall was papered with pink roses, the others in a bold orange geometric design and purple nylon curtains completed the schizophrenic decor. Beds are often too short, usually of orthopaedic hardness and bedding consists of blankets in a duvet-cover. Other equipment in the room includes a colour television and a telephone. Wake-up calls may be arranged at the reception desk.

Bathrooms

All bedrooms for foreigners (except those for student tour groups) are equipped with bathrooms of a sort. They feature broken fittings, dripping taps, a lavatory with a dislocated and usually cracked seat and no plugs in either bath or basin. The manager of the Olgina Hotel where I stayed in Leningrad was obviously trying to give his establishment an air of American efficiency and cleanliness - I found a long paper notice that read 'Sanitized', suspended over the un-flushed loo in my bathroom! The hot water system is generally reliable in Moscow and Leningrad but not in Siberia. Here you should have a bath or shower whenever you find hot water. Don't forget your universal bathplug, soap and loo paper.

INTOURIST

Although the state tourist organisation lost its monopoly status in 1990 it is so large a company (owning most of the hotels) that it is likely to control the destiny of the majority of visitors for many years to come. Intourist will attempt to cater for your every whim while you are here. The relationship between the western tourist (or 'guest' as Intourist calls you) and the organisation is not always the symbiotic and happy relationship that both sides might wish for. However, many tourists find Intourist and their guides perfectly charming and get on well with them. The best advice is to make good use of the organisation when you need it (for changing travel arrangements) and avoid it when you don't.

Intourist services
From the Service Bureau in their hotels Intourist offers set tours of local sights, books theatre tickets, arranges guides and interpreters and orders taxis and arranges other transport for you. Most services must be paid for in foreign currency. The tours tend to cover a lot of ground in quite a short space of time and are a mixture of what Intourist feels you would like to be shown and of what the organisation feels would be good for you to see. Many tours, therefore, still include a visit to the war memorial and there are tours which concentrate specifically on factories or co-operative farms. As far as Intourist is concerned, your visit is as much an educational experience as a holiday.

Tours, guides and interpreters
In Moscow and Leningrad, where you've got a limited amount of time and a vast number of sights, it's probably worth taking a tour. Prices are around US$10 for a city tour. In other cities you will probably see just as much by wandering round on your own. Details of tour programmes for each city are listed in the appropriate section in Part 4: City Guides and Plans

Sputnik
Basically junior Intourist, Sputnik is the International Youth Travel Bureau of the USSR. The organisation runs hotels, holiday camps and tours where the young of the West can meet the young of the Communist East. Tours are booked through Intourist and specialist travel agencies outside the USSR.

LOCAL TRANSPORT

When you are arranging your trip you may be encouraged to purchase 'transfers' which mean you will be met at airport or station and taken to your hotel. The prices charged for this service can be astronomical (£25 + for one to three people, although most transfers are less than this) and in many cases they are not necessary. If you're arriving at an airport there's bound to be a tour group that you can tag along with, and there are often Intourist buses waiting to meet trains. If your hotel is near a metro station you can get there for a mere 15 kopecks. However, if you want to take a taxi from the station, beware of drivers who meet you on the platform and offer you their services at extortionate rates, usually in hard currency.

Taxis

The desire for hard currency has now made it almost impossible for visitors in tourist areas to pay in roubles - US$ or Marlboro cigarettes are the required taxi currency. If you refuse to pay in hard currency and point out to the driver that he is breaking the law you'll probably find yourself on the pavement. The way to find a rouble-accepting taxi driver is to go to the places where local people catch taxis (ie not outside Intourist hotels). In Moscow and Leningrad you'll probably have to pay in hard currency wherever you get your taxi but in Siberian towns the bus station is often a good place to find uncorrupted taxi-drivers. You can also flag one down in the street (a green light indicates that it is free), or join a taxi queue, identified by a sign and a crowd of people. They are usually supervised by a woman who will ask you in advance for your destination and then shout it to the driver when he arrives. If someone else is going your way you can share the cab. If they get out before you, make sure you get a reduction on the fare. All taxis have a meter, prices are very low and tips are not given by locals. You may even get people in private cars offering you lifts to make a little money on the side. Agree on a price before getting in. As in any Western city it is inadvisable for women to do this alone.

Metro

A very cheap and quick way to get around with a flat fare of 15 kopecks and trains every few minutes. In Moscow it's worth using the metro just to see the stations which are more like subterranean stately homes with ornate ceilings, gilded statues and enormous chandeliers. There are no tickets, just put a 15 kopeck coin into the turnstile to get in (change machines are provided). Be careful not to fall over getting on the escalator - they move at least twice as fast as those in the West. Soviet metro systems are built rather deeper underground than their western counterparts, some say to act as shelters in case of nuclear attack. Because they're so far down, escalators need to be extremely long as well as swift. You will therefore not be surprised to learn that the world's longest escalator (Lenin Square station, Leningrad) has 729 steps and rises 59 metres.

In the street, metro stations are indicated by a large blue M. If you need translations of the maps, these are provided for in Part 4. In the stations, lines are named by the terminal stations, as on the Paris metro. One peculiarity you will notice is that, where two lines intersect, the station is given two names, one for each line. As the train moves off, the next station is announced over the intercom. A metro system is being built in Novosibirsk and some stations are already open. There is, however, no metro in Irkutsk or Khabarovsk.

Bus

In all cities there is a bus service (often very crowded) and sometimes also trolley-buses and trams. The fare is the same as for the metro: 15 kopecks per journey. Some buses have conductors, some ticket machines and in others tickets are purchased from the driver in booklets of 6. In buses without conductors, you must punch the ticket yourself, using one of the machines by the windows. If the bus is crowded and you can't reach, hand the ticket to someone near the machine and they will do it for you. If you happen to be standing near a ticket puncher, you will probably spend the journey being passed tickets. Occasionally, inspectors get on the buses to check tickets, imposing on-the-spot fines for those without punched tickets.

Internal flights

These usually involve long delays and far too much sitting around in airports. I would avoid flying in the USSR, not because I think it unsafe but because it leaves you with no control over changed circumstances. If you're travelling on the ground there are always alternatives if one form of transport fails. However some places in Siberia (Yakutsk for example) are accessible to the tourist only by air. If you do fly, watch out for the flies...'There's always one hovering around, whether you're Aeroflotting in Europe, Central Asia or Siberia and I now feel that having one on board is a good omen for the holiday. On the odd occasion you might even have a whole family of flies on board - then you're in for the holiday of a lifetime!' Kathy Olley (UK)

TRAILBLAZER feedback 'When we went to present our tickets at Khabarovsk for our Flight SU811 to Niigata the Aeroflot official there refused point-blank to accept our tickets (which were issued by Intourist London and British Airways) on the flimsy excuse that our air travel started in the USSR, and that such tickets must be issued by Aeroflot. To say all hell broke loose would be an understatement, but the only way we could leave Khabarovsk was to purchase new tickets. My wife was in tears, there were people shouting, gesticulating and threatening us as we continued to hold up the queue in order to try to justify our rights. The furore lasted nearly an hour'. Bill Edwards (NZ).

Boat

Most of the cities you will visit are built on rivers and short trips on the water are usually possible. In Leningrad the best way to reach Petrodvorets is by jet-boat. You can also get to Lake Baikal by boat up the Angara from Irkutsk. Possibly the most exciting river trip you can make is from Yakutsk to the Lena Pillars.

Car Rental

In Leningrad and Moscow it is possible to rent a self-drive car. Charges are high and you will need an international driving-licence (as well as your normal licence).

ELECTRICITY

In most cities in the USSR this is 220v. 50 cycles AC. Sockets require a continental-type plug or adapter. In some places the voltage is 127v so you should enquire at the reception desk before using your own electrical appliances. Sockets are provided on the train for electric razors.

TIME

The Soviet Union spans eleven time zones and on the Trans-Siberian you will be adjusting your watch an hour almost every day. The railway runs on Moscow time and timetables do not list local time. It can be disconcerting to cross the border from China at breakfast-time to be informed by station clocks that it is really only 2.00am. Moscow time (MT) is three hours ahead of Greenwich Mean Time. Siberian time zones are listed throughout the route guide and the main cities are in the following zones: Novosibirsk (MT+4), Irkutsk (MT+5), Khabarovsk (MT+7).

MONEY

The rouble is the basic unit of Soviet currency and this is divided into 100 kopecks. Notes are in denominations of 1, 3, 5, 10, and 25 roubles and there are coins of 1, 2, 3, 5, 10, 15, 20, 50 kopecks, and 1 rouble. Note that 50 and 100 rouble notes were withdrawn from circulation in early 1991 and are now worthless. Black marketeers may try and palm them off on you.

There are two rates of exchange for tourists, one for Intourist Services and for use in Beriozka shops (although prices are marked in roubles you must pay in hard currency) and another for roubles to be spent in non hard-currency shops. The first rate has been approximately 1 rouble to £1 for many years. The second rate has jumped from 1 rouble to £1 in 1989, to 10 roubles to £1 in 1990, to almost 50 roubles to £1 in 1991 in order to try to kill off the Black Market.

Banks

You will not usually need to go further than your hotel *Bureau de Change* as the rate of exchange is the same wherever you cash your travellers' cheques. The service charge is one per cent for each transaction and you must make sure you get the currency declaration form (handed out on entering the country) stamped each time. Don't change too much money at a time as you will find there's not an awful lot to spend it on. Keep small denomination foreign notes for foreign currency bars and Beriozka shops. If you're crossing Mongolia note that US$ are required for the restaurant-car.

Tipping

The official policy is against tipping. It is seen as nothing less than bribery: the thin end of the corruption wedge. *Glasnost* has been at work here too, though, and you'll find that now certain people (taxi-drivers and waiters in co-operative restaurants) have come to accept the practice. It's really up to you but the Russians don't. If you want to thank your guide or your carriage attendant on the train, the best way of doing so is not with money but with a small gift of some kind, preferably something that is obviously Western and, therefore, to the Russian, rather exotic. Scented soap, perfume, cosmetics, tights, cigarettes, chewing gum or any Western food product will all go down well.

POST AND TELEPHONES

Postal needs are also satisfied by your hotel, which sells post-cards, writing paper and stamps. Stamps cost 45 kopecks for an air letter, 35 kopecks for a post-card to Western countries. Telegrams cost about 10 roubles and are sent from the central telegraph office in each city. International telephone calls cost about 10 roubles to West Europe, 15 roubles to Japan and 18 roubles to the USA. For further details see under the appropriate city heading in Part 4.

BROCHURES AND NEWSPAPERS

The hotel will supply you with glossy brochures detailing local sights. Most hotels also have a small bookshop where you can now buy a range of Western papers and magazines as well as *Pravda* (English translations available); local guide-books; and (sometimes) maps. Newspaper kiosks in most towns also stock these maps when available, and a good range of postcards.

NATIONAL HOLIDAYS

- 01 Jan: New Year's Day
- 06 Jan: Russian Orthodox Christmas Day. Declared a holiday by the Russian parliament in 1991 for the first time since 1917.

- 08 Mar: International Women's Day.
- 01 May: International Working People's Solidarity Day
- 09 May: Victory Day, to commemorate the end of World War II
     (the 1941-45 Great Patriotic War)
- 07 Oct: Constitution Day
- 07 Nov: Anniversary of the Great October Socialist Revolution

FESTIVALS

Annual arts festivals in Moscow include Moscow Stars (05 - 15 May) and Russian Winter (25 Dec to 05 Jan). Prices for tours and hotels are reduced by 10-20 per cent in winter. The most interesting festival is Leningrad's White Nights, held around the summer solstice when the sun does not set. The days are separated by only a few hours of silvery light: a combined dusk and dawn. The theatres and concert halls save their best performances for this time and a festival is also held at Petrodvorets.

FOOD

In spite of the recent food shortages in the country visitors are well taken care of, although the general standard of hotel food has fallen over the last five years. No one ever came to the Soviet Union for the food alone but that doesn't mean you won't have some really good meals. There's rather more to Russian cuisine than borsch and chicken Kiev but as you'll be eating most of your meals on the train, you will not have many chances of finding this out. You will probably leave with the idea that Russian cooking is of the school dinner variety, with large hunks of meat, piles of potatoes and one veg (the interminable cabbage), followed by ice-cream. If you are stopping along the way you should try some of the local restaurants.

You will realise from the generous proportions of the average Russian, male or female, that these people like their food, or at least they certainly get more of it than they need. A substantial breakfast (served at around 08.00) will provide you with enough energy to tackle even the heaviest sight-seeing schedule. The first meal of the day consists of fruit juice (good if it's apple juice), cold meat or cheese, eggs, bread, jam and *kefir* (thin, sour yoghurt). Lunch (13.00 - 14.30) and dinner (from 19.00) will be of similarly large size, consisting of at least three courses. Meat dishes can be good but there is a shortage of fresh fruit and vegetables.

Zakuski

This is the Russian name for hors d'oeuvres, which consist of some or all of the following: a selection of cold meat, sausages, salmon, pickled herring, paté, various vegetables, sturgeon and caviare (see below). Large quantities of vodka are usually drunk with *zakuski*.

Soups

Soviet soups seem to be uniformly good and filling - meals in themselves with a stack of brown bread. Best known is *borsch*: beetroot soup which often includes other vegetables (potatoes, cabbage and onion) chopped ham and a swirl of sour cream (*smetana*). Cabbage soup or *shchi* is the traditional soup of the proletariat and was a favourite of the last Tsar. Nicholas II is said to have detested caviare, since it gave him severe indigestion. He preferred plain peasant cooking (to the great disappointment of his excellent French chef). *Akroshka* is a chilled soup made from meat, vegetables and *kvas* (thin beer). *Rassolnik* is a soup of pickled vegetables.

Fish

These include herring, halibut, salmon and sturgeon. These last two may be served with a creamy sauce of vegetables. In Irkutsk you should try *omul*, the famous Lake Baikal fish which has a deliciously delicate flavour.

Meat

Everyone's heard of chicken Kiev (fried breast of chicken filled with garlic and butter). This delicious, cholesterol-rich dish (famous for the way in which it spurts butter at you as you cut into it) has become so well-known in Britain that you can even get it in ready-to-cook packs from your local supermarket. Almost as famous is *boeuf* Stroganov, beef stew with sour cream and mushrooms. It is named after the great merchant family who financed the first Siberian military expedition in the 1580s. The most popular regional specialities come from the southern republic of Georgia and include *shashlik* (kebab), chicken *tabaka* (chicken with garlic sauce) and *pilaf* (rice with spiced meat). From Siberia come *pelmeni*, which are small dumplings filled with meat and served in soup or as a main course. If you're expecting a thick hunk of sirloin when you order *beefstek* you will be disappointed - it's just a compressed lump of minced meat.

Caviare

This exotic delicacy, the roe of the sturgeon, becomes more expensive as it gets rarer. There are four species which are acknowledged to produce the best caviare: beluga, sterlet, osetra and sevruga. They are all to be found in the Caspian and the Black Sea. To produce its characteristic flavour (which should not be too 'fishy') a complicated process is involved. First the female fish is stunned with a mallet. Her belly is slit open and the roe sacs removed. The eggs are washed and put through strainers to grade them into batches of a similar size. The master-taster then samples the roe and decides how much salt to add for preservation.

Processed caviare varies in colour (black, red or golden) and also in the size of the roe. It is eaten either with brown bread and butter or else served with sour cream in *blinis* (thin pancakes). You can get it in most tourist hotels but is difficult to buy outside the Beriozka shops. On the train red caviare is occasionally available. Black marketeers (often hotel waiters who will sidle up to your table with a jar hidden under a dishcloth) often try to swap caviare for Western goods.

Puddings

Very often the choice is limited to ice-cream (*morozhenoye* - uniformly good and available everywhere) and fruit compôte (a disappointing fruit salad of a few pieces of tinned fruit floating in a large dish of syrup). You may, however, be offered *blinis* with sour cream and fruit jam; *vareniki* (sweet dumplings filled with fruit) or rice pudding. There is very little fresh fruit, unless you are staying in one of the more expensive hotels.

Bread

Russian bread is wholesome and filling and on your restaurant table you will find a plate piled with a stack of white or sour brown slices. Soviet tourist literature claims that over one hundred different types of bread are baked in Moscow. Russian 'bread technology' is said to be so much in demand in the West that Soviet experts have had to build a brown bread factory in Finland.

Drinks

● **Non alcoholic** Most popular is tea, traditionally served black in a tall glass with a spoonful of fruit jam or sugar. Milk is not always available so you are advised to take some of the powdered variety with you. Coffee (introduced by Peter the Great at the end of the 17th century) is also available although its quality tends to be variable. It's worth taking a jar of instant coffee with you. Bottled mineral water is available everywhere but it often tastes rather too strongly of all those natural minerals that are supposed to be so good for you. There are several varieties of bottled fruit juice, of which apple seems to be the most consistently good. The Soviets finally capitulated to American fizzy drink companies and until recently allowed only one cola manufacturer (Pepsi) to avoid competition. Coke is becoming available in some places now as is Fanta Orange.

● **Alcoholic** Vodka predominates, of course, but the Russians will be disgusted if you start putting tonic water or lime juice into it. It should be drunk neat in small single shot glasses which are drained in one. It is usual to eat while you drink, indeed *zakuski* (see above) should never be served without vodka. The spirit has its origins in twelfth century Poland and Russia (although some say it was brought back from Holland by Peter the Great) and the word vodka means 'little water', something of an understatement. If you tire of the original product, there are several flavoured vodkas to sample: lemon, cherry, blackberry or pepper. Wines tend to be rather too sweet for the Western palate. Russian champagne is surprisingly good and cheap. Beer is available in most hotels and restaurants. You should also try *kvas* a fermented mixture of stale brown bread, malt sugar and water. A popular drink, sold on the streets during the summer, its alcohol content is so low it's hardly noticeable at all.

One of the biggest problems about alcoholic drinks in the USSR is that, outside the hotels, they are difficult to find. Vodka is not sold on trains (except occasionally by Black Marketeers), so if you wish to glide across Siberia in an alcoholic stupor, you will have to bring your own. Beer is sometimes available, though only very occasionally. If you're on the Chinese train, the Chinese carriage attendants often have a good supply for around US$1 per can.

Alcoholism in the USSR

This has been a serious problem here since long before the Revolution. Drink was virtually the only way in which the Russian peasant could escape his oppressed position for a few hours. Travelling through Russia in 1895, R.L. Jefferson reported: 'Drunkenness as we know it is as a flea-bite to a Russian drunk. In one of the towns I passed through I was surprised to see twenty or thirty men lying in the road-way outside a *gostinitca* dead drunk - and they would remain until the effects of the vodki had evaporated from their brains and they could get home.'

Siberian colonists in the eighteenth and nineteenth centuries set up vodka distilleries in their remote outposts and the native tribes quickly became addicted. Early explorers in the Yakutsk area reported that native babies were insensible most of the time, owing to the fact that their mothers fed them liquor in large quantities. The men who drove sledges and *tarantasses* (carriages) across Siberia, in the days before the railway, were perpetually drunk, it being the only way to fight the cold. Most of the accidents that frequently occurred along the post road, were the result of drivers who were very much 'under the influence'. In 1914, Tsar Nicholas II banned the production of vodka but a flourishing black market grew up quickly.

The situation as far as alcohol dependency goes has hardly changed since then. The average life expectancy of male Soviet citizens is said to have fallen from 68 years in the mid 1970s to 64 in 1985. When Mikhail Gorbachev came to power in March 1985 he was determined to crack the problem which was by then costing the country millions of roubles in lost working days and additional health care each year. In May 1985 the crackdown was announced with severely reduced licensing hours and a ban on the sale of alcohol on trains. The reduced licensing hours has resulted only in longer queues. There is a popular Moscow joke which tells of Brezhnev returning from the dead and, upon seeing the great crowd of people outside the liquor shop he says: 'So people are drinking more vodka now than they did when I was Party Secretary'. The difficulty in obtaining one of life's little essentials in the USSR has led to a many people resorting to making alcohol and beer at home, which is illegal. Since Gorbachev has been in power more than 200,000 people have been punished for home-brewing, with more than 1,000 sent to prison.

RESTAURANTS

The restaurant scene over the last few years has been revolutionised by the co-operatives that mushroomed after Gorbachev's Individual Enterprise Law (May 1987) allowed groups of people to set up in business on money borrowed from the state. The problem now is that they are being so heavily taxed that their prices are escalating and they're no longer a viable alternative for the budget traveller, unless payment can be made in roubles, which is becoming more difficult these days. Some co-operatives accept roubles for lunch only, credit cards or hard currency only for dinner. Advance bookings are necessary for dinner.

As well as these co-operatives there are restaurants run by the local city council some of which are good, serving regional specialities. However, the two problems here are language and the fact that local restaurants are usually very popular with local people and it is often difficult to get in. The Service Bureau in your hotel may be able to book a table for you, otherwise the only way is to join the queue outside the restaurant.

The first obstacle to get past is the doorman who usually tries to turn all custom away, whether or not there are places in the restaurant. Next you must leave your coat with the cloakroom attendant as it is considered unhygienic to take it into the dining room. Next approach the woman behind the desk near the door who will assign you a table or shake her head and inform you that there are no free tables as you gaze across the empty room. If she tries to turn you away, this is the time to start acting the crass, pushy foreigner. Don't allow yourself to be turned away too easily. In these state-run establishments they seem to regard an unheralded extra customer as an imposition.

Once you have been shown to your table you will have more than enough time to try and interpret the menu. Many of the dishes that have prices pencilled against them will in fact be unavailable. Once you have ordered, you face an even longer wait for your food to arrive. When Russians go to a restaurant, they go in large groups and they like to make a meal last the evening. Waiters do their best to ensure no dish arrives too quickly and a dance-band entertains customers, with folk-songs and Western hits from the sixties at so high a volume that you can't ignore them. Nevertheless a visit to a local restaurant can be an entertaining and drunken affair especially if you get invited to join a Russian party. Note that tsarist traditions die hard: if a man wishes to invite a woman from another table to dance he will ask permission of the men at her table before she joins him on the dance-floor

If you're able to pay in roubles Soviet restaurants can be ridiculously cheap by Western standards. However, if you have to pay with hard currency and have had a large meal with vodka and champagne you can easily run up a very large bill. Check that you have not been overcharged as this happens quite often.

The cheapest places to go are the self-service cafés found in most shopping streets and these are also your best bet if you're in a hurry.

WHAT TO DO IN THE EVENING

If you're expecting a wild nightlife during your stay in the USSR, you may be disappointed. There are a few late-night foreign-currency bars in the better hotels but for most people it's lights out before midnight. Apart from going to a restaurant (which, as indicated above, will take up most of the evening), entertainment in the evening is basically of a cultural nature. You can visit the opera, theatre, ballet or circus and tickets can be arranged through the Service Bureau in your hotel (for hard currency). It is also possible to buy them from the kiosks in the street or at the box-office (for roubles) on the day of the performance. For more popular shows you are more likely to get a ticket if you let the hotel make the arrangements. Performances tend to start early: usually between 18.00 and 19.00.

Ballet

The season lasts from September to May and you should not miss the experience of a night at the Bolshoi in Moscow or the Kirov in Leningrad. Apart from the quality of the dancing, famous throughout the world, tickets cost far less than Covent Garden prices and the buildings themselves are magnificent. Black Marketeers sell tickets for the Bolshoi on the steps before the performance but you should make sure you're being sold a valid ticket. Note that many touring groups dance at the Bolshoi so it may not be the famous company you see the night you go. You may be interested to know that Rudolf Nureyev, Russia's most famous star, was 'shaken out' of his mother's womb on the Trans-Siberian as it was rattling along towards Lake Baikal.

Opera and theatre

In the past opera was encouraged more than the theatre as it was seen as politically neutral. *Glasnost* has encouraged playwrights to produce drama that reflects Soviet life as it is, rather than as the government would like people to see it. This has led to several successful new theatre groups opening in Moscow and Leningrad. Details of plays and operas are available from the Service Bureau. There are also several puppet theatres which are highly recommended if you have the time.

Cinema and video

In the 1980s the Soviet film industry also benefited from the greater freedoms that came with *glasnost*. In early 1987, one of the most controversial films (and a considerable box-office success) was *Is It Easy To Be Young?*, which was deeply critical of the Soviet war in Afghanistan. In the 1990s the pessimism of the people towards life under Gorbachev is reflected in films made here. *Little Vera* (1990) is the story of a provincial girl who sinks into small-time prostitution and finally drowns herself. Gorbachev walked out of it saying he disapproved of the sex scenes. In *Executioner* (1991) a woman journalist takes on the Mafia in Leningrad and doesn't win. More Western and American movies are being allowed into the country and censorship laws have been relaxed. In Jan 1991 *Gone with the Wind* was one of the most popular films to see. There are cinemas in every town and shows start early in the evening. Films are shown as a whole programme with a couple of short educational films before the main feature.

'Video Bars' are becoming very popular now and to be seen even in Siberia.

An incident at the cinema

It's interesting to go to a film in the Soviet Union as much to watch the audience's reactions to it as for the film itself. In Irkutsk our programme started with a long, boring 'short' about an artist who produced the kind of glassware that Woolworths would reject. Then followed another film in which an old war veteran walked around a field beside a railway track and reminisced about his experiences. The camera hardly moved for twenty minutes and the audience was becoming noticeably bored. Three lads in the back row cracked a joke and started laughing, whereupon a woman in uniform stood up and shouted angrily that it was men like this veteran who had given their lives for the country and they deserved respect for the sacrifices they had made. She might not have got away with it in European Russia or the Baltic Republics but here in Siberia the effect was startling and instantaneous: utter silence while the veteran droned on. The main film was about adulterous goings-on in an army camp and ended with the moral of the story heavily hammered home as jealous husband knifed his wife's lover while the credits rolled.

SHOPPING

This can be a complicated and frustrating affair in the Soviet Union. The shops are very crowded and if they're not, this is usually a sign that there's nothing worth buying in them. There is the story of the wife of a Soviet official, who, accompanying her husband on a visit to London, went shopping in Oxford Street. She was greatly impressed by the quality and attractive packaging of the goods. However, she came home with the idea that because the shops did not seem to be as tightly packed with people as in Moscow, it was obvious that the people couldn't afford the tempting things offered for sale.

Queues

In Soviet shops demand far exceeds supply for most goods. You will see people queuing for things but the queues are usually not as long as reports in the Western press would lead you to believe. Nevertheless most Russians carry a small string bag called an *avoska* (a just-in-case bag) and are quick to notice a queue forming, joining it even before they know what the queue is for. The reasoning is that, even if they don't want the article, if they can get hold of one thing that is in short supply, they will be able to swap it for something they want that someone else has bought.

Making a purchase

The procedure for buying something is rather more complicated than in the West and exactly the same as the outmoded purchasing process that still exists in the department stores of New Delhi. First you must decide what you want to buy and find out the price (the assistant may write this down on a ticket for you). Then go to the cash desk (where an abacus may be used to calculate the purchase price of the goods you want) and pay, getting a receipt. This must then be taken back to the first counter and exchanged for your purchases.

Department stores

No visit to Moscow would be complete without a visit to GUM, the largest department store in the USSR. It comprises an enormous collection of arcades housed in an impressive glass-roofed building, rather like a giant greenhouse. The store claims to serve 146 million people per year, accounting for 10 per cent of the capital's non-food retail trade. There is another chain of department stores: TSUM, which has branches in most of the larger cities.

Beriozka shops and hard-currency stores

While local shops are interesting to visit, you will soon find that they contain very little you would actually want to take home as presents or souvenirs. The best I could come up with in GUM one Christmas was a tube of Sputnik After Shave Cream and some packets of Red Star Brand biscuits. Foreign consumers will find their desires best served by the Beriozka shops - branches in most Intourist hotels and in all cities that are open to tourists. Come prepared with small denomination notes and be warned that your change will come in whatever currency is in the till. If you are after vodka and caviare then the Beriozka shop is the only place you will be able to find them easily. Joint-venture hard-currency shops, stocking a wide range of Western products, are being opened in some of the hotels in Moscow and Leningrad.

Opening Hours

Large department stores are open from 08.00 to 21.00 Monday to Saturday. Smaller stores have a wide range of opening times, anywhere between 08.00 and 11.00, closing between 20.00 and 23.00, with an hour's lunch-break either from 13.00 to 14.00 or 14.00 to 15.00. Most shops are closed on Sundays.

THINGS TO BUY

Handicrafts

These include the attractively decorated black lacquer *palekh* boxes (that the icon-makers started producing when their religious art lost popularity after the Revolution); enamelled bowls and ornaments; embroidered blouses and tablecloths from the Ukraine; large black printed scarves; guitars and balalaikas; lace tablecloths and handkerchieves; jewellery and gemstones from Siberia and the Urals; rugs from the southern republics and painted wooden ornaments (including the ubiquitous *matrioshka* dolls which fit one inside the other). Modern variations on the *matrioshka* doll include leaders of the USSR ('Gorby' dolls) and the Beatles. Badges and plaster busts of Lenin are rapidly losing shelf-space to the above.

Until recently the best quality items were to be found only in the Beriozka shops but now the craft markets in Moscow and Leningrad are producing some very high quality crafts.

Books

The only English-language books you will find are the range of guide-books produced by Progress Publishers, Lenin's works and a few other edifying tomes. Some of the Russian-language art books are worth buying for their photographs and they're not expensive. Some shops stock large, colourful posters which are popular amongst Westerners. There are branches of Dom Knigi (House of Books) in Moscow and Leningrad.

Records

Whilst the records themselves are not as high quality as in the West, they are still cheap. There is a fairly wide range of classical records and folk music as well as local pop groups blossoming under *glasnost*. One of the most popular stars in the Soviet pop world was Dean Reed, an American who 'defected' to the East and died under mysterious circumstances in June 1986. Melodiya (the state-run label) also produces, under licence, records by several Western groups famous outside the USSR in the sixties and seventies. The Beatles have always had a large following in the USSR but it was only in March 1986 that their records went on sale outside the black market.

Clothes

Most are over-priced and shoddy and unless you have a penchant for wide ties, nylon shirts and terylene trousers there are few clothes you would want to buy during your visit. If you are interested in fur hats and coats these are available but may be expensive; this depends on which exchange rate you're working with. Try GUM in Moscow or the Beriozka shops, especially in Siberia. Black Marketeers may offer you rabbit-fur hats as well as Soviet military clothing which you should keep out of sight as you leave the country or it might be confiscated by the customs officials.

Food and Drink

Vodka and caviare are as popular with tourists as with Russians and more easily available in the Beriozka shops. Caviare is about a quarter of the Beriozka price if bought on the Black Market (from a hotel waiter). Soviet chocolate bars and chocolate covered sweets are very good and sometimes available outside the Beriozkas.

SPECULATION

The days are gone when you could finance your day-to-day needs in the USSR from a pair of Levis swapped on the street-corner for a fistful of roubles. It's not that people aren't keen to buy almost anything Western off you, rather that there's less to spend your roubles on (many restaurants now demanding hard currency while most travel arrangements may no longer be paid for in roubles). With foreign travel restrictions on Soviets lifted, US dollars are what the people are after to fund their trips and also to spend in hard currency shops. For a while many travellers changed money on the black market at up to three times the bank rate. To counter this, in 1991 the bank rate for foreign currencies went up to five times what it had been previously, (£1 now buys around 50 roubles) and no doubt this will increase again. The situation is changing so fast that the best advice on how to change your money is to check the bank rate (in your hotel) and the black market rate (from other travellers and from the touts) and decide whether the (small) risk involved in dealing on the black market is worth it.

● **Speculators**   You will have no difficulty in meeting people wanting to buy clothes and dollars from you. They hang around the places tourists are most likely to go to: hotels, Red Square in Moscow and Nevsky Prospect in Leningrad. From your clothes, they will recognise you as a potential source of Western goods and will sidle up and ask you something in Russian. Your blank look satisfies them that you are indeed a genuine tourist. They then ask if you speak English and there may be a few more pleasantries exchanged before the line of conversation is abruptly altered and a price is suggested for the shirt you are wearing, or perhaps a swap for the 'Gorby' watch, rabbit-fur hat or *matrioshka* dolls they happen to have with them. There seem to be two types of speculators, the black market touts who want a quick exchange of roubles or rabbit-fur hats and the younger speculators who are often students. They are happy to show you around, help you get into a restaurant or may even offer you floorspace in their flat for the night if you've got no hotel booked. It's definitely worth spending some time with these people even if you're not making anything in the exchange of your T-shirt or dollars with them. See page 33 for what to bring into the country.

• **Spending your roubles** How ever you come by your roubles you should be aware that there are now fewer things you can do with them. There's very little in the shops (liquor and caviare rarely available except from Beriozka shops); tourist shops (Beriozkas) take hard currency only; it's not easy to get taxi-drivers to abide by the law and take your roubles; it's getting more difficult to pay for travel arrangements in the country in roubles and many restaurants now demand hard currency.

• **The Black Market** is an integral part of life in the Soviet Union and involves much more than the purchase of dollars from Western tourists. It is often the only way to get spare parts for machines in industry, fresh fruit and more exotic vegetables, and a whole range of household goods. Ten per cent of the population of Moscow are said to be involved to some extent in this lucrative private sector but Gorbachev has recently introduced new laws to combat corruption and speculation. This may not be one of his wiser policies, given the contribution the black market makes to keeping many of the machines in industry working and people supplied with products that have no other source. Needless to say the Mafia are heavily involved.

CRIME

Along with the harmless black-marketeering has grown a disturbing protection racketeer movement. These gangs, using 'heavies' recruited from the army use violence to extort money from black marketeers and the new private enterprises. The owners of co-operatives are forced to pay protection money running into tens of thousands of roubles or face their properties being set on fire. Taxi-drivers have been threatened with having their cars damaged or families attacked. There are several gangs operating in the cities and there have even been reports of shoot-outs between rival gangs in the streets of Moscow and Leningrad likened to Chicago in the 1920s. Local people will tell you that it is not the local council that runs their city but the Mafia.

The Soviet Union is still a safe place for tourists to visit but a little more care should be taken these days. Crimes against tourists are something that were almost unimaginable ten years ago but now a new branch of the police force has had to be set up to protect tourists. The situation is not as bad as in New York or even some other European capitals but you shouldn't wander around late at night, especially in Moscow or Leningrad. It also helps not to dress too ostentatiously or wear expensive jewellery or watches.

Travellers have reported that petty pilfering from hotel rooms has increased quite considerably over the last few years - mainly small things like chocolate bars and biscuits. Don't take valuables on holiday with you and leave your passport at the hotel reception desk. A money-belt for travellers' cheques and foreign currency you'll be carrying with you is worth considering.

An unnamed Soviet man fined in Yalta for illegal dealing in cigarettes took revenge by setting fire to the court building with Molotov cocktails, destroying part of the building. (Reuter) The *Times* 19 Mar 1991.

PART 3: SIBERIA AND THE RAILWAY

Historical outline

EARLY HISTORY

Prehistory: the first Siberians

Recent discoveries at Dering Yuryakh (100km south of Yakutsk) have indicated that man may have lived in Siberia for far longer than had previously been thought. Unconfirmed evidence from this site suggests human habitation stretching back as far as 1-2 million years ago, which would place the site on a par with Professor Leakey's discoveries in East Africa. There is rather more recent evidence of man in the Lake Baikal area. In the thirteenth millennium BC Stone Age nomads were roaming round the shores of the lake, hunting mammoths and carving their tusks into the tubby fertility goddesses that can been seen in the museums of Irkutsk today. Several of these sites in the Baikal area have been discovered and the railway passes through one at the village of Malta, 45 miles west of Irkutsk, where a camp dating back to this early period has been excavated.

By the Neolithic Age (twelfth to fifth millennia BC) there is far more archaeological evidence and it shows that the nomadic tribes had reached the Arctic Circle and moved into North America through Alaska. These northern tribes trained dogs to pull their sledges but were left behind technologically, remaining in the Stone Age until Russian colonists arrived in the mid-seventeenth century.

In the south, however, several Bronze Age cultures emerged around the central parts of the Yenisei River. Afanassevskaya, south of Krasnoyarsk, has given its name to the culture of the people who lived in this area in the second millennium BC. They made pottery and decorated it with a herring-bone pattern. The first evidence of permanent buildings has been found near Achinsk, where the Andronovo people built huge log cabins in the first millennium BC. Excavations of sites of the Karassuk culture, also dated to the first millennium BC, have yielded Chinese artifacts, indicating trade between these two peoples.

Early civilisations

The Iron Age sites show evidence of more complex and organised societies. The clear air of the Altai Mountains has preserved the contents of numerous graves of the Tagar Culture which existed here in the second century BC. Their leaders were embalmed and buried like Egyptian pharaohs with all that they might need in the after-life. In their burial mounds archaeologists have found perfectly preserved woollen blankets, decorated leather saddles and the complete skeletons of horses, probably buried alive when their master died.

The Huns moved into the region south of Lake Baikal in the third century BC where the Buryats, their descendants, now live. Their move west continued slowly over the next five centuries when their infamous leader Attila, the 'Scourge of God', having pillaged his way across Europe, reached Paris where he was defeated in 452 AD.

The ancestors of the Kirghiz people of West Siberia were the Tashtyks, who built large houses of clay (one found near Abakan even has an underfloor central heating system), moulded the features of their dead in clay death masks and decorated their bodies with elaborate tattoos. The tiny modern Kirghiz Republic in the extreme south of the country is all that remains of a once mighty empire that stretched from Samarkand to Manchuria in the twelfth century AD. In the following century, the Kirghiz were taken over by the rapidly advancing Mongols. Genghis Khan's Mongol empire grew to become the largest empire ever, including the Tartars of South Russia, and the peoples of North Asia, Mongolia and China.

The first Russian expeditions to Siberia

In mediaeval times, Siberia was known to Russians only as a distant land of valuable fur-bearing animals. There were occasional expeditions from Novgorod in the fifteenth century. These became more frequent in the sixteenth century, once the lands of South Russia had been released from the grip of the Mongols by Tsar Ivan the Terrible who seized Kazan and Astrakhan, opening the way to Siberia. Yediger, the leader of a small Siberian kingdom just over the Urals, realised his vulnerability and sent Ivan a large tribute of furs, declaring himself a vassal of the Tsar.

Yediger's son, Kuchum, was of a more independent mind and, having murdered his father, he put an end to the annual tribute of furs, proclaiming himself Tsar of Siberia. Since Ivan's armies were occupied on his western frontiers, he allowed the powerful Stroganov family to raise a private army to annex the rebel lands. In 1574 he granted them a twenty-year lease on the land over the Urals as far east as the Tobol River, the centre of Kuchum's kingdom.

Yermak: the founder of Siberia

The Stroganovs' army was a wild bunch of mercenaries led by ex-pirate Yermak, the man now recognised as the founder of Siberia. They crossed the Urals and challenged Kuchum, gaining control of his lands after a struggle that was surprisingly long, since the Russians were armed with muskets, the enemy with swords and bows and arrows. On 5th November 1581, Yermak raised the Russian flag in Isker (near modern Tobolsk) and sent the Tsar a tribute of over 2500 furs. In return Ivan pardoned him for his past crimes, sent him a a fur-lined cape that had once graced the royal shoulders and a magnificent suit of armour. Over the next few years Yermak was constantly harassed by Kuchum. On 16th August 1584, the enemy ambushed them when they were asleep on an island in the Irtysh. The story goes that Yermak drowned in the river, dragged under by the weight of the armour given him by the Tsar. His name lives on as the top brand of Soviet rucksack.

The quest for furs

Over the next fifty years Cossack forces moved rapidly across Siberia, establishing *ostrogs* (military outposts) as they went and gathering tributes of fur for the Tsar. Tyumen was founded in 1586, Tomsk in 1604, Krasnoyarsk in 1628, Yakutsk in 1633 and by 1639 the Cossacks had crossed the width of the country reaching the east coast. Like the Spanish Conquistadors in South America they dealt roughly with the native tribes they met, who were no match for their muskets and cannons. The prize they lusted after was not gold (as it was for the Spaniards in Peru and for later Russian adventurers in Siberia) but furs. In the days before fur farms certain pelts were worth far more than they are today. From the proceeds of a season's trapping in Siberia a man could buy and stock a large farm with cattle and sheep. The chances that such a man would be successful in finding his way into or out of the dark, swampy forests of the *taiga* were not very high but quite a few did.

Khabarov and the Amur

In 1650, a Russian fur merchant named Khabarov set out from Yakutsk to explore the Amur region in what is now the Far Eastern Territories. He found the local tribes extremely hostile as the Russians' reputation for rape and pillage had spread before him. The land was fertile and rich in fur-bearing animals and Khabarov and his men committed such atrocities that the news reached the ears of the Tsar, who ordered him back to the capital to explain himself. Bearing gifts of fur, he convinced the Tsar that he had won valuable new lands which would enrich his empire. The local tribes, however, appealed to the Manchus, their southern neighbours, who sent an army to help them fight off the Russians. The Tsar's men were gradually beaten back but periodic fighting went on until 1689, when the Russians were forced out of Manchuria and the Amur by the Treaty of Nerchinsk.

Eighteenth-century explorers

Peter the Great became Tsar in 1696 and initiated a new era of exploration in the Far East. By the following year the explorer, Atlassov, had claimed Kamchatka for Russia. In 1719 the first scientific expedition set out for Siberia. Peter commissioned the Danish seaman, Vitus Bering, to try to find a northern sea-passage to Kamchatka and the Sea of Okhotsk (unaware that the route had been discovered by Deshnev eighty years before). However, the Tsar did not live to see Bering set out in 1725.

Between 1733 and 1743 another scientific expedition, comprising naval officers, topographers, geodesic surveyors, naturalists and astronomers, made detailed charts of Russians lands in the Far East. Fur traders reached the Aleutian Islands and the first colony in Alaska (on Kodiak Island) was founded in 1784 by Gregory Shelekhov. (His grave is in the cemetery of the Church of the Holy Saviour in Irkutsk.) The Russian colony of Alaska was sold to the United States in 1868 for the bargain price of two cents an acre.

THE NINETEENTH CENTURY

There were two developments in Siberia in the nineteenth century which had a tremendous effect upon its history. First, the practice of sentencing criminals to a life of exile or hard labour in Siberia was increased to provide labour for the mines and to establish communities around the military outposts. The exile system, which caused a great deal of human misery, (see page 73) greatly increased the population in this vast and empty region. Secondly, and of far greater importance was the building of the Trans-Siberian Railway in the 1890s (described in a later section).

Colonisation

By the end of the eighteenth century, the population of Siberia was estimated to be about one and a half million people, most of whom belonged to nomadic native tribes. The policy of populating the region through the exile system swelled the numbers of settlers but criminals did not make the best colonists. As a result, voluntary emigration from overcrowded European Russia was encouraged by the government. Peasant settlers could escape the bonds of serfdom by crossing the Urals but Siberia's reputation as a place of exile was not much of an incentive for them to move.

As the railway penetrated Siberia, the transport of colonists was facilitated. Tsar Alexander's emigration representatives were sent to many thickly-populated regions in Russia in the 1880s. They offered prospective colonists incentives including a reduced rail fare (6 roubles for the 2,000km journey) and a free allotment of twenty-seven acres of land. Prices in Siberia were high for most things and colonists could expect get up to 100 per cent more than in European Russia for produce grown on this land. Many peasants left Europe for Siberia after the great famine of 1890-91.

Further exploration and expansion

Throughout the century scientists and explorers continued to make expeditions to Siberia, recording their discoveries in the region. The lands of the Kirghiz in south-west Siberia were explored by geologists and naturalists and annexed by the Tsar. In 1829, an expedition led by the German scientist Baron von Humboldt, who had become famous for his scientific explorations in South America, investigated the geological structure of the Altai plateau (southern Siberia).

In 1840, the estuary of the Amur was discovered and colonisation encouraged, after Count Muraviev-Amursky, Governor General of Eastern Siberia, had annexed the entire Amur territory for Russia. This was in flagrant violation of the Russo-Chinese Treaty of Nerchinsk, which had been signed in 1689. However, the Chinese were in no position to argue, being threatened by the French and English as well as by internal troubles in Peking. By the Treaty of Peking (1860) they ceded the territory north of the Amur to Russia, and also the land east of the Ussuri, including the valuable Pacific port of Vladivostok.

THE EXILE SYSTEM

The word 'Siberia' meant only one thing in Victorian England and nineteenth century Russia - an inhospitable land of exiled murderers and other evil criminals who paid for their sins by working in the infamous salt mines. To a great extent this was a true picture of Siberia except that the prisoners were mining gold, silver and coal rather than salt. Some of the first exiles sent over the Urals did indeed work in salt mines which may be why people associated Siberia with salt. By the year 1900, over one million people had been exiled and made the long march over the Urals to the squalid and overcrowded prisons of Siberia.

George Kennan

In 1891 a book entitled *Siberia and the Exile System* written by George Kennan, was published in America. It exposed the truly horrific conditions under which prisoners were kept in Siberia and aroused public opinion in both America and Britain. Kennan was a journalist working for the New York *Century Magazine*. He knew Siberia well, having previously spent two years there. He was then unaware, however, of quite how badly the convicts were treated and in a series of lectures before the American Geographical Society he defended the Tsarist government and the exile system. When his editor commissioned him to investigate the system more thoroughly, the bureaucrats in St Petersburg were happy to give him the letters of introduction which allowed him to venture into the very worst of the prisons and to meet the governors and convicts. The government hoped, no doubt, that Kennan would champion their cause. Such had been the case with the Rev Dr Henry Landsell who had travelled in Siberia in 1879. In his account of the journey *Through Siberia*, he wrote that 'on the whole, if a Russian exile behaves himself decently well, he may in Siberia be more comfortable than in many, and as comfortable as in most of the prisons of the world.' After the year he spent visiting Siberian prisons, Kennan could not agree with Landsell and the inhumanity of the exile system, the convict mines and the terrible conditions in the overcrowded prisons were all revealed in his book.

The first exiles

The earliest mention of exile in Russian documents of law is in 1648. In the seventeenth century, exile was used as a way of getting rid of criminals who had already been punished. In Kennan's words: 'The Russian criminal code of that age was almost incredibly cruel and barbarous. Men were impaled on sharp stakes, hanged and beheaded by the hundred for crimes that would not now be regarded as criminal in any civilised country in the world, while lesser offenders were flogged with the *knut* (a whip of leather and metal thongs, which could break a man's back with a single blow) and *bastinado* (cane), branded with hot irons, mutilated by amputation of one or more of their limbs, deprived of their tongues, and suspended in the air by hooks passed under two of their ribs until they died a lingering and miserable death.' Those who survived these ordeals were too mutilated to be of any use so they were then driven out of their villages to the lands beyond the Urals.

Exile as a punishment: the convict mines

With the discovery of valuable minerals in Siberia and the shortage of labourers available to mine them, the government began to use criminals to work them. Exile was thus developed into a form of punishment and extended to cover a range of crimes including desertion, assault with intent to kill and vagrancy (when the vagrant was of no use to the army or the community). It was also the punishment for offences that now seem nothing short of ridiculous. According to Kennan, exile became the punishment for fortune-telling, prize-fighting, snuff-taking (the snuff-taker was not only banished to Siberia but also had the septum between his nostrils torn out) and driving with reins. (The old Russian driver had been accustomed to ride his horse or run beside it - using reins was regarded as too Western, too European.)

Abolition of the death penalty

In the eighteenth century demand for labour for the mines continued to grow and the list of exilable crimes was further extended to include drunkenness and wife-beating, the cutting down of trees by serfs, begging with a pretence to being in distress, and setting fire to property accidentally. In 1753, the death penalty was abolished (for all crimes except an attempt on the life of the Tsar) and replaced by exile with hard labour. No attention was given to the treatment of exiles en route, they were simply herded like animals over the Urals, many dying on the way. The system was chaotically corrupt and disorganised, with hardened murderers being set free in Siberia while people convicted of relatively insignificant offences perished down the mines.

Reorganisation in the nineteenth century

In the nineteenth century the system became more organised but no less corrupt. In 1817 a series of *étapes* (exile stations) was built along the way to provide overnight shelter for the marching parties. They were nothing more than crude log cabins with wooden sleeping platforms. Forwarding prisons were established at Tyumen and Tomsk, from where prisoners were sent to their final place of exile. From Tyumen, convicts travelled by barge in specially designed cages to Tomsk. From here some would be directed on to Krasnoyarsk or else to Irkutsk, a 1040 mile, three-month march away. The prisoners would be sent from these large centres to smaller prisons, penal colonies and to the mines. The most infamous mines were on the island of Sakhalin, off the east coast, where convicts dug

The Siberian Boundary Post (circa 1880) In this melancholy scene, friends and relatives bid exiled prisoners farewell by the brick pillar that marked the western border of Siberia, on the Great Post Road.

for coal; the mines at Kara, which Kennan states were producing an annual average of 3,600 pounds of pure gold in the late nineteenth century; and the silver mines of Nerchinsk.

Records were started in 1823 and between this date and 1887, when Kennan consulted the books in Tomsk, 772,979 prisoners had passed through on their way to Siberia. They comprised *katorzhniki* (hard labour convicts) who were distinguishable by their half-shaved heads; *poselentsi* (penal colonists); *silni* (persons simply banished and allowed to return to Russia after serving their sentence), and *dobrovolni* (women and children voluntarily accompanying their husbands or fathers). Until the 1850s hard-labour convicts and penal colonists would be branded on the cheek with a letter to indicate the nature of their crime. More than half of those who crossed the Urals had had no proper trial but were exiled by 'administrative process'. As Kennan states: 'Every village commune has the right to banish any of its members who, through bad conduct or general worthlessness, have proved themselves obnoxious to their fellow citizens.'

Life in the cells

The first prison Kennan was shown round on his trip in 1887, was the Tyumen forwarding prison. He records the experience thus: 'As we entered the cell, the convicts, with a sudden jingling of chains, sprang to their feet, removed their caps and stood in a dense throng around the *nari* (wooden sleeping platforms)...."The prison" said the warden,"is terribly overcrowded. This cell for example is only 35 feet long by 25 wide, and has air space for 35, or at most 40 men. How many men slept here last night?" he inquired, turning to the prisoners. "A hundred and sixty, your high nobility", shouted half a dozen hoarse voices.....I looked around the cell. There was practically no ventilation and the air was so poisoned and foul that I could hardly force myself to breathe it in.'

The hospital cells

None of these dreadful experiences could prepare Kennan for the hospital cells, filled with prisoners suffering from typhus, scurvy, pneumonia, smallpox, diphtheria, dysentery and syphilis. He wrote afterwards: 'Never before in my life had I seen faces so white, haggard, and ghastly as those that lay on the gray pillows in the hospital cells....As I breathed that heavy, stifling atmosphere, poisoned with the breaths of syphilitic and fever-stricken patients, loaded and saturated with the odor of excrement, disease germs, exhalations from unclean human bodies, and foulness inconceivable. It seemed to me that over the hospital doors should be written "All hope abandon, ye who enter here".' From the records he discovered that almost 30 per cent of the patients in the prison hospital died each year. This he compared with 3.8 per cent for French prisons of the time, 2 per cent for American and 1.4 per cent for English prisons.

Corruption

As well as the grossly inhuman conditions he saw in the prisons, Kennan found that the whole exile system was riddled with corruption. Bribes were regularly accepted by warders and other officials. One provincial administrator boasted that his governor, the Governor of Tobolsk, was so careless that he could get him to sign any document he was given. As a wager he wrote out 'The Lord's Prayer' on an official form and placed it before the Governor who blindly signed it. The government in St Petersburg was too far away to know what was going on in the lands beyond the Urals.

Many high-ranking officials in Siberia were so tightly bound by bureaucratic ties that change was impossible, even if they desired it. An officer in the Tomsk prison confided in Kennan: 'I would gladly resign tomorrow if I could see the (exile) system abolished. It is disastrous to Siberia, it is ruinous to the criminal, and it causes an immense amount of misery; but what can be done? If we say anything to our superiors in St Petersburg, they strike us in the face; and they strike hard - it hurts!'

Political exiles

Life for the so-called 'politicals' and 'nihilists', banished to prevent them infecting European Russians with their criticisms of the autocratic political system that was choking the country to death, was luxury compared to that of the prisoners. Many came from rich aristocratic families and, after the move to Siberia, life for them continued in much the same way as it had west of the Urals. The most famous political exiles were the 'Decembrists': the men who took part in the unsuccessful coup in 1825. Some of the houses in which they lived are now preserved as *'Dom'* (house) museums in Irkutsk (see page 160).

Kennan secretly visited many of the 'politicals' in Siberia and was convinced that they did not deserve being exiled. He wrote later: 'If such men are in exile in a lonely Siberian village on the frontier of Mongolia, instead of being at home in the service of the state - so much the worse for the state.' A few politicals were sentenced to exile with the native Yakut tribe within the Arctic Circle. Escape was impossible and life with a Stone Age tribe unbearable for cultured men who had until recently been part of the St Petersburg court circle.

Temporary abolition of the exile system

The exile system was abolished in 1900. However corrupt the system and inhuman the conditions in these early Siberian prisons, worse was to come only thirty years later. Under Stalin's regime, vast concentration camps (in European Russia as well as in Siberia) were set up to provide a huge slave-labour force to build roads, railways and factories in the 1930s and '40s. The camps were strictly off-limits to twentieth century George Kennans but former inmates have reported that the prisoners were grossly overworked and undernourished. The mortality rate in some of these camps is said to have been as high as thirty per cent. Reports of the number of people sentenced to these slave labour camps range from between three million and twenty million. Some reports place the death toll up to the late 1950s as high as eighteen million. Prison labour is still used in the Soviet Union today with prisoners being kept in Corrective Labour Camps, administered by the KGB but conditions are far less severe.

Political exiles (circa 1880), many of whom came from aristocratic families, were free to adopt whatever lifestyle they could afford within the confines of Siberia.

Early travellers

VICTORIAN ADVENTURERS

This was the great age of the gentleman (and woman) adventurer. These upper-class travellers spent the greater part of their lives exploring the lesser-known regions of the world, writing long and usually highly-readable accounts of their adventures and encounters with the natives. Siberia attracted almost as many of this brave breed as did Africa and India. Once they had travelled across the great Siberian plain using the normal forms of transport of the time (carriage and sledge) they resorted to such new-fangled inventions as the bicycle (R.L.Jefferson in 1896), the train (from 1900) and then the car (the Italian Prince Borghese in an Itala in 1907). Some even crossed the country entirely on foot.

THE GREAT SIBERIAN POST ROAD

Before the railway was built, there was but one way for convicts, colonists and adventurers to cross this region: a rough road known as the Post Road or *Trakt*. Posting stations were set up at approximately 25 mile intervals along the route, where travellers could rent horses and drivers. Murray, in his *Handbook for Russia, Poland and Finland* (1865 edition) told his travellers: 'Three kinds of conveyances are available: the *telega*, or cart without springs, which has to be changed at every station, and for which a charge of about 8d is made at every stage; the *kibitka* or cart (in winter a sledge) with a hood; and the *tarantass*, a kind of carriage on wooden springs which admits of the traveller lying down full length and which can be made very comfortable at night. The two latter vehicles have to be purchased at Perm, if the *telega*, or postal conveyance be not accepted. A *tarantass* may be bought from £12 to £15.'

George Kennan called the Imperial Russian Post System 'the most perfectly organised horse express service in the world'.

(Opposite) Post Houses (Posting Stations) were set up at twenty-five mile intervals along the Great Post Road in the nineteenth century. They provided travellers with fresh horses, carriages or sledges (although most people travelled in their own), inedible meals and squalid accommodation. This is a fortified example (*ostrog*) to be seen at the open-air museum near Irkutsk.

The discomforts of Siberian travel

Since a visit to Siberia could rarely be completed in a single season, most travellers experienced the different modes of transport used in summer and winter. They found the sledge more comfortable than the *tarantass* and indeed no nineteenth century travelogue would be complete without a detailed description of this unique vehicle. The *tarantass* had a large boat-shaped body and travellers stored their belongings on the floor, covering them with straw and mattresses on top of which they lay. Although this may sound comfortable, when experienced at speed over atrocious roads and for great distances, by contemporary accounts it was not. S.S.Hill wrote in 1854: 'The worst of the inconveniences arose from the deep ruts which were everywhere...and from the necessity of galloping down the declivities to force the carriage upon the bridges. And often our carriage fell with such force against the bridges that it was unsafe to retain our accustomed reclining position...'

Kate Marsden, a nurse travelling in 1894, recalled the agony of days spent in a *tarantass* in the following way: 'Your limbs ache, your muscles ache, your head aches, and, worst of all, your inside aches terribly. "*Tarantass* rheumatism" internal and external, chronic, or rather perpetual, is the complaint.'

The yamshchiki

The driver (*yamshchik*) of the *tarantass* or sledge, was invariably drunk. He had to be bribed with vodka to make good time between the post stations and Murray's 1865 guide-book thoughtfully includes in its 'Useful Russian Phrases' section, the words 'Dam na vodki' (I will give you drink money). Accidents were commonplace and R.L. Jefferson (on a trip without his bicycle in 1895) wrote that his *yamshchik* became so inebriated that he fell off the sledge and died. The same fate befell one of Kate Marsden's sledge-drivers who had gone to sleep with the reins tied around his wrists. She wrote: 'And there was the poor fellow being tossed to and fro amongst the legs of the horses, which, now terrified, tore down the hill like mad creatures.... In a few minutes there was a fearful crash. We had come into collision with another *tarantass* and the six horses and the two *tarantasses* were mixed up in a chaotic mass'.

(Opposite) Top: Yaroslavl Station. Trans-Siberian trains depart from and arrive at this station in Moscow. **Bottom:** Winter in Red Square, Moscow, with the sinister bulk of Lenin's mausoleum on the left.

The horses

Sledges and *tarantasses* were pulled by a *troika*, a group of three horses. These were small furry specimens, 'not much larger than the average English donkey', noted R.L.Jefferson. They were rented between post stations and usually belonged to the *yamshchik*. S.S.Hill was shocked at the way in which these animals were treated. He remarked: 'The Arab is the friend of his horse. The Russian or Siberian peasant is his severe master who exacts every grain of his strength by blows accompanied with curses....lodges him badly or not at all, cares little how he feeds him, and never cleans him or clips a hair of his body from the hour of his birth to that of his death.'

Horses were worked literally until they died. R.L.Jefferson recalls that two of his animals dropped dead in harness and had to be cut free.

Dangers

Travel in Siberia was not only uncomfortable, it was also dangerous. Wolves and bears roamed the forests and when food was scarce would attack a horse or man (although you were safe in a *tarantass*). In the Amur region lived the world's largest tiger, the Amur tiger. Just as wild as these animals, and probably more dangerous, were the *brodyagi*, escaped convicts in search of money and a passport to readmit them to Europe.

Dirt and disease

As well as the discomfort of the 'conveyance' and the dangers along the *Trakt*, travellers were warned about the dirt and disease they could encounter. R.L.Jefferson wrote: 'No wonder that Siberia is looked upon by the traveller with abhorrence. Apart from its inhabitants, no one can say that Siberia is not a land of beauty, plenty and promise; but it is the nature of its inhabitants which make it the terrible place it is. The independence, the filth and general want of comfort which characterize every effort of the community, serve to make a visit to any Siberian centre a thing to be remembered for many years and an experience not desirable to repeat.'

Hotel rooms were universally squalid. Kate Marsden gives the following advice to anyone entering a hotel bedroom in Siberia: 'Have your pocket handkerchief ready...and place it close to your nostrils the moment the door is opened. The hinges creak and your first greeting is a gust of hot, foetid air.'

(**Above**) Until the building of the Trans-Siberian, the Great Post Road formed the life-line for hundreds of tiny communities such as this. (**Below**) There were few bridges on the Road — crossing frozen rivers and lakes was treacherous in early winter and spring.

Insects

Especially in the summer months, travellers were plagued by flies and mosquitoes. Kate Marsden wrote: 'After a few days the body swells from their bites into a form that can neither be imagined nor described. They attack your eyes and your face, so that you would hardly be recognised by your dearest friend.'

At night, travellers who had stopped in the dirty hotels or posting stations were kept awake by lice, bed-bugs and a variety of other insects with which the bedding was infested. R.L.Jefferson met a man who never travelled without four saucers and a can of kerosene. In a hotel at night he would put a saucer filled with kerosene under each bed-leg, to stop the bugs reaching him in bed. However, Jefferson noted that: 'With a sagacity which one would hardly credit so small an insect, it would make a detour by getting up the wall on to the ceiling, and then, having accurately poised, drop down upon the victim - no doubt to his extreme discomfort.'

Bovril and Jaeger underwear: essential provisions

R.L.Jefferson, who made several trips to Russia (three of which were on his Imperial Rover bicycle) never travelled without a large supply of Bovril and a change of Jaeger 'Cellular' underwear - 'capital stuff for lightness and durability' he wrote after one long ride. Kate Marsden shared his enthusiasm for Dr Jaeger's products: 'without which it would have been quite impossible to go through all the changes of climate; and to remain for weeks together without changing my clothes', she wrote. On the subject of provisions for the trip, Murray recommended taking along basic foodstuffs. Miss Marsden packed into her *tarantass* 'a few boxes of sardines, biscuits, some bread, tea and one or two other trifles which included forty pounds of plum pudding'.

S.S.HILL'S 'TRAVELS IN SIBERIA'

This two-volume account of Hill's Siberian adventures was the result of a journey made in the early 1850s to Irkutsk and then Yakutsk (now in the Far Eastern Territories). Armed with a pistol loaded with goose-shot (for the law forbade a foreigner to shoot at a Russian, even in self defence), he travelled by *tarantass* and existed on *shchi* (soup) and tea for most of the time. He makes some interesting observations upon the culinary habits of the Siberians he met along the way.

He records that on one occasion, when settling down to a bowl of *shchi* after a long winter's journey 'we found the taste of our accustomed dish, however, today peculiar'. He was made aware of the main ingredient of their soup later, 'by the *yamshchik* pointing out to us the marks of the axe upon the frozen carcass of a horse lying within a quarter of a verst of the site of our feast'. In some places even tea and *shchi* were unavailable and they could find only cedar nuts ('a favourite food article with the peasants of Eastern Siberia').

He ate better in Irkutsk, where, at a dinner party, he was treated to *comba* fish, six feet in length and served whole. 'I confess I never before saw so enormous an animal served or cooked whole save once, an ox roasted at a 'mop' in Worcestershire', he wrote later. He was shocked by the behaviour of the ladies at the table, who, when bored, displayed 'a very droll habit of rolling the damp crumb of rye bread... into pills'. He remarks with surprise that in Siberian society ' a glass of milk terminates the dinner'.

KATE MARSDEN VISITS SIBERIAN LEPERS

Miss Marsden was a nurse with a definite mission in Siberia. In the 1880s she learnt, through travellers' accounts, of the numerous leper colonies to the north of Yakutsk. There were rumours of a special herb found there, that could alleviate the symptoms of the disease. After an audience with Queen Victoria, during which she was given useful letters of introduction, she travelled to Moscow. She arrived, in mid-winter, wearing her thin cotton nurses' uniform and a white bonnet, which she immediately exchanged for thick Russian clothes.

Crossing Siberia

When she had met the Empress, who gave her a thousand roubles for her relief fund, she started on her long sledge ride. It was not a dignified send-off - 'three muscular policemen attempted to lift me into the sledge; but their combined strength was futile under the load'. She got aboard eventually and was soon experiencing the extreme discomfort of Siberian travel. She said it made her feel more like 'a battered old log of mahogany than a gently nurtured English-woman'.

Distributing tea, sugar and copies of the Gospel to convicts in the marching parties she encountered along the *Trakt*, she reached Irkutsk in the summer. She boarded a leaky barge on the Lena River, north of Lake Baikal and drifted down to Yakutsk, sitting on the sacks of potatoes with which the boat was filled. Of this part of the journey she wrote: 'Fortunately we had only about 3,000 miles of this but 3,000 miles were enough'. Her goal was still a 2,000 mile ride away when she reached Yakutsk. Although she had never been on a horse before, this brave woman arranged an escort of fifteen men and rode with them through insect infested swamps and across a fiery plain, below which the earth was in a constant state of combustion, until she reached the settlement of Viluisk.

The Lepers of Viluisk

On her arrival, the local priest informed her that 'On the whole of the earth you will not find men in so miserable a condition as the Smedni Viluisk lepers'. She found them dressed in rags, living in hovels and barely existing on a diet of rotten fish. This was in an area where, in winter, some of the lowest temperatures in the world have been recorded. Unfortunately she did not find the herb rumoured to exist there but she left all the more convinced that finances must be raised for a hospital.

Although she managed to raise 25,000 roubles towards the enterprise, her task was not made any easier by several individuals who took exception to her breezy style of writing, accusing her of having undertaken the journey for her own fame and fortune. Some even suggested that the journey was a fiction invented so that Miss Marsden could collect charitable sums for her own use. In the end she was forced to sue one of her attackers who wrote a letter to the *Times* describing her journey as 'only a little pleasure trip'. Nevertheless she achieved her aim and a hospital was opened in Viluisk in 1897.

JEFFERSON'S BICYCLE TRIPS

R.L.Jefferson was an enthusiastic cyclist and traveller who made several journeys to Siberia in the 1890s. A year after bicycling from London to Constantinople and back, he set out again from Kennington Oval for Moscow on his Imperial Rover bicycle. Twelve hours out of Moscow, a speeding *tarantass* knocked him down, squashing the back wheel of his 'machine'. Repairs took a few days but he still managed to set a cycling speed record of just under fifty days for the 4,281 mile journey from London to Moscow and back.

His next ride was to the decaying capital of the Khanate of Khiva, now in Soviet Uzbekistan. The 6,000 mile journey took him across the Kirghiz Steppes in south-west Siberia, along the coast of the Aral Sea and over the Kara Kum Desert. When the bicycle's wheels sank up to their axles in the sand he had the Rover lashed to the back of a camel for the rest of the journey. While in Central Asia he lived on a diet of boiled mutton and *koumis* (fermented mares' milk). He travelled in a camel-hair suit (Jaeger) and top boots, with a white cork helmet to complete the outfit.

Across Siberia

Jefferson then made two more trips to Siberia. In *Across Siberia by Bicycle* (1896), he wrote that he left Moscow and 'Sleeping the night in some woodman's hut, subsisting on occasional lumps of black bread, bitten to desperation by fearful insects, and tormented out of my life during the day by swarms of mosquitoes, I arrived in Perm jaded and disgusted...'. He then cycled over the Urals and through the mud of the Great Post Road to Yekaterinburg (now Sverdlovsk). Here he was entertained by the Yekaterinburg Cyclists' Club whom he described as 'friends of the wheel - jolly good fellows all'.

Declaring that 'From a cyclist's point of view, Russian roads cannot be recommended', he left his Imperial Rover behind in 1897 for the adventure described in *Roughing it in Siberia*. With three other men, he went on the train to the end of the line (Krasnoyarsk) and thence by sledge 'jerking about like peas in a frying pan'. They travelled up the frozen Yenisei to visit the gold mines in the Minusinsk district, where they spent several weeks prospecting in the Syansk Mountains.

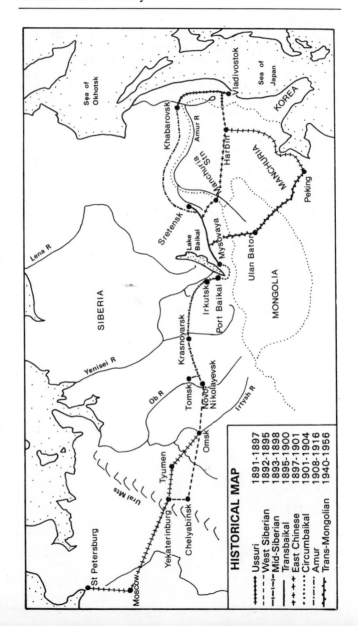

Building the railway

The first railway to be built in Russia was Tsar Nicholas I's private line (opened in 1836) which ran the ten miles from his capital, St Petersburg, to his summer palace at Tsarkoye Selo (now Pushkin). The Tsar was said to have been most impressed with this new form of transport and over the next thirty years several lines were laid in European Russia, linking the main cities and towns. Siberia, however, was really too far away to deserve serious consideration since most people only went there if they were forced to as exiles. And as far as the Tsar was concerned, traditional methods of transport kept him supplied with all the gold and furs he needed.

PLANS FOR A TRANS-SIBERIAN RAILWAY

The earliest plans for long distance railways in Siberia came from a number of foreigners. Most books which include a history of the Trans-Siberian give a passing mention to an English engineer, if only because of his wildly eccentric ideas and his unfortunate name. Thus a Mr Dull has gone down in history as the man who seriously suggested the building of a line from Perm across Siberia to the Pacific, with carriages being pulled by wild horses (of which there were a great many in the region at the time). He is said to have formally proposed his plan to the Ministry of Ways of Communication, who turned it down.

The Englishman's name was, in fact, not Dull but Duff and it is not only his name that has been distorted through time. His descendants (John Howell and William Lawrie) have requested that the story be set straight. Thomas Duff was an enterprising adventurer who went out to China to seek his fortune in the 1850s. He returned to England via Siberia, spending some time in St Petersburg with wealthy aristocratic friends. Here he was introduced to the Minister of Ways of Communication and it was probably during their conversation that he remarked on the vast numbers of wild horses he had encountered on his journey. Could they not be put to some use? Perhaps they might be trained to pull the trains that people were saying would soon run across Siberia. It is unlikely that this remark was intended to be serious but it has gone down in history as a formal proposal for a horse-powered Trans-Siberian Express.

At around this time the American Perry McDonough Collins was exploring the Amur river, having persuaded the US government to appoint him as their commercial agent in the region. He had been given an enthusiastic welcome by Count Amurski Muravyev, the Governor-General of Siberia, before setting off to descend the Amur in a small boat. Collins envisaged a trade link between America and Siberia with vessels sailing up the Amur and Shika rivers to Chita, where a railway link would shuttle goods to and from Irkutsk. He sent his plans for the building and financing of such a line to the government but these too were rejected. Collins' next venture, a telegraph link between America and Russia, also failed but not before he had made himself a considerable fortune.

It took a further twenty years for the government to become interested enough in the idea of a railway in Siberia to send surveyors to investigate the feasibility of such a project. Plans were considered for the building of lines to link the great Siberian rivers, so that future travellers could cross Siberia in relative comfort by a combination of rail and ship. European lines were extended from Perm over the Urals, reaching Yekaterinburg in 1878.

Tsar Alexander III : the railway's founder

In 1881 Alexander III became Tsar and in 1886 gave the Trans-Siberian project his official sanction, with the words: 'I have read many reports of the Governors-General of Siberia and must own with grief and shame that until now the government has done scarcely anything towards satisfying the needs of this rich, but neglected country! It is time, high time!'

He was thus able to add 'Most August Founder of The Great Siberian Railway' to his many other titles. He rightly saw the railway as both the key to developing the land beyond the Urals and also as the means to transport his troops to the Amur region which was being threatened by the Chinese. When the commission looking into the building of the new line declared that the country did not have the money to pay for it, the Tsar solved the problem by simply forming a new committee, dismissing the first.

THE DECISION TO BUILD

The new commission took note of the petitions from Count Ignatyev and Baron Korf, the Governors-General of Irkutsk and the Amur territories, respectively. They proposed rail links between Tomsk and Irkutsk, Lake Baikal and Sretensk (where passengers could board ships for the journey down the Shilka and Amur Rivers to the coast) and for the Ussuri line to Vladivostok. Baron Korf considered that it was imperative for the Ussuri line to be built as soon as possible if the valuable port of Vladivostok was not to be cut off by the advancing Chinese. The Tsar took note and declared: 'I hope the Ministry will practically prove the possibility of the quick and cheap construction of the line'.

Surveys were commissioned and detailed plans prepared. In 1891 it was announced that the Trans-Siberian Railway would indeed be built and work would start immediately. It was, however, to be constructed as cheaply as possible using thinner rails, shorter sleepers and timber (rather than stone) for the smaller bridges.

The route

The railway committee decided that the great project should be divided into several sections with work commencing simultaneously on a number of them. The West Siberian Railway would run from Chelyabinsk (the railway over the Urals reached this town in 1892) to the Ob River where the settlement of Novo Nikolayevsk (now Novosibirsk) was being built. The Mid-Siberian Railway would link the Ob to Irkutsk, the capital of Eastern Siberia. Passengers would cross Lake Baikal on ferries to Mysovaya, the start of the Transbaikal Railway to Sretensk. From here they would continue to use the Shilka and Amur River for the journey to Khabarovsk, until the Amur Railway could be built between these towns. The Ussuri Railway would link Khabarovsk with Vladivostok. There were also plans for a shortcut from the Transbaikal area to Vladivostok, across Manchuria. This would be known as the East Chinese Railway.

Nicholas lays the foundation stone

After the decision to start work, the Tsar wrote the following letter to his son, the Tsarevich, who had just reached Vladivostok at the end of a tour around the world: 'Having given the order to build a continuous line of railway across Siberia, which is to unite the rich Siberian provinces with the railway system of the interior, I entrust you to declare My will, upon your entering the Russian dominions after your inspection of the foreign countries of the East. At the same time I desire you to lay the first stone at Vladivostok for the construction of the Ussuri line forming part of the Siberian Railway...'

On 31 May 1891, Nicholas carried out his father's wishes, filling a wheelbarrow with earth and emptying it onto what was to become part of the embankment for the Ussuri Railway. He then laid the foundation stone for the station.

RAILWAY CONSTRUCTION: PHASE 1 (1891-1901)

● **The Ussuri, West Siberian & Mid-Siberian Railways (1891-98)**
Work started on the Ussuri line (Vladivostok to Khabarovsk) some
time after the inauguration ceremony and proceeded slowly. In July
1892, the construction of the West Siberian (Chelyabinsk to the west
bank of the Ob River) was begun. In July 1893 work started on the
Mid-Siberian (east bank of the Ob to Irkutsk). The West Siberian
reached Omsk in 1894 and was completed when the rails reached the
Ob in October 1895. The Ussuri railway was completed in 1897 and
in the following year the final rails of the Mid-Siberian were laid and
Irkutsk was linked to Moscow and St Petersburg.

● **The Transbaikal Railway (1895-1900)** The rail link between the
Lake Baikal port of Mysovaya and Sretensk on the Shilka River was
begun in 1895. In spite of a flood which swept part of the track away
in 1897, the line was completed by the beginning of 1900. Passengers could now travel to Irkutsk by train, take the ferry across Lake
Baikal and the train again from Mysovaya to Srtensk, where steamers would take them to Khabarovsk.

● **The East Chinese Railway (1897-1901)** Surveys showed that the
proposed Amur Railway between Sretensk and Khabarovsk would be
expensive to build because of the mountainous region it would have
to pass through and the large supplies of explosives required to deal
with the permafrost. In 1894 the Russian government granted China
a generous loan to help her pay off her debts to Japan. In exchange
for this financial help, a secret treaty was signed between Russia and
China allowing the former to build and control a rail link between
the Transbaikal region and Vladivostok, across the Chinese territory
of Manchuria. Every difficulty encountered in building railways in
Siberia (severe winters, mountains, rivers, floods, disease and bandits) were part of the construction of the East Chinese Railway,
begun in 1897 and open to light traffic in 1901.

The labour force
The greater part of the Trans-Siberian Railway was built without
heavy machinery by men with nothing more than wooden shovels.
They nevertheless managed to lay up to two and a half miles of rail
on a good day. Most of the labour force had to be imported as the
local peasants were already fully employed on the land. They came
not only from European Russia but also from as far away as Italy
and Turkey. Chinese coolies were employed on the Ussuri Railway
but overseers found them unreliable and terrified of the Amur tigers

with which the area was infested. The government soon turned to the prisons to relieve the shortage of labour and gangs of convicts were put to work on the lines. They were paid twenty-five kopecks a day and had their sentences reduced - eight months on the railways counted for a year in prison. The 1500 convicts employed on the Mid-Siberian worked hard but those brought in from Sakhalin Island to work on the Ussuri line ran riot and terrorised the inhabitants of Vladivostok.

Shortage of materials
On many parts of the Siberian Plain engineers discovered that although there were vast forests of trees, none of them were suitable for using as sleepers (ties). Timber had to be imported over great distances. Rails came from European Russia and some were bought from England. They were either shipped via the Kara Sea (a southern part of the Arctic Ocean) and up the Yenisei River to Krasnoyarsk, or else right around the continent by boat to Vladivostok (which took about two months). From here, when work started on the Transbaikal line in 1895, materials had to be shipped up the Ussuri, Amur and Shilka Rivers to Sretensk (a distance of well over a thousand miles). Horses and carts were scarce in Siberia and these, too, had to be brought in from Europe.

Difficult terrain
When the railway between St Petersburg and Moscow was being planned, the Tsar took ruler and pencil and drew a straight line between the two cities, declaring that this was the route to be followed, with almost every town by-passed. For the Trans-Siberian, Alexander ordered that it be built as cheaply as possible which is why in some places the route twists and turns so that expensive tunnelling might be avoided.

There were few problems in laying foundations for the rails across the open steppe land of the Siberian plain but cutting through the almost impenetrable forests of the *taiga* proved extremely difficult. Much of this area was not only thickly forested but swampy in summer and frozen in winter until July. Consequently the building season lasted no more than four months in most places.

In eastern Siberia parts of the ground were locked in permafrost and, even in mid-summer, had to be dynamited or warmed with fires before rails could be laid. The most difficult terrain was the short line around the southern end of Lake Baikal, the Circumbaikal Loop, which required over two hundred trestles and bridges and thirty-three tunnels.

Conditions

For the workers who laboured in Siberia, conditions were hardly the most enjoyable. All were far from home, living in isolated log cabins that were not much cleaner or more comfortable than the squalid prison in Tyumen, graphically described by George Kennan in *Siberia and the Exile System*. Winters were very long and extremely cold. The brief summer brought relief from the cold but the added discomfort of plagues of black flies and mosquitoes in the swamps of the *taiga*. There were numerous outbreaks of disease. Workers on the East Chinese Railway were struck first by an outbreak of bubonic plague in 1899 and cholera in 1902. In many places the horses were wiped out by Siberian anthrax.

There were other dangers in addition to disease. In Manchuria and the Amur and Ussuri regions, the forests were filled with Amur tigers for whom the occasional railway labourer made a pleasant snack. In Manchuria construction camps were frequently raided by bandits (*hunghutzes*) who roamed around the country in gangs of up to seven hundred men. As a result, the Russian government was obliged to allocate considerable sums of money and men to the policing of the region.

There were several set-backs that no one could have foreseen. In July 1897 severe flooding swept away or damaged over two hundred miles of track near Lake Baikal on the Transbaikal line, also destroying settlements and livestock. Damage was estimated at six million roubles. In other areas landslides were caused by torrential rainfall.

RAILWAY CONSTRUCTION: PHASE 2 (1898-1916)

Reconstruction

As the first trains began to travel over the newly-laid tracks, the shortsightedness of the policy of building the railway as cheaply as possible soon became clear. Many of the materials used in its construction were either sub-standard or unsuitable to the conditions they were expected to withstand. The rails were under half the weight of those used in America and fashioned of iron of an inferior quality. They soon bent and buckled and needed replacing. The ballast under the sleepers was far thinner than that put down on the major railways of Europe. As a result, the ride in the carriages was bumpy and uncomfortable and speed had to be kept down to 13 mph for passenger trains, 8 mph for freight. Foreign engineers proclaimed the whole system unsafe and were proved correct by the frequent derailments which took place.

In 1895 Prince Khilkov became Minister of Ways of Communication. He went on a tour of inspection along the West and Mid-Siberian lines and quickly realised that a massive rebuilding programme would have to be put into operation. Extra trains were also needed to transport the hundreds of thousands of emigrants who were now flooding over the Urals. In 1899 about 100 million roubles were allocated for repairs, work which would have been unnecessary had sufficient funds been made available from the start.

● **The Circumbaikal Loop Line (1901-1904)** In 1901 work began on the 260km Circumbaikal Loop line around Lake Baikal's southern shores. The initial project had been shelved in 1893, since the terrain was considered too difficult. Passengers used the ferry service across the lake but it was soon found that the ships couldn't cope with the increased traffic. The situation became critical at the start of the Russo-Japanese war in 1904, when troops and machinery being sent to the East by rail were delayed at the lake. Construction of the new line continued as fast as possible and by the end of the year the final section of the Trans-Siberian was opened. Passengers were at last able to travel from Calais to Vladivostok entirely by train.

● **The Amur Railway (1907-1916)** The original plans for a railway from Sretensk to Khabarovsk along the Shilka and Amur Rivers were abandoned because the route would entail expensive engineering work. After the Russo-Japanese war in 1904-5, the St Petersburg government realised that there was a danger of Japan taking control of Manchuria and the East Chinese Railway. This was the only rail-link to Russia's naval base at Vladivostok. It was therefore decided that the Amur Railway must indeed be built.

Work began at Kuenga in 1908. There were the usual problems of insects, disease and permafrost but with the rest of the railway operational, it was easier to transport men and materials to the Amur area. When the bridge over the Amur at Khabarovsk was finished in 1916, the Trans-Siberian Railway was at last complete. Over 1000 million roubles had been spent on building all the sections (including the East Chinese line) since 1891.

THE FIRST RAILWAY TRAVELLERS

Rail service begins
As each of the sectors of the Trans-Siberian was completed, a rail service was begun. To say that there were teething troubles would be a gross understatement; there was a shortage of engines and carriages, most of the system operated without a timetable and there

were frequent delays and derailments along the shoddily constructed line. Nevertheless, in order to attract foreign travellers, luxury trains and 'Expresses' were introduced. Those run by the government were known as Russian State Expresses while another service was operated by the Belgian 'Compagnie Internationale des Wagons-Lits'. In 1900 the Ministry of Ways of Communication published their detailed *Guide to The Great Siberian Railway* in English.

The Paris Exhibition

The Russian government was keen to show off to the world the country's great engineering feat and at the Paris 'Exposition Universelle' of 1900, a comprehensive Trans-Siberian exhibit was organised. Amongst photographs and maps of Siberia, and Khirghiz, Buryat and Goldi robes and artifacts, there were several carriages to be operated by the Wagons-Lits Company on the Great Siberian Railway. They were decorated and furnished in the most sumptuous style. There were just four spacious compartments in the sleeping carriages, each with a connecting lavatory. The other carriages contained a smoking-room done up in Chinese style, a library and music-room complete with piano.

In the two restaurant cars, decorated with mahogany panelling and heavy curtains, visitors to the exhibition could dine on the luxurious fare that was promised on the journey itself. To give diners the feeling of crossing Siberia, a length of canvas on which was painted a Siberian panorama of wide steppes, thick *taiga* and little villages of log cabins, could be seen through the windows. In order to complete the illusion that the train was actually chugging across the Great Siberian Plain, the painted panorama was made to move past the windows by mechanical means. Visitors were intrigued and impressed and more than a few soon set off on the epic trip. The reality, they were to discover, was a little different from what they experienced at the exhibition.

Early rail travellers

When R.L.Jefferson set out to investigate the Minusinsk gold-mining region in 1897, he was able to take the train (travelling for once without his Imperial Rover bicycle but no doubt taking along a good supply of Bovril and 'Cellular' underwear) as far as Krasnoyarsk. East of here the line was not yet open.

The first English woman to travel to Japan along this route was Annette Meakin, who took her aged mother for company on the journey made in 1900. They travelled first to Paris where they visited the Siberian display at the Paris Exhibition. Having crossed Siberia, they went by ship to Japan and then to North America, crossing that continent by train too. Having circumnavigated the globe by rail, Miss Meakin recorded her experiences in the book she called *A Ribbon of Iron*.

Two years later, in 1902, Michael Myres Shoemaker took *The Great Siberian Railway from St Petersburg to Pekin* (the name of his account of the journey). He was impressed and wrote enthusiastically: 'This Railway will take its place amongst the most important works of the world....Russia is awakening at last and moving forward.'

It is interesting to compare the descriptions these travellers give of the trains they took, with the carriages displayed at the Paris Exhibition as well as with the service operated today by Soviet Railways.

The carriages

Advertising brochures informed prospective Trans-Siberian travellers, in gushing prose, that the carriages in which they were to be conveyed would be of a standard equal to those used by European royalty. In addition to the luxurious sleeping compartments and dining cars shown at the Paris Exhibition, there would be a bathroom with marble bath-tub, a gymnasium equipped with a stationary bicycle and other exercising machines, a fire-proof safe, a hair-dressing salon and a darkroom equipped with all the chemicals a photographer would need. The carriages would be lit by electric lighting, individually heated in winter and cooled by under-floor ice-boxes in summer.

Although more than a few of those luxurious appointments, which they had seen in the carriages of the Siberian exhibit in Paris, were missing on their train, Annette Meakin and her mother found their accommodation entirely satisfactory. She wrote: 'The Siberian express is a kind of "Liberty Hall", where you can shut your door and sleep all day if you prefer it, or eat and drink, smoke and play cards if you like that better. An electric bell summons a serving-man to make your bed or sweep your floor, as the case may be, while a bell on the other side summons a waiter from the buffet....Time passes very pleasantly on such a train.'

The ride was not so comfortable for the Meakins from Mysovaya on the Transbaikal Railway. Only fourth class carriages were provided and they were forced to take their travelling rugs and picnic hamper to the luggage van, where they spent the next four days.

'On the Siberian and Chinese Eastern Railways a passenger is allowed to carry gunpowder up to 3 *funts*, ie about 1kg, (carefully kept in a metal box). *The Imperial Japanese Government Railway Guide to East Asia* (1913).

Travelling in 1902, Michael Myres Shoemaker was very impressed with the bathing arrangements on the train and wrote: 'I have just discovered that there is a fine bathroom in the restaurant car, large and tiled, with all sorts of sprays, plunges and douches. This bath has its separate attendant and all the bath towels you may demand.'

He was less enthusiastic about his travelling companions, a French Consul and family whose fox terrier 'promptly domesticated itself in my compartment'.

The restaurant car

At the Paris Exhibition visitors were led to believe that a good part of the enjoyment of travelling on the Trans-Siberian would be the cordon bleu cuisine served in the restaurant car. It was claimed that the kitchens were even equipped with water tanks filled with live fish. The waiters would be multi-lingual and a truly international service was promised.

Travellers found the above description to be something of an exaggeration. Annette Meakin reported the existence of a Bechstein piano and a library of Russian novels in the restaurant car. Shoemaker wrote: 'The restaurant car is just like all those on the trains of Europe. There is a piano, generally used to hold dirty dishes. There are three very stupid waiters who speak nothing save Russian. The food is very poor.'

Travellers were warned by their guide-books that there were occasional food shortages and advised to take along a picnic hamper. The Meakins found theirs invaluable on their four-day jaunt in the luggage van. In fact, for the first few years after the service began, there had been no restaurant cars. R.L.Jefferson wrote that at mealtimes, the train would stop at a convenient station and all the passengers (and the engine-driver) would get off for a meal in the station buffet.

The church car

Behind the baggage car was a peculiar carriage known as the church car. It was a Russian Orthodox Church on wheels, complete with icons and candelabra inside, church bells and a cross on the roof, and a peripatetic priest who dispensed blessings along the way. This carriage was detached at stations and settlements where churches had not yet been built and services were conducted for railway workers and their families.

Transport of emigrants

While foreign visitors discussed whether or not their accommodation was all that the Siberian exhibit in Paris had led them to believe, emigrants travelled in the unenviable conditions described by R.L.Jefferson: 'The emigrants' train is simply one of the cattle trucks, each car being marked on the side "Forty men or eight horses". There are no seats or lights provided, and into each of these pens forty men, women and children have to herd over a dreary journey of fourteen or fifteen days...They have to provide their own food but at every station a large samovar is kept boiling in order to provide them with hot water for their tea.'

By the end of the century they were crossing the Urals to Siberia at the rate of about a quarter of a million peasants each year.

Stations

Little wooden station buildings mushroomed along the railway. Russian stations were traditionally given a class number from one to five. Of the stations listed in the official *Guide to the Great Siberian Railway*, none was of the first class and the majority were no more than fifth class. Beside most stations there towered a water-tank to supply the steam engines. Many of these towers, their eaves decorated with ornate fretwork, can still be seen today. Most of the larger stations also had their own churches and resident priests. If the train did not have a church car, stops would be made for lengthy services at these railside churches, especially on the eve of an important saint's day.

R.L.Jefferson found that in the early years of the railways, the arrival and departure of every train at a Siberian station was quite an event, being 'attended with an amount of excitement that it is hard to associate with the usually stolid Russian. Particularly is this so in Eastern Russia where railways are new and interesting.' A man ' performs a terrific tintinabulation on a large suspended bell. All the conductors blow whistles.' Jefferson goes on to explain that none of the passengers was allowed out of the train until the engine driver had got down and shaken hands with the station-master and all his staff.

Delays

Because the original line was so badly laid, the ride in the carriages was rough and uncomfortable and speed had to be kept down. There were frequent derailments and long delays. Annette Meakin complained: 'We stopped at a great many stations; indeed on some parts of the route we seemed to get into a chronic state of stopping'. 'All day long at a dog trot,' wrote Shoemaker, 'Certainly no more than ten miles an hour.' Over some sections the train went so slowly passengers could get out and pick flowers as they walked along beside it. Still, the delays did give one time to catch up on current affairs, as Miss Meakin observes when her train was delayed for four hours at Taiga ('a mere nothing in Siberia'). She writes: 'As we sat waiting in the station the good news was brought that Mafeking had been relieved.'

Bridges
Although the rails were badly laid and of poor quality, the bridges that were made of stone were built to such a high standard that many are still in use today. They were largely the work of Italian masons, who laboured throughout the winter months, the bridge-building season, since no work could be done on the snow-covered line. Many of these labourers caught hypothermia while they worked in temperatures as low as -40°C, dropping to their death on the ice below.

If a bridge was not finished in the winter when the railway lines reached it, engineers had the brilliant idea of laying rails across the ice. The sleepers were literally frozen onto the surface of the river by large amounts of water being poured over them. When R.L.Jefferson's train reached the track laid across the Chulim River, passengers were made to get out and walk, in case the train proved too great a weight for the ice to bear. He wrote: 'As it passed us we felt the ice quiver, and heard innumerable cracks, like the reports of pistols in the distance, but the train got across the centre safely.'

Breakdowns
These were all too frequent. A wait of twenty-four hours for a new engine was not regarded as a long delay. Annette Meakin recorded the following incident: 'Outside Kainsk the train stopped. "The engine has smashed up," said a jolly Russian sailor in broken English. "She is sixty years old and was made in Glasgow. She is no use any more"....The poor old engine was now towed to her last berth....I had whipped out my "Kodak" and taken her photograph, thinking of Turner's "Fighting Temeraire".'

Cost of the journey
The *Guide to the Great Siberian Railway* informed its readers that, for the journey from London to Shanghai: 'The conveyance by the Siberian Railway will be over twice as quick and two and a half times cheaper than that now existing' (the sea passage via the Suez Canal). The cost of a first class ticket for the sixteen day journey was to be 319 roubles. From Moscow to Vladivostok the price was 114 roubles. Travellers again found the reality somewhat different. Shoemaker had to pay 111 roubles for his relatively short journey from St Petersburg to Irkutsk.

THE RAILWAY IN THE TWENTIETH CENTURY

After the Revolution
'When the trains stop, that will be the end,' announced Lenin and the trains continued to run, the Trans-Siberian included, throughout these troubled times. When the new Bolshevik government pulled out of the First World War in early 1918, a Czech force of 50,000 well-armed men found themselves marooned in Russia, German forces preventing them getting back to western Europe. Receiving permission to leave Russia via Vladivostok, they set off on the Trans-Siberian. Their passage was not a smooth one for the Bolsheviks suspected that the Czechs would join the White Russian resistance movement; the Czechs suspected that the Bolsheviks were not going to allow them to leave. Violence erupted, several Czechs were arrested and the rest of the legion decided they would shoot their way out of Russia. They took over the Trans-Siberian line from the Urals to Lake Baikal and travelled the railway in armour-plated carriages.

The Civil War in Siberia (1918-20)
At this time Siberia was divided amongst a number of forces, all fighting against the Bolsheviks, but not as a combined unit. Many of the leaders were nothing more than gangsters. East Siberia and Manchuria were controlled by the evil Ataman Semenov, half-Russian, half Buryat and supported by the Japanese. He charged around Transbaikalia murdering whole villages and, to alleviate the boredom of these mass executions, a different method of death was adopted each day. Then there was Baron General von Ungern Sternberg, one of the White Russian commanders whose cruelty rivalled that of Semenov. The Americans, French, English and Japanese all brought troops into Siberia to evacuate the Czech legions and to help Admiral Kolchak, the Supreme Ruler of the White Government which was based at Omsk. Kolchak, however, failed to win the support of the people in the Siberian towns, his troops were ill-disciplined and in November 1919 he lost Omsk to the Bolsheviks. He was executed in Irkutsk in early 1920 and the Allies abandoned the White Russian cause. The Japanese gave up Vladivostok in 1922 and all Siberia was then in Communist hands.

Reconstruction
After the Civil War the Soviet Union set about rebuilding its battered economy. High on the priority list was the repair of the Trans-Siberian line, so that raw materials like iron ore could be transported to European Russia. The First Five Year Plan (1928) set ambitious goals for the expansion of industry and agriculture. It also included

new railway projects, the double-tracking of the Trans-Siberian and the building of the Turk-Sib, the line built between Turkestan and Novosibirsk. Work began on two giant industrial complexes known as the Ural-Kuznetsk Combine. Iron ore from the Urals was taken by rail to the Kuznetsk in Siberia, where it was exchanged for coal to take back to the Ural blast furnaces. For all these giant projects an enormous, controllable labour force was needed and this was to a large extent provided by prisoners from the corrective labour camps. ·

The Second World War
Siberia played an important backstage role in the Great Patriotic War. Many factories were moved from European Russia to Siberian cities and the populations of places like Novosibirsk rose dramatically. The Trans-Siberian's part was a vital one and loads of coal and food were continuously despatched over the Urals to Europe throughout the war years.

The Trans-Siberian today

THE TRAIN

Engines

If you imagined you would be hauled across Siberia by a puffing
steam locomotive you will be sadly disappointed. The Soviet Union
Railways (SZD) has, since 1927, been converting to electricity
(1.5kV dc on suburban routes; 3kV dc 25kV ac 50Hz elsewhere).
Between Moscow and Irkutsk the Trans-Siberian is pulled by electric
locos. These engines are usually Czechoslovakian-built Skoda
ChS2's (line voltage 3kV dc; max output 4620kW; max speed
160kph; weight 126 tonnes) and ChS4T's (25kV 50 Hz; 5200kW;
180kph; 126 tonnes). The latest Czech-built engines used for passenger trains are the CS200 (3kV dc; 8400kW; 200kph; 157 tonnes) and
the CS7 being developed from it. The line is almost entirely electrified, and where electrification has yet to be completed (Eastern Siberia) diesel, rather than steam, engines are used. They are usually
Soviet-built TEP70's (4,000 hp; 160kph; 129 tonnes; first built in
1973) and TEP75's (6,000 hp; 160kph; 138 tonnes; first built in
1975). If you're continuing on the Trans-Mongolian or Trans-
Manchurian routes to Beijing, it is quite likely that a steam loco will
be hitched to your carriages, at least for shunting duties. Although
steam engines have officially been phased out in the USSR, they
have not all been scrapped yet, many lining the tracks in several
stations along the way. See below for identification information and
class numbers.

Carriages and carriage attendants

Most of the carriages now used are of East German origin, solidly-
built, warm in winter and each staffed by an attendant (*pro-
vodnitsa/si* (female) *provodnik/i* (male) in Russian, *fuwuyuen* in
Chinese), whose 'den' is situated at one end of the carriage. Their
duties include collecting your tickets, letting down the carriage steps
at stations, coming round with the vacuum-cleaner each day and
providing you with tea (good but without milk) or coffee (utterly
disgusting). You pay for what you've drunk on your trip just before
you reach your destination but the bill is rarely more than a couple of
roubles. The *provodnitsi* also stoke the solid-fuel boiler which heats
the carriage and the samovar. The Chinese attendants often have

things to sell (cans of beer ($1.00), or slippers ($1-2.00). The stove-samovar (*batchok*) is situated opposite the *provodnitsa's* compartment at one end of the carriage and provides a continuous supply of boiling water. There are doors at both ends of the carriages and if you are a smoker the only place on the train where you will be allowed to indulge your habit is in this area between the carriages (unheated in winter).

Carriages are air-conditioned in summer but in order to operate all windows (and doors) must be kept shut, since the system operates on the pressure difference between the inside and outside of the carriage and takes about an hour to get going. The initial instinct (and certainly that of the Soviet passengers) is to open all the windows, and the carriage attendant wages a constant battle with everyone to keep them closed. Music (either radio or cassettes) is piped to the compartments from the *provodnitsa's* den and the knob above the window controls the volume.

TRAILBLAZER feedback 'On both sectors of the journey we had two *provodniks* and both were husband and wife. A small gift early on smoothed the way and they were all very friendly, helpful and efficient. An example of this was when I discovered one of my small gold earrings was missing. Valia had just hoovered our compartment so she put on rubber gloves, emptied out the contents and found it among the dust'. Joan Nicholls (UK).

Compartments

● **Deluxe First Class (Chinese train only)** The closest you can get to luxury accommodation while crossing Siberia, these two berth compartments have attached shower-rooms (the only showers on any of the trains), wider bunks, wood panelling, a wind-down window, armchair, table-lamp with frilly shade and plush green carpet. See photo opposite page 112.

● **Soft/First Class** Can be two berths and a washbasin or else the standard hard class four berth compartment, with only two berths used (no wash-basin but more space). On the Chinese train there's a choice between Deluxe First Class (see above) and standard first class which is four people in a hard class compartment with seat covers - not really worth the extra money. Make sure you know what you're getting - I met a honeymooning couple who found themselves sharing a four-berth first class compartment.

● **Hard/Tourist/Second Class** All four berths are used. There is adequate stowage space under the lower bunks and over the door. Bedding is provided and sheets are supposed to be changed every three days. Most travellers find Hard Class clean and comfortable.

● **Dormitory/Third class** Not available to travellers booking through Intourist abroad (yet) but if you're buying a ticket in the USSR you may be able to travel in this class. Open-plan carriage similar to Hard Class in China - doorless compartments containing four bunks in tiers of two with another bunk opposite, beside the corridor.

TRAILBLAZER feedback 'Our sheets were not changed during the six days and we were even refused clean towels. The towels were mini hand-towels and even when we demonstrated their greying colour, no clean ones were forthcoming. The sheets were not even clean when we boarded in Moscow and we had to demand clean sheets and pillow-cases.' - Joan Eriksson (Finland). Another reader travelling in early 1991 also complained about the sheets. They were clean but still very damp from the laundry. It might be worth taking your own sheets or a sheet sleeping-bag.

Bathroom

Sadly the marble bath-tub (ingeniously designed so that the water would not spill as the train rounded a corner) and the copious supplies of hot water and towels that Michael Myres Shoemaker enthused over on his trip in 1902 are no more. The lack of proper bathing facilities is usually the biggest grumble from people who've done the trip. There are no showers on the train - a ridiculous oversight. With most of the rail system now electrified there is a cheap power source for heated shower units but no doubt it will be years before they are installed. In all carriages there's a 'bathroom' at each end. This small cubicle contains a basin and a lavatory with a seat that springs up. To flush the lavatory - fully depress the foot pedal, hold it down and lean back out of the way, as the contents have a nasty habit of going the wrong way if the train is moving fast. The taps on the basin are operated by pushing up the little lever situated in the water outlet. In some carriages a foot pedal operates the taps. There is usually hot water but it takes a while to warm up. If you don't know which tap is which, the one marked with the Russian word beginning with the letter 'T' is hot, the other (beginning with 'X') cold. Don't forget to bring along a universal plug for the basin, soap and a supply of lavatory paper. One of these items is usually available but never all three together. There's a socket for an electric razor but you may need to ask the *provodnitsa* to turn it on. Best time to visit is early in the morning when the bathroom's just been cleaned. Note that it's locked for the several hours it takes to get across the borders.

Restaurant cars

You may be feasting on caviare and champagne as you rattle across the Siberian steppes but this will be only if you've brought along a well-stocked picnic hamper. When the restaurant-car does have caviare, it is never beluga, just the cheaper red variety and there's unlikely to be any champagne as it's not usually sold on trains. The waiter may have a black-market bottle for a price. The nationality of the restaurant-car depends on the country in which you're travelling. You're stuck with the Soviet one (even if you're in the Chinese train) as long as you're in the USSR. The Mongolian restaurant-car is attached at Ulan Bator and stays only as far as the border, where it is replaced by a Chinese dining-car.

● **Soviet Railways restaurant-car** The food never was much to write home about and as life gets tougher in the Soviet Union railway cuisine reflects it. Still, you can always rely on the bread and soups (*shchi* and *solyanka*) to be good and filling. On entering the restaurant-car (having averted your eyes from the grubby kitchen to preserve your appetite) you may be presented with the foreign menu. This is no different from the Russian one apart from being written in English, French, German and Chinese. You will notice that even though it runs to about sixteen pages there will rarely be more than one item on offer per page and these are indicated by a pencilled-in price. The 'choice' includes egg or tomato salad (the white sauce is not mayonnaise but sour cream - actually rather good), *shchi* (thick cabbage soup with meat in it), *solyanka* (meat soup, thick and nourishing), meat-balls and mash or macaroni, smoked *teshka* fish (like hunks of smoked salmon), *skumbria* fish (usually fried and quite good), beef Stroganov with potatoes, boiled chicken or duck, tea and coffee, and occasionally cakes. Piles of sour black bread and various fizzy drinks (*napitok*) and fruit juice (*sok*) are also on sale. Depending on the exchange rate prices vary from the very reasonable to the absurdly cheap (£0.50-£1.50 for a full meal). The cashier sometimes has snacks and bars of chocolate for sale and you should do as the Russians do and buy whenever things become available.

There are usually two waiters, who have their own halves of the car and will not serve you if you're in the other half. A packet of Marlboro given early on will encourage attentive service. Open 09.00-19.00 but these times are variable.

● **Mongolian restaurant-car** Have your US$ ready here as Mongolian *tugriks* are not accepted. The food is better than in the Russian dining-car but there's not a great range. Alcohol and 'duty-free' is available as well as postcards, stamps and souvenirs. See page 251.

- **Chinese restaurant-car** The food is much better than what you've become used to in the USSR but considerably more expensive. Payment is in FEC's and you must pay before you eat. Breakfast: scrambled eggs, bread, jam and tea (£0.75). Lunch and supper consist of tomato salad (£0.50), cold chicken or sauté chicken with hot sauce and peanuts (£1.50), fish (£1.25), sweet & sour pork (£1.50), saute beef or egg plant with dried shrimp. Drinks include beer (£0.35), cola (£0.40) and mineral water (£0.50). The single-tot measures of Chinese vodka are not good value even at the equivalent of £0.15!

LIFE ON THE TRAIN

Most people imagine they'd get bored on so long a journey but you may be surprised at how quickly the time flies by. Pack a good supply of books, *War and Peace* weighing in at 1,444 pages is a frequent choice, although I know only one person who actually managed to finish it on the trip. There are so many other things to do apart from reading. You can have monosyllabic conversations with inquisitive Russians, meet the other Westerners on the train, play cards or chess, visit the restaurant car or hop off at the stations for a little exercise. The Trans-Siberian is, as Annette Meakin wrote in 1900, a veritable 'Liberty Hall', and 'time passes very pleasantly on such a train'.

Bathing in a Chinese spittoon
A week was a short time to go without a bath in Siberia, we were told, but this didn't make the prospect any more appealing. I read somewhere that in pre-Revolution days most Russian peasants spent the whole winter without having a bath. Shopping for supplies on a freezing December afternoon in Beijing before we left, we resolved to find some kind of bucket or basin to facilitate washing on the train. In one shop we found weighty china buckets with bamboo handles and in another a plastic bath designed for a large baby and complete with a little holder for the soap. In the end we settled for something smaller, an enamel spittoon (diameter 9ins/23mm) which turned out to exactly fit the basin in the train. It could be filled from the samovar in the corridor (to the astonishment of the Chinese passengers who knew the true purpose of the utensil we employed for bathing purposes) and it greatly simplified the difficult process of washing on the train.

Meeting the locals

Russian passengers are extremely friendly and genuinely interested in foreign travellers. Sharing her compartment with three Russians on a recent journey from Khabarovsk, a winter traveller writes: 'Inside the carriage there's interest on both sides. Five hours ago my Walkman was borrowed (with only one tape inside it). It has just been returned with a helpless gesture - the battery (surprise, surprise) has run out. Great concern all round about my travelling unaccompanied and questions as to the whereabouts of my parents. Much shaking of heads and 'tutting'. There's plenty for me to find out. The thin man (with cold eyes that have gradually thawed over the last two days) has five children and is going to Moscow to get stomach medicine for one of them (or for himself?). The large motherly *babushka* in the corner who has been so kind to me is an artist, going to visit her son (or is the son an artist?). The fourth member of the compartment played chess with me last night, totally baffled by my tactics (there weren't any) so that we ended with a stalemate. He hasn't offered again. So much can be achieved with not a word of language in common.' Heather Oxley (UK)

Other foreigners

Fellow travellers are an equally interesting bunch, certainly not your run-of-the-mill tourists: 'Since I was starting the trip in Yokohama, I had expected at least an English teacher or two and the usual back-packing globetrotter. Nothing of the sort. A Finnish welding instructor and I were the only foreigners to go straight through to Moscow. (He spent the journey selling off all the presents he'd been given on his business trip in Japan.) In the next compartment (as far as Irkutsk) was a Frenchman who'd been leading a tour-group around Thailand.

'I was right to expect a back-packer but I never thought he'd be an old age pensioner as well. Leaving his wife to look after the farm in America, he spent an average of six months a year on the road and was accompanied on this trip by his 70-year-old brother. They'd brought a large pot of jam with them and purchased a loaf of black bread at one of the stops. The dining-car's menu was always rather limited but one could rely on supplies of sour cream so I proposed a cream tea. What better way to spend an afternoon crossing the wilds of Siberia!' Anna Udagawa (UK).

Stops

Getting enough exercise on so long a journey can be a problem and most people make full use of the brief stops: 'We even managed to persuade our carriage attendant (never seen out of her pink woollen hat) to take part in our efforts to keep fit on the platforms. Several Russian passengers were happy to participate in our foreign antics while others, dressed in the ubiquitous blue track-suits, watched from the windows of the train. However, if your conductress indicates that you shouldn't get off at a stop, take her advice. At some stops another train pulls in between the platform and yours, making it almost impossible for you to get back on board.' Jane Bull (UK).

Steve Oxley, travelling in June 1990 missed his connection in Irkutsk after being 'helped out by a friendly local' who told him the train had been delayed two hours. The hotel service bureau managed to book him onto another train the next day and rewrote one of his Moscow hotel vouchers for another night in Irkutsk.

Time

During his trip on the Great Siberian Railway in 1902, Michael Myres Shoemaker wrote: 'There is an odd state of affairs as regards time over here. Though Irkutsk is 2,400 miles from St Petersburg, the trains all run on the time of the latter city, therefore arriving in Irkutsk at 5pm when the sun would make it 9pm. The confusion en route is amusing; one never knows when to go to bed or when to eat. Today I should make it now about 8.30 - these clocks say 10.30 and some of these people are eating their luncheon.'

You will be pleased to know that this is something that hasn't changed, although the system now operates on Moscow time (which is no different from St Petersburg/Leningrad time). Crossing the border from China after breakfast, the first Russian station clock you see tells you that it's actually 01.00 hours. All timetables quote Moscow time. The restaurant car, however, runs on local time. Passing through anything up to seven time-zones, things can get rather confusing. The answer is to ignore Moscow time and reset your watch as you cross into new time zones (details given in the Route Guide). A watch that can show the time in two zones might be useful, otherwise just add or subtract the appropriate number of hours every time you consult the timetable in the carriage corridor.

RUSSIAN STEAM LOCOMOTIVES

In 1956, the USSR stopped producing steam engines, and the official policy was to phase out these locomotives by 1970. As with most official plans in the USSR, this one overran a little and a second official end of steam was announced for the end of 1987, when the number of locos stood at over 6000. Many are now stored as a 'strategic reserve' in the yards of larger stations, occasionally being used for shunting work and other light duties. Although Soviet Central Asia is reputed to be the best place to see steam engines, there are quite a few along the Trans-Siberian line (see Route Guide for locations). Many of the 1500 remaining Ye 2-10-0s have been stored at stations east of Irkutsk. In Northern China there are large numbers still at work.

In 1837, the first locomotive arrived in St Petersburg, a Hawthorn 2-2-0 to pull the Tsar's private carriages over the fourteen miles of six-foot gauge track to his palace at Tsarskoye Selo. The Russians have always been (and still are) conservative in nature when it comes to buying or building engines. Usually large numbers of a few standard locomotives have been ordered so there's not much of a range to be seen today. They seem to be uniformly large, standing up to 17 feet high, and larger than British locos (partly owing to the Russian gauge being 3½ inches wider than that used in Britain). They are numbered separately by classes, not in a single series as in Britain and not by railway regions. If variations of the class have been built, they are given an additional letter to follow the main class letter. Thus, for example, a 0-10-0 freight locomotive is Class E and those of this class built in Germany are Class Eg. The classes you might see in Siberia should include some of the following (Roman alphabet class letters given in brackets); * = very rare now:

● **Class O (O)*** The first freight trains on the Trans-Siberian route were pulled by these long-boilered 0-8-0 locos (55 tons) which date back to 1889. The 'O' in the class name stands for *Osnovnoi Tip* meaning 'basic type'. Although production ceased in 1923, as late as 1958 there were 1,500 of these locomotives still at work. You would be very lucky to see one of these now though.

● **Classes Б (B)*** and **Г (G)*** These were 4-6-0 passenger engines (63 tons) used at the turn of the century.

● **Class Щ (Shch)*** 2-8-0 Used on East Chinese Railway and later in Siberia. Came into production in 1906.

● **Class Ф (F)*** Mallet 0-6-0 + 0-6-0 First built in 1908.

● **Class C (S)*** 2-6-2 (75 tons) A highly successful passenger engine. 'S' stands for Sormovo, where these locos were built. First produced in 1911. **Class Cy (Su)** ('u' for *usileny*, meaning 'strengthened') was developed from the former class and in production from 1926-51.

● **Class Э (E)** 2-10-0 (imported from the USA in 1914) and 0-10-0 (80 tons, was built in Russia from 1926-52 and also produced in Germany and Sweden). Large numbers still around.

● **Class И (I)*** 2-10-2 Built by Skoda in Czechoslovakia (1929) and used on the mountain section of East Chinese Railway.

- **Class CO (SO)** 2-10-0 (97 tons) Built between 1934-54, in Ulan Ude from 1938 (watch out for SO17u at Ulan Ude station) and in Krasnoyarsk from 1943.

- **Class Ea (Yea)** 2-10-0 (90 tons) In production between 1944 and 1947, during which time several thousand were produced.

- **Class ФД (Fd)** 2-10-2 There's a magnificent example (FD21-3000) preserved on a plinth beside the track in Novosibirsk (km3333-S). See photograph opposite page 112.

- **Class Л (L)** 2-10-0

Class letters are, of course, shown in Cyrillic on the locomotives.

BAM: A SECOND TRANS-SIBERIAN

It was in the 1930s that another Herculean undertaking was begun. The project was named the Baikal-Amur-Magistral: a second Trans-Siberian railway, 3,140km long, running parallel but to the north of the existing line. It was to run through the rich mining districts of northern Siberia and provide an east-west communications back-up to the main line. Work began in Taishet and the track reached Ust Kut on the Lena River when the project was officially abandoned at the end of the war. Much of the 700km of track that had been laid was torn up to replace war-damaged lines in the west. Construction continued in secret, using slave labour until the *gulags* were closed by Khrushchev in 1954.

In 1976 it was announced that work on the BAM was recommencing. Incentives were offered to labourers to collect the 100,000 strong work-force needed for so large a project. For eight years they laboured heroically, dynamiting their way through the permafrost which covers almost half the route, across a region where temperatures fall as low as -60°C in winter. In October 1984 it was announced that the way was open from Taishet to Komsomolsk-na-Amur. Although track-laying had been completed, only the eastern half of the system was operational (from Komsomolsk to BAM station, where traffic joined the old Trans-Siberian route).

By 1991 the whole system was still not fully operational (1993 is the new date), the main obstacle being the Severomuisk Tunnel, at present bypassed by an unsatisfactory detour with a 1 in 25 gradient. The tunnel will be almost 10 miles long, and it has taken the last 10 years to drill 8 miles in the most difficult of conditions. Many are now questioning the point of a railway that is looking more and more like a white elephant. It's true that when the tunnelling is completed the new line will be able to compete with shipping routes for the tranfer of freight. However there has been considerable ecological damage, workers complain of poor housing and there is no money left now for the extraction of the minerals that was the other reason for the building of the railway in the first place.

In 1990 the first tourists managed to ride part of the BAM line although it is still supposed to be off-limits. If you wish to go you will have to join a special tour (see page 24), otherwise content yourself with a pack of post-cards available from most stations along the Trans-Siberian. They show smiling female railway workers, happy children in the new towns along the way, vast expanses of birch trees and heroic 'Bamovtsi' labourers hammering in the last sleepers on the 'Baikal-Amur-Magistral: The Road of Courage and Heroism'.

YAKUTIA RAILWAY

Work has been being carried out simultaneously on this branch line from the BAM (at Tynda) pushing north eventually to Yakutsk, to transport the huge reserves of coal to be found in Yakutia. The project was scheduled for completion at the same time as the BAM but has been severely delayed. It will be many years before readers will be able to purchase a return ticket from London's Victoria Station to Yakutsk.

SAKHALIN RAILWAY

It is reported that SZD is planning rail cruises on the 3ft 6in-gauge system on the island of Sakhalin (in the Sea of Okhotsk north of Japan). For the first 80km out of Kholmsk the special train is hauled by a 2-8-2 (of JNR's D51 type), then by a diesel for the remaining 600km. (Continental Railway Journal, Summer 1990)

(Opposite) Top: This preserved Class Fd steam engine stands at Km3333(S), just west of Novosibirsk station. **Bottom:** The most luxurious way to travel across Siberia is in Deluxe First Class on the 'Chinese' train. These are the only compartments on the whole railway system that have showers (photo: Bernard Taylor).

018
10837

РОССИЯ
МОСКВА - ВЛАДИВОСТОК

ASIA-EUROPE LAND BRIDGE

By the end of 1992 it may be possible to travel from the Chinese Pacific port of Lianyungang back to Europe on a new route along the ancient Silk Road in China, crossing into Soviet Central Asia. In September 1990 the rail link between Urumchi in China and the Soviet border (Kazakhstan Republic) was completed but bogie-changing sheds, customs facilities and signalling and telecommunications links have yet to be installed. The new route is being hailed as the shortest rail-link (2000kms shorter than the Trans-Siberian) between countries on the western Pacific coast and the eastern Atlantic coast, enabling freight to be transported faster and more cheaply than by ship. It may be many years before it is able to operate efficiently, though, because much of the Chinese part is still only single-tracked. For travellers it will offer an interesting alternative to the Trans-Siberian.

(Opposite) Top: Destination plates are fixed to the sides of carriages. In Russian, the Trans-Siberian is known as the *Rossiya*.   **Bottom:** The *Rossiya* at Novosibirsk station, one of the major stops on the line.

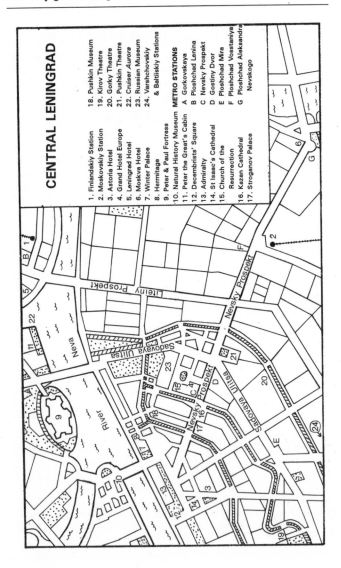

CENTRAL LENINGRAD

1. Finlandskiy Station
2. Moskovskiy Station
3. Astoria Hotel
4. Grand Hotel Europe
5. Leningrad Hotel
6. Moskva Hotel
7. Winter Palace
8. Hermitage
9. Peter & Paul Fortress
10. Natural History Museum
11. Peter the Great's Cabin
12. Decembrists' Square
13. Admiralty
14. St Isaac's Cathedral
15. Church of the
    Resurrection
16. Kazan Cathedral
17. Stroganov Palace

18. Pushkin Museum
19. Kirov Theatre
20. Gorky Theatre
21. Pushkin Theatre
22. Cruiser *Aurora*
23. Russian Museum
24. Varshavskiy
    & Baltiiskiy Stations

METRO STATIONS

A Gorkovskaya
B Ploshchad Lenina
C Nevsky Prospekt
D Gostiny Dvor
E Ploshchad Mira
F Ploshchad Vosstaniya
G Ploshchad Aleksandra
    Nevskogo

Liteiny Prospekt

Nevsky Prospekt

Sadovaya Ulitsa

Neva

River

PART 4: CITY GUIDES AND PLANS

Leningrad

Less than 300 years old, Leningrad is a young city compared to Moscow and yet there is probably as much, if not more, to see here. Many visitors prefer this northern city, perhaps because it is of more manageable proportions than the sprawling capital. It is certainly more beautiful, having been laid out in eighteenth-century Classical style on a grand scale by Peter the Great. A trip to Leningrad is well worth it if only for a visit to the famous Hermitage Museum, one of the world's most spectacular collections of European paintings, partly housed in the fabulously ornate building that was once the Tsars' Winter Palace.

You can visit Manchester's twin city by taking a side-trip from Moscow on the overnight train and staying a night or two but you really need at least four days to do justice to the sights. Alternatively, you can route your Trans-Siberian journey through Leningrad by starting (or ending) your trip in Helsinki (200km from Leningrad) or by travelling directly between Leningrad and Warsaw (bypassing Moscow). The city is especially attractive in winter, when the snow shows up the brightly painted facades of the buildings. In summer, the most important cultural festival in the USSR, 'White Nights', is held here in the last week of June.

HISTORY

'Window on Europe'
Peter the Great decided to build his new capital here to give Russia a 'window on Europe', to secure a European port for the country. He felt that his country was becoming introverted and backward, with its capital isolated from the rest of Europe. The building of this European capital, St Petersburg, was the first step in Peter's crusade for the Westernisation and modernisation of Russia. The site selected for the new capital was particularly inhospitable: the marshy estuary of the River Neva. Work began on the Peter and Paul Fortress in May 1703 and in 1712 the capital was moved here from Moscow. St

Petersburg grew quickly and stylishly, for Peter employed the finest Italian architects for the palaces and many other important buildings.

Cultural and revolutionary centre

St Petersburg soon developed into the cultural centre of Russia and in the nineteenth century was one of the great cultural centres of Europe. It has been the home of such composers as Tchaikovsky, Glinka, Mussorgsky, Rimsky-Korsakov and Shostakovich, and writers such as Gorky, Pushkin, Turgenev and Dostoyevsky. It was a centre of new ideas and among them, inevitably, were revolutionary thoughts. On 14 December 1825, these thoughts were translated into actions for the first time in the history of Russia, when a group of revolutionaries from the nobility (who came to be known as the Decembrists) led their troops into Senate Square having refused to swear allegiance to Nicholas I on his accession. The revolutionaries were quickly disarmed and exiled to Siberia.

The Revolutions of 1905 and 1917

The second revolution took place in 1905 when, on 22 January (the day that came to be known as 'Bloody Sunday'), the Tsar's troops fired on a crowd that had marched to the Winter Palace to ask his help in improving their working conditions. Ninety-two people were killed, several hundred wounded but more tragic for the country was the fact that the people's faith in their Tsar was finally shattered. Strikes and civil disorder followed and on 25 October 1917 the shot was fired from the cruiser *Aurora* that was the signal for the Revolution that changed the course of Russian history.

'Hero City'

In 1914 the Tsar Nicholas II had changed the city's name to the more Russian-sounding Petrograd. Ten years later it was renamed Leningrad (and there is now talk of a return to one of the old names). In 1945 it gained the title 'Hero City' for its stand against the Germans during the Second World War. During the Siege of Leningrad, from September 1941 to January 1943, the starving inhabitants were bombarded with an average of 250 shells a day. In fact most of the 641,803 Leningraders who died during the blockade died of hunger. During the winter of 1941/2 the daily bread ration was reduced to 250g for labourers, 125g for everyone else. People ate dogs, cats and rats; they chewed paper and glue to dull the hunger pains and made coffee from acorns. The streets were littered with piles of frozen corpses waiting until the ground was soft enough for mass graves to be dug.

Postwar years

Leningrad has been practically rebuilt since the war and fortunately the planners opted for restoration of many of the historic buildings, rather than replacement. The building programme continued until the 1980s but is now slowing down owing to a severe shortage of funds. In 1777, 1824, 1924 and 1984 the waters of the Neva rose three metres, engulfing the city and an ambitious flood barrier 25km long around the edge of the Gulf of Finland was begun but has recently been halted in its final stages, a billion roubles having been spent.

The modern city is in a chaotic state of flux. There is terrible pollution from the factories, chemical plants and inefficient sewage system (on no account should you drink the tap-water), a severe housing crisis with many people still living in communal flats while local industry is out of touch with market demands. Eighty per cent of industry is defence-related at a time when military spending is being cut back.

Leningrad's City Council has revolutionary plans: to turn the city into a free economic zone, establish a stock exchange and restore the historic centre. There may also be a referendum to decide whether to rename the city (St Petersburg or Petrograd). Many of the street names are in the process of being changed but Leningraders still tend to use the old names.

ARRIVAL AND DEPARTURE

By 'plane There are two airports: **Pulkovo II** (20km south of the city) for international and some domestic flights (bus 13 from Moskovskiy metro station) and **Pulkovo I** for domestic flights (bus 39 from Moskovskiy metro station or express bus from the Aeroflot terminal just off Nevsky Prospekt at 13, Ul. Gertsena). If you're travelling independently you can probably join one of the groups going by bus from your hotel if you ask at the Service Bureau. Although the flight between Moscow and Leningrad takes only one hour and costs about the same as the overnight train, what with getting to and from airports and the usual delays you are better off taking the train.

By train

There are five stations, three of interest to foreign travellers. Their names are self-explanatory: **Finlandskiy Voksal** (metro station: Ploshchad Lenina) for trains to and from Helsinki; **Moskovskiy Voksal**, (metro station: Ploshchad Vosstaniya) for Moscow trains; and **Varshchovskiy Voksal** (metro station: Frunzenskaya) for trains to Warsaw, Berlin and other Western cities. Do not confuse this last

station with Baltiiskiy Station next door to it. Check departure times
with the hotel Service Bureau and arrive half an hour before the train
is due to leave. Soviet trains rarely depart late and have been known
to roll out of the station a few minutes ahead of schedule.

ORIENTATION AND HOTELS

Central

The two most centrally located hotels have both been completely
renovated as luxury hotels (with luxury prices). The **Astoria**, which
opened in 1913 with beautiful Art Nouveau decor, has now reopened
after four years of rebuilding by a Finnish-Soviet joint venture to
restore it to its former grandeur. It is opposite St Isaac's Cathedral at
39 Ul. Gertsena (Herzen Street). A claimed US$100 million will
have been lavished on the **Grand Hotel Europe/Yevropeiskaya**
(opening Nov 1991) by the Swedish-Soviet joint venture to make it
the first five-star hotel in the city. It is conveniently located just off
Nevsky Prospekt at 1/7 Ul Brodskogo and will be run by RESO, the
Swedish hotel chain already managing the luxury floating hotel,
Olympia (see below).

Middle zone

The next group comprises five hotels each located a few stops on the
metro from the centre. Due west, on Vasilyevsky Island, is what was
Leningrad's top hotel (until the renovations of the Astoria and Grand
Hotel Europe), the **Pribaltiskaya**. Built by the Swedes and opened in
1979 the hotel has beds for 2,400 people. Nearest metro station:
Primorskaya; buses 7, 30, 128. In the same area is the luxury floating hotel **Olympia** (formerly an oil rig platform), moored at the sea
passenger terminal beside Ploshchad Morskoi Slavy (metro: Primorskaya then trolley-bus 10a). The **Leningrad Hotel**, at 5/2 Pirogov-
skaya Nabezhnaya, was built in 1970 and decorated by the Finns. It
overlooks the river and is convenient if you're arriving from (or
going to) Helsinki as it's two blocks from the station. Nearest metro:
Ploshchad Lenina; trams: 6, 25, 30, 51. The **Moskva**, at 2 Ploshchad Aleksandra Nevskogo, is also modern (with quirky little touch-
es like a key-fob doubling as a bath-plug!). Nearest metro: Ploshchad
Aleksandra Nevskogo; trolley-buses 1, 14, 22; trams 7, 13, 29, 38,
44, 49; buses 8, 26, 155, 160. South of the centre at 1 Ploshchad
Pobedy is the **Pulkovskaya**, opened in 1981 (metro: Moskovskaya).

Outskirts

As one might expect the two cheaper hotels are not centrally located.
The **Karelia** is north-west of the centre at 27/2 Ul. Tukhachevskogo.

There is no metro station near it but trolley-buses 3, 12, 19 and buses 102, 106, and 131 ply this route. The most inconvenient hotel to land up in, if you have no transport, is the **Olgino Camping Motel**, 19km from the centre on the road to Finland. There are buses into Leningrad (forty minutes) from the stop on the main highway outside the entrance (buses 11 and 16, every ten minutes). There is supposed to be a complimentary shuttle bus to the city centre but this is not to be relied upon. It's also possible to get there by train from Finlandskiy Station, getting off at Olgina Station and walking south across the two main roads.

Alternative hotels (middle zone)

The above are the places usually used by Intourist but it may become possible to arrange accommodation in cheaper hotels, as the regulations are eased. Other hotels include: **Chaika** (38, Serebristi Boulevard, tel 395 30 85, metro: Pionerskaya); **Gavan** (88, Sredny Prospekt, tel 356 85 52, bus 30); **Druzhba** (4, Ulitsa Chapygina, tel 234 18 44, metro: Petrogradskaya); **Kievskaya** (49 Ulitsa Dnepropetrovskaya, tel 166 04 56, bus: 14,57); **Ladoga** (26 Prospekt Shaumyana, tel 528 56 28, metro Krasnogvardeivskaya); **Morskaya** (1, Ploshchad Morskoi Slavy, tel 355 14 17, metro Primorskaya, then trolley-bus 10a); **Oktyabrskaya** (10, Ligovsky Prospekt, tel 277 63 30, metro Ploshchad Vosstaniya); **Rossiya** (11, Ploshchad Chernyeshevskogo, tel 296 76 49, metro Park Pobedy); **Sovyetskaya** (43, Lermontovsky Prospekt, tel 259 20 70, metro Baltiiskaya); **Sputnik** (34 Prospekt Toreza, tel 552 56 32, metro Ploshchad Muzhestva); **Vyborgskaya** (3, Ulitsa Torzhkovskaya, tel 246 23 19, metro Chernaya Rechka).

TRANSPORT

In this city of canals and rivers, that has been called the 'Venice of the North' you might expect the local transportation system to be dominated by gondolas or punts but it's just like any other city in the USSR for getting around. There is a good metro system and the buses, trams and trolley-buses are less crowded than those in Moscow. The metro stations rival Moscow's in their Soviet Baroque decor and trains run from 05.35 to 01.00. The fare on the metro, on trolley-buses, buses and trams is a flat 15 kopecks. Taxis are difficult to get unless you are prepared to pay hard currency at US$1 a ride or so, although drivers are supposed by law to accept roubles only. Jet boats for excursions to the palace of Petrodvorets go from Pier No. 2 near Decembrists' Square.

TOURS

The Service Bureau in your hotel can arrange the following tours:
the Hermitage, daily (except Mon) at 14.15, 2½hrs US$13.00; city
tour, daily at 10.00, 3hrs, US$8.00; Peter & Paul Fortress, Mon and
Thurs at 14.45, 3hrs, US$11.50; also an architecture tour, a metro
station tour, boat trips along the river and canals, and excursions to
Petrodvorets (US$13.00), Pushkin and Pavlovsk (each US$12.00).
Between May and Sep, boats leave Anichkov Bridge Pier (just off
Nevsky Prospekt) from 10.00 (next departure time is listed on the
kiosk by the pier) for the 70-minute tour. During the 'White Nights'
festival (midsummer) boats leave the pier near Decembrists' Square
at 21.00 and passengers are entertained by musicians during the trip.
You can get full details about tours and make bookings at the Service
Bureau in your hotel.

LENINGRAD METRO PLAN (ENGLISH)

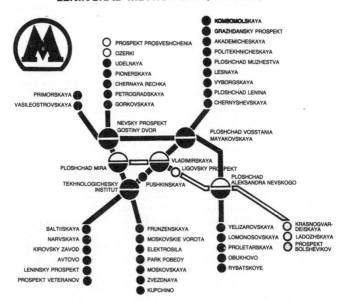

WHAT TO SEE

The State Hermitage Museum

Rivalling the British Museum and the Louvre in size, this museum surpasses all others in the lavishness of its setting, and the comprehensiveness of its collection of paintings. It comprises two huge buildings, the **Winter Palace** and the **Hermitage**. The Winter Palace, designed by the Italian architect, Rastrelli, was completed in 1762. The thousand rooms and halls contained within its Baroque exterior were decorated in the reign of Catherine the Great who favoured the Classical style. Catherine ordered the building of the Hermitage next door to her palace, as a place of retreat where she could contemplate the art collection she had begun.

The Hermitage is so large it would be impossible to see more than a small part of it in one visit.

LENINGRAD METRO PLAN (RUSSIAN)

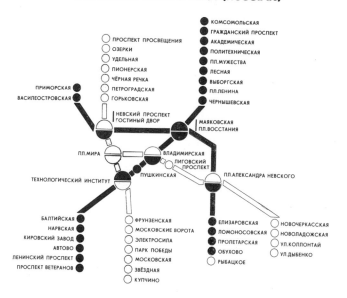

КОМСОМОЛЬСКАЯ
ГРАЖДАНСКИЙ ПРОСПЕКТ
АКАДЕМИЧЕСКАЯ
ПОЛИТЕХНИЧЕСКАЯ
ПЛ.МУЖЕСТВА
ЛЕСНАЯ
ВЫБОРГСКАЯ
ПЛ.ЛЕНИНА
ЧЕРНЫШЕВСКАЯ

ПРОСПЕКТ ПРОСВЕЩЕНИЯ
ОЗЕРКИ
УДЕЛЬНАЯ
ПИОНЕРСКАЯ
ЧЁРНАЯ РЕЧКА
ПЕТРОГРАДСКАЯ
ГОРЬКОВСКАЯ

ПРИМОРСКАЯ
ВАСИЛЕОСТРОВСКАЯ

НЕВСКИЙ ПРОСПЕКТ
ГОСТИНЫЙ ДВОР

МАЯКОВСКАЯ
ПЛ.ВОССТАНИЯ

ПЛ.МИРА
ВЛАДИМИРСКАЯ
ЛИГОВСКИЙ ПРОСПЕКТ
ПУШКИНСКАЯ
ПЛ.АЛЕКСАНДРА НЕВСКОГО
ТЕХНОЛОГИЧЕСКИЙ ИНСТИТУТ

БАЛТИЙСКАЯ
НАРВСКАЯ
КИРОВСКИЙ ЗАВОД
АВТОВО
ЛЕНИНСКИЙ ПРОСПЕКТ
ПРОСПЕКТ ВЕТЕРАНОВ

ФРУНЗЕНСКАЯ
МОСКОВСКИЕ ВОРОТА
ЭЛЕКТРОСИЛА
ПАРК ПОБЕДЫ
МОСКОВСКАЯ
ЗВЁЗДНАЯ
КУПЧИНО

ЕЛИЗАРОВСКАЯ
ЛОМОНОСОВСКАЯ
ПРОЛЕТАРСКАЯ
ОБУХОВО
РЫБАЦКОЕ

НОВОЧЕРКАССКАЯ
НОВОЛАДОЖСКАЯ
УЛ.КОЛЛОНТАЙ
УЛ.ДЫБЕНКО

The departments of the Hermitage Museum are as follows:

1. The History of Russian Culture

2. Ancient History (Do not miss the exquisite goldwork in the Scythian collection although you will only be allowed in if you are with a tour group.)

3. Central Asian Department

4. The Middle East, China and Japan

5. Ancient Greece and Rome

6. European Art. This is the section that draws the tourists to Leningrad. There are works by Leonardo da Vinci, Raphael and Michelangelo (Halls 207-30); El Greco, Velazquez, Murillo and Goya (Halls 239-40); Van Dyck, Rembrandt and Rubens (Halls 245-54). French artists are well represented in Halls 272-297 and the Impressionists can be seen in Halls 317-345. The works of Reynolds, Gainsborough and other English artists are displayed in Halls 289-303.

The setting for these masterpieces could not be more magnificent - grand halls with gilded columns, walls of marble, mosaic floors and vast crystal chandeliers. If you have the time, it is better to make several short visits to the Hermitage, rather than one extended one. Even if you're not on a guided tour you should try to follow a tour-group into the museum through the foreign visitors' entrance round the back. The main reason for doing this is not that you will avoid paying the entrance fee but (far more important) you will not waste valuable viewing time standing in the long queue for tickets at the front entrance (not too bad around 12.30, though). The square outside the Winter Palace swarms with black-marketeers (selling 'mee-leetaree watches' etc) but the police are paid off and seem to turn a

---

Rules for social conduct in the Hermitage
When Catherine the Great held a dinner party in her Hermitage the lucky few who were honoured with an invitation were bound by a list of social rules displayed by the doors to the dining room. Guests were ordered to 'put off their title and rank as well as their hats and swords'. Pretensions were to be left outside; guests were to 'enjoy themselves but break nothing and spoil nothing'; be sparing with their words; eat and drink with moderation and avoid yawning. Those who violated the above rules were obliged to undergo the following punishment - the drinking of one glass of fresh water (ladies not excepted) and the recital of a page of poetry.

blind eye. Their commercialism extends even to rides in a horse-drawn carriage around the Alexander Column for US$1.00! The Hermitage is open daily (except Mon) 10.30 to 18.00 but entrances close at 17.00.

TRAILBLAZER feedback 'In Leningrad we were told by the hotel service bureau that the 'Gold Room' (Scythian Collection) was closed for repairs. With the help of Black Marketeers, whom we befriended, we obtained tickets via some friends in security'. Robert Bray (UK).

Decembrists' Square and St Isaac's Cathedral

In this square that was the scene of the uprising by the group of officers who came to be known as the Decembrists (and were sent to Siberia for their treachery) stands the **Bronze Horseman**, the monument to Peter the Great. The statue was commissioned by Catherine the Great and the work carried out by the French sculptor Falconet, in 1782. South of the Square is **St Isaac's Cathedral** (built between 1819 and 1859) with its vast gilded dome and ornate interior. You can climb part of the way up the dome for a good view over the city. In pre-Revolutionary days, the Cathedral would be packed with up to 14,000 people for major celebrations like Easter and the Saint's birthday. Now it's a museum, open from 11.00 to 19.00 but it may soon be reconsecrated.

A walk down Nevsky Prospekt

This has been the main shopping street and most fashionable place to be seen in the city since the foundation of St Petersburg. A walk along this once grand street past palaces and churches, over canals and beside faded buildings that once housed international banks and companies is a walk through the history of the city itself. There are numerous cafés, bakeries and food-shops (including several newly-opened hard-currency cafés) lining the avenue to provide you with refreshment along the way. The Nevsky Prospekt starts near the Admiralty Building and as you walk east from here, you can identify the buildings by the numbers beside the doors. The following buildings may be of interest:

7 Gogol wrote *The Government Inspector* here in the 1830s, the lower floors now house a large **Beriozka** shop.
9 This building was modelled on the Doges' Palace in Venice, for the Swedish banker, Wawelberg. Now the **Aeroflot** office and air terminal.
14 Note the blue and white sign here which dates from the Siege of

Leningrad in World War Two and advises pedestrians to walk on the other side of the street during shelling.

17 This impressive building, designed by Rastrelli and built in 1754, was once the palace of the wealthy Stroganov family. Although they are more famous for the beef stew named after them, it was the Stroganovs who initiated the conquest and colonisation of Siberia by sending their private army to the Urals in the 1570s.

20 The former **Dutch Church**, built in 1837, now a library.

22 Good pizzas and snacks from the basement café here.

24 Once the showrooms of the court jewellers Fabergé (creators of the golden Easter eggs now on display in the Kremlin).

27 'Nevsky 27' Café (hard currency only – beer US$2.50, expresso US$2.50, pastries US$1.50). German-Soviet joint venture.

28 The former showrooms of the Singer Sewing Machine Co. with their trademark (a glass globe) still on the roof. Now the **Dom Knigi** (House of Books), the largest bookshop in the city.

● **Kazan Cathedral** was designed by Voronikhin and completed in 1811. This large, domed cathedral is approached by an impressive, semi-circular colonnade. There is a statue at each end of the colonnade, that on the left being of Mikhail Kutuzov, who prayed here before leading the army to battle against Napoleon. After the victory over the French in 1812, the Cathedral became a monument to Russia's military glory. In an act of supreme tastelessness, the Soviets turned it into a Museum of Atheism. This is now closed and the Cathedral is about to be reconsecrated.

● Looking north along the Griboyedov Canal, you will see the onion-domed **Church of the Resurrection** (looking rather like St Basil's in Moscow). It was built on the spot where Tsar Alexander II was assassinated in 1881.

31 This housed the City Duma (Municipal Council) in tsarist times. The tower was used as a fire-lookout. The little portico around the corner is the **theatre box-office**. Foreigners may buy tickets here. Opposite the Duma, Ul. Brodskogo runs north into Arts Square (Ploshchad Iskusstv) where the **Russian Museum** (in the Mikhailovsky Palace (this is one of the largest art galleries with 300,000 paintings, drawings and sculptures; open 10.00-18.00, closed Tue), the **Maly Opera House** and the **Leningrad State Philharmonia** are situated. The **Grand Hotel Europe/Yevropeiskaya** is a short distance down Ul. Brodskogo.

32 The **Church of St Catherine**. Stanislaw Poniatowski, the last king of Poland and one of the lovers of Catherine the Great, is buried here.

40 'Nevsky 40' café. This is a branch of the bar 'Nevsky 27' above.

- **Gostiny Dvor** fills the whole of the next block (south side). This is the largest department store in the city and Intourist guides claim that 300,000 people pass through the arcades each day. It has even started to compete with the touts that hang around your hotel (trying to buy things off you) with the sign in English: 'Dear Guests! Our supermarket Gostiny Dvor is buying new things (clothes etc) on nonfixed prices, from 10am till 4pm every day but Saturday and Sunday. Paying of money just immediately.'
- The **statue of Catherine the Great**, surrounded by her lovers (or 'associates' as an Intourist guide coyly put it) and other famous people of the time, stands in a park in front of the Pushkin Theatre. There is a large craft market (*palekh* boxes (180-3000 roubles), *matrioshka* dolls (from 20 roubles), shawls, paintings and samovars (US$20-30)) here. Bargain hard; many tourists come here so the prices are not low but there are some bargains and a very wide selection.

54 Gastronom Number One is a mere shadow of its former glorious self when it was run by Mr Yeliseyev and rivalled the food hall at Harrods. The ornate interior survived the Revolution and the Siege but the shelves and cabinets that were built to display exotic fare are now lined with drab tins of fruit juice and stacks of bottled vegetables.

The building on the south side of the street beside the Fontanka Canal became known as the **Anichkov Palace** (after the nearby **Anichkov Bridge** with its famous equestrian statues). Continuing east along the Nevsky Prospekt, it's 1km from here to Ploshchad Vosstaniya where Moskovskiy Railway Station (trains to Moscow) is situated. From Ploshchad Vosstaniya it's a further 2km to the end of the avenue at Ploshchad Aleksandra Nevskogo. The **Alexander Nevsky Monastery**, with seven churches in the grounds, is situated here, across the square from the **Moskva Hotel**.

Peter and Paul Fortress

Work began on this fortress, situated on an island at the very heart of the city, in 1703. It was used as a maximum security prison until 1921, when it was turned into a museum. If you're here at mid-day don't be surprised by the sound of a cannon. It's the daily noon-day cannon that Leningraders check their watches by. At the centre of the fortress is the **St Peter and St Paul Cathedral**, with its soaring, needle-like spire (122m). It now serves as a mausoleum for Peter the Great and his successors and is positively littered with their ornate tombs. A memorial to Russia's last king, Nicholas II, is planned. Leaving the fortress, crossing the bridge and walking east along the river (see map) you will come to a small brick building amongst the trees in a square. This outer shell protects **Peter the Great's log cabin**, the earliest surviving building in the city (built in 1703) and now preserved as an interesting little museum (closed Tue).

Other sights

Since the city boasts a total of sixty museums, it is impossible to give details of more than a few in a guide of this type. As well as those places of interest listed above there are art museums (**Monastery of the Holy Trinity and Alexander Nevsky**); museums of social history (the **cruiser** *Aurora* from which was fired the signal for the Revolution, open to groups only; the **Smolny Institute** and many other places connected with the Revolution); literary museums (homes of **Dostoyevsky** and **Pushkin**); scientific museums (the history of rail transport in the USSR at the **Railway Museum** at 50 Ul.Sadovaya; the **Arctic and Antarctic Museum**; the **Natural History Museum**, where a fully preserved mammoth dug out of the permafrost, is on display).

Excursions

Thirty kilometres west of the city lies **Petrodvorets** (Peterhof), built as Peter the Great's Versailles by the sea. It is most famous for its spectacular fountains whose gilded figures appear in all the tourist literature. Open daily (though main palace is closed on Mon) from 11.00-20.00. In the summer you can get there by jet-boat from the landing stage near the Hermitage (several boats each hour, 1.20 roubles each way) or go by train from Baltiiskiy Voksal (metro: Baltiiskaya). At **Pushkin** (25km outside Leningrad) is the grand palace (closed Tue) that was the home of the Imperial family. Set in a beautiful park, it was formerly known as Tsarskoye Selo (the Tsar's village). Four kilometres south of here is **Pavlovsk**, built by Catherine the Great for her son Paul. Trains for Pushkin and Pavlovsk leave from Vitebskiy Voksal (metro: Pushkinskaya). **Lomonosov (Oranienbaum) Palace** with its beautiful park attracts far fewer tourists than the above three and is a peaceful place to visit. Trains from Baltiiskiy Voksal (metro: Baltiiskaya). Ilya Repin's house **Penaty** (closed Tue) is at Repino and can be reached by train from Finlandskiy Voksal.

RESTAURANTS

Things are changing fast on the Leningrad food scene - so much so that it's now even possible to call 29 22 666 and have **Pizza Express** deliver to your hotel room! The co-operative restaurant 'movement' and the numerous joint-ventures now appearing have given visitors more choice. However, it seems to be no less difficult to get a table in a restaurant, with all the Leningraders looking for a night out. There are also fewer culinary bargains around as many places are now demanding payment in hard currency: either in cash (preferably US$) or by credit card.

The hotel restaurants which have been recommended include the **Pribaltiyskaya** for Russian cuisine; **Karelia** for Karelian (once part of Finland) food; **Sovyetskaya** for Russian food; the restaurants in the luxurious new **Astoria** Hotel and the Grand Hotel Europe/Yevropeiskaya (**Yevropeiskaya** and **Sadko** restaurants) should be good but expensive.

Outside the hotels you could try **Troika** which has traditional cuisine and a floor-show (27, Zagorodny Prospekt, metro: Vladimirskaya then trolley-bus 3,8 or 15) or some of the numerous cafés and restaurants along Nevsky Prospekt. **Literaturnoye Kafe** (18 Nevsky Prospekt) has been the traditional meeting place for writers, artists and intellectuals since the last century. This was where Pushkin had his last meal before his fatal duel. **Kavkazsky**, (25, Nevsky Prospekt) is famous for its Caucasian cuisine. **Metropol**, 22 Ul.Sadovaya (south of Nevsky Prospekt), is often recommended but reservations must be made in advance (tel 310 18 45). You can eat in Leningrad's largest restaurant, the **Neva**, (with seating for more than 1,000 but not particularly recommended) at No.44; try the cakes and pastries at the **Sever Kafe** at No.46 and sip champagne (if available) with your ice-cream at the **Kafe Morozhenoye** at No.24.

If you're on a tight budget, check that the restaurant you wish to eat at is not hard currency only. Alternatively try the numerous snack bars (hamburgers and pizzas) along Nevsky Prospekt, many of which accept roubles.

NIGHTLIFE

Leningrad is probably the most interesting city in the USSR for things to do in the evening. Ask at the Service Bureau for a programme of **ballet** (Kirov and Maly), **opera**, **concerts** and the **circus**. They sell tickets for hard currency (Kirov and Maly: US$50 and US$20 each) but you can buy tickets, if they are available, for roubles at the kiosk off Nevsky Prospekt (near the City Duma - see page 124). There is also the **Jazz Club** (weekends only) 27 Zagorodny Prospekt, near Troika restaurant (above). If none of this appeals you could try the Wild West theme **disco** (US$5.00, including drink) in the Karelia Hotel.

SHOPPING

The Nevsky Prospekt is the main shopping street where you will find the **Beriozka** shop (No.7-9); the largest department store **Gostiny Dvor** (No.35) and **Dom Knigi** (the House of the Book, for good-value art books and Revolutionary posters). There is also quite a good **craft market** around the park in front of the Pushkin Theatre. The larger hotels now all operate **hard-currency shops** such as the Baltic Star at the Astoria and the Neva Star at the Moskva. Typical prices: Marlboro 100s (US$16), Stolichnaya vodka (US$10), red caviar 140g (US$18), black caviar 56g (US$30).

(Opposite) Top: Outside the Hermitage Museum in Leningrad all the commercial possibilities for tourists are being exploited in the new Russia. You can now have a ride in a horse-drawn carriage round the Alexander Column.
Bottom: Variations on the *matrioshka* theme for sale on Nevsky Prospekt.

Moscow

All railway lines in the USSR lead to the capital, so you'll be spending some time here, even if it's just a quick visit to Red Square as you change stations. Most travellers stay at least one night but to see the main sights you would need a minimum of three days. Unless you've managed to arrange alternative accommodation, the high cost of hotel rooms is the limiting factor. If you don't have a place to stay, it's still possible (even on a transit visa) to spend a night here on your way from Siberia, since your visa allows you a little extra time to catch the connecting train to Europe. You may be invited home by students who hang around in the station looking for Westerners with things to sell, otherwise you can sleep either in the 'hotel' train waiting in Belorusskaya Station or in the waiting-room. Details given below.

HISTORY

The archaeological record shows that Moscow has been inhabited since Neolithic times. However, the first written mention of the city was not until 1147, when Prince Yuri Dolguruky was said to have founded the city by building a fort on a site beside the Moskva River, in the principality of Vladimir. The settlement which grew up around the wooden fort soon developed into a major trading centre. Disaster struck the Russian principalities in the early thirteenth century in the form of the Mongol invasion. Moscow was razed to the ground in 1238 and for the next two and a half centuries was obliged to pay an annual tribute to the Mongol Khan. During this time the principality of Muscovy (of which Moscow was capital) emerged as the most important princely state in Russia. In 1326, Moscow became the seat of the Russian Orthodox Church. Prince Dimitri Donskoi strengthened the city's defences and built a stone wall around the Kremlin. In 1380 he defeated a Mongol-Tatar army at Kulikovo but it was not until 1476 that tributes to the Khan ceased.

(Opposite) St Basil's Cathedral, Moscow's most famous landmark, is situated on Red Square. A museum for many years, it has now been given back to the Orthodox Church.

The years of growth
The reign of Ivan III (the Great) (1462-1505) was a period of inten-
sive construction in the city. Italian architects were invited to rede-
sign the Kremlin, and many of the cathedrals and churches date from
this period. Prosperity continued into the sixteenth century under
Ivan IV (the Terrible) and it was in his time that St Basil's Cathedral
in Red Square was built.

The early seventeenth century was a time of civil disorder with a
revolt of the peasants which culminated in the invasion of Moscow
by Polish and Lithuanian forces. When they were driven out in 1612
the city was, for the second time in its history, burnt to the ground.
Rebuilt in stone, Moscow became the leading industrial city in
Russia by the end of the century. It remained an important economic
and cultural centre even after 1712 when Peter the Great transferred
the capital of Russia to St Petersburg.

The third and final sacking of the city occurred in 1812 when
Napoleon invaded Russia. As much of the damage was probably
done by retreating Muscovites as by the French armies but three
quarters of all the buildings were destroyed. Recovery was swift and
trade increased after the abolition of serfdom in 1861.

Revolution
Towards the end of the century Moscow became a revolutionary
centre and factories were hit by a series of strikes and riots. Michael
Myres Shoemaker, who was here in 1903, wrote in *The Great Siberian Railway from St Petersburg to Peking*: 'Up to the present day
the dissatisfaction has arisen from the middle classes especially the
students, but now for the first time in Russia's history it is spreading
downward to the peasants... but it will be a century at least before
that vast inert mass awakens to life.' In 1905 there was an armed
uprising and twelve years later 'that vast inert mass' had stormed the
Kremlin and Soviet power was established in the city. There were
terrible food shortages and great loss of life during the civil war.

The capital once more
In March 1918 Lenin transferred the government back to Moscow.
As well as being the country's capital, it is now also the capital of
the Russian Republic (RSFSR). In the years between the two world
wars the city embarked on an ambitious programme of industrial
development and the population doubled to four million in 1939.
During the Second World War many of the factories in the European
part of the USSR were evacuated to towns over the Urals, a sensible
move as it turned out, for by October 1941 the German army had
surrounded the city and the two-month Siege of Moscow had begun.

Moscow today

Since the war the capital has continued to grow and is now very much the industrial, political, scientific and cultural centre of the USSR. The population stands at over eight million and the majority of workers are employed in industry. The largest factories are the Likhachkov and Lenin Komsomol Automobile Plants, where half the employees are women. (In fact there are three quarters of a million more women than men in Moscow). Your guide may supply you with a plethora of statistical information including the fact that the city produces 39 per cent of the USSR's vacuum cleaners and 3,000 different types of ball-bearing.

The city has a certain dynamism about it, being at the epicentre of all the revolutionary changes currently sweeping the country. It could be argued that its problems are not quite as acute as those of Leningrad but there is still a chronic housing shortage here (1.8 million people on the council waiting list), severe pollution and always a shortage of some basic foodstuff or other. Crime, ranging from petty pilfering to gang warfare on the streets is on the increase. Facing bankruptcy in early 1991, Moscow's City Council (Mossoviet) was forced to raise prices of many essential services, including the metro system. Dominated by radicals, the Council has announced a wide range of reforms, some as revolutionary as the privatisation of virtually all the homes in the city.

Many of the streets are being renamed - Gorky St (Ul.Gorkogo) has now reverted to its name of Tver St (Ul.Tverskaya) although many people still call it Ul.Gorkogo. Kalinin Ave is now New Arbat Prospekt.

ARRIVAL AND DEPARTURE

By 'plane

International flights land at **Sheremetyevo International Airport** which is 20 miles from the city centre. There are taxis but drivers will refuse to take you unless you pay in dollars. There is also an airport bus - ask at the Intourist Information Office in the airport. To get to the airport from Moscow your hotel may operate a bus service or you can go to the air terminal office at 37 Leningradsky Prospect (metro stations Aeroport and Dinamo) where you can get a bus or helicopter (!).

By train

There are nine railway stations, the four you are most likely to use being: **Belorusskaya** (trains to and from Western Europe); **Leningrad** (Helsinki and Leningrad) and (next door to it) **Yaroslavl**

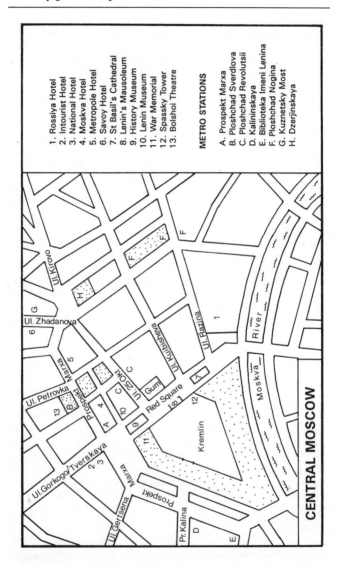

1. Rossiya Hotel
2. Intourist Hotel
3. National Hotel
4. Moskva Hotel
5. Metropole Hotel
6. Savoy Hotel
7. St Basil's Cathedral
8. Lenin's Mausoleum
9. History Museum
10. Lenin Museum
11. War Memorial
12. Spassky Tower
13. Bolshoi Theatre

METRO STATIONS

A. Prospekt Marxa
B. Ploshchad Sverdlova
C. Ploshchad Revolutsii
D. Kalininskaya
E. Biblioteka Imeni Lenina
F. Ploshchad Nogina
G. Kuznetsky Most
H. Dzerjinskaya

CENTRAL MOSCOW

(Trans-Siberian trains, except No 26 to Novosibirsk via Kazan) and **Kazanskogo** (opposite Leningrad Station) for the *Sibiriak* to Novosibirsk. **Kiev** Station is for trains to Budapest.

Arrival on Trans-Siberian (transit passengers)

Trains coming from Siberia arrive at Yaraslavl station and if you're on a transit visa you are supposed to go directly to the station for your onward train (Belorusskaya for Berlin , Kiev for Budapest, Leningrad for Helsinki) to make your reservations for departures the same day. Take the metro. To make a reservation for non 'same-day' departures or to purchase a ticket for any other destination go (as soon as possible as the queues can be long) to the Intourist Travel Office on 15 Ulitsa Petrovka. Take the metro to Ploshchad Sverdlova, then pass the Bolshoi Theatre and turn left along Ul. Petrovka. The office is on the left, after a 7-10 minute walk. Go to the second floor for reservations on tickets already bought or to the third floor to buy tickets. If they won't take roubles, you could try to get a Russian to buy you a same-day ticket at the station. Train times for **Budapest** (35hrs) - No 29 (Fri): 10.51; No 69: 21.21; No 15: 22.37. For **Helsinki** (15½hrs) - No 32: 21.30. For **Berlin** (28hrs) and **Warsaw** (16hrs) - No 125: 12.21; No 13: 16.59; No 33: 18.35; No 15 also to **Hoek van Holland for UK**: 20.11. Note: 'If you only have a ticket as far as Berlin and wish to go to Hook of Holland try to arrange an upgrade on the train before Rzepin where the Hook carriage is detached from the Berlin portion of the train', Keith Watson (UK). 'It's possible to go to Belorusskaya Station and bribe the guard to let you on the train'. Sophie Mackenzie-Ross (UK).

There are left luggage rooms and lockers in all stations. For accommodation advice, see 'No hotel booked?' below.

Visa extension It may become easier to extend/convert your visa from transit to tourist and is worth trying. The office is at 42, Ulitsa Chernyshevskovo (metro Ploshchad Nogina, then bus No 45 or a 20min walk). Some people have managed this, taking their passports in in the morning and collecting them in the afternoon.

ORIENTATION AND HOTELS

Central

At the very centre of the city are the Kremlin and Red Square and the most conveniently placed hotels are in this area. The **Rossiya** at 6 Ulitsa Razina is the world's largest hotel and there are good views from the restaurant at the top (metro: Ploshchad Nogina). The luxurious and expensive **Metropole** (1 Prospekt Marxa) is as much a

historic monument as a hotel for it was here that Rasputin is said to
have dined, and Lenin to have made several speeches. Its beautiful
Art Nouveau interior featured in the film of *Dr Zhivago* and has
recently been completely renovated in a Finnish-Soviet joint venture.
The **Moskva** is at 7 Prospekt Marxa but it is not an Intourist hotel.
The **National** (14 Prospekt Marxa), built at the same time as the
Metropole, will be closing soon for extensive renovations. The
Intourist (3 Ulitsa Gorkogo/Tverskaya) is large and modern, next
door to the National. The nearest metro station for the Metropole,
National and Intourist is Prospect Marxa. The **Savoy**, at 3 Rozhdest-
venka (formerly Ul. Zhdanova), is the old Berlin restored to its
former glory in a joint venture between Finnair and Intourist. It is a
luxurious hotel popular with business people (metro: Kuznetsky
Most).

Middle zone
At about 5kms from Red Square, the Sadovoye (Garden) Ring Road
encircles the city centre and there are several other hotels beyond
this ring. The run-down **Belgrade II** on the Sadovoye (near Smolen-
skaya Ploshchad metro station) is where many independent travellers
get lodged. Then there are the two Stalinist 'wedding-cake' sky-
scraper-hotels: across the river is the **Ukraina**, 2 Prospekt Kutuzov-
sky, not far from Kiev Railway Station and the **Leningradskaya** is
near Komsomolskaya metro station, so it's convenient for trains to
Siberia or Leningrad. The **Mezhdunarodnaya** ('Mezh' for short),
inconveniently located at 12, Krasnopresnenskaya Nab. is a 500m
walk from Ulitsa 1905 metro. The luxurious **Cosmos**, built by the
French is 10km from the centre, near the Exhibition of Economic
Achievements (metro: VDNK). The **Sevastopol**, opened in 1979, is
about 20km out and not recommended (metro: Sevastopolskaya or
Kakhovskaya). Other hotels occasionally used for foreigners include
Akademicheskaya I (Leninsky Prospekt), **Akademicheskaya II**
(Donskaya Ulitsa), the **Druzhba** (53, Prospekt Verdanskogo; metro:
Prospekt Verdanskogo) and the **Molodyozhnaya** (27, Dmilvovskoye
Shosse).

Outskirts
Beyond the outer ring road (Moscow's equivalent of London's M25)
there are two hotels that are cheaper but inconveniently distant from
the centre. The **Mozhaiskaya** is about 21km out (165 Mozhaiskaya
Highway) and the **Solnechny Hotel and Campsite** (21 Varshav-
skoye Highway) is 27km from the centre on the main road to
Warsaw. Both have complimentary buses to and from Red Square
(every couple of hours - check at Service Bureau for times. Note that

neither of these hotels has facilities for money-changing. If you're only staying one night it's worth paying a bit more to be closer to Red Square and the main sights.

No hotel booked?

There are several ways round this problem. At Belorusskaya station a 'hotel' train is brought into the station each evening and you can buy a ticket for a berth for 2 roubles. You buy tickets at counter No 4 in the booking office. They're not too keen to sell these tickets to foreigners so try to look as Russian as possible or get someone else to buy the ticket for you. Failing this a hard-currency bribe may work. In extremis you can spend the night in the waiting-room upstairs which is at least warm. You may be approached by students who are happy to put you up for the night in their flat in exchange for a small gift of western origin.

TRAILBLAZER feedback 'It's worth explaining how to use the combination-lock luggage lockers at all Russian stations because they're not as straight-forward as they look. Find an empty locker and put your luggage in it, taking care not to leave any valuables. Before you close the door set the dials (1 letter, 3 numbers) on the inside of the door to your desired combination, insert required change (usually 15 kopecks) and close door. Note down the number of the locker as well as the number of the combination'.

TRANSPORT

The best way to get around is on the palatial metro system. It's cheap (15 kopecks per ride) and fast (trains every 90 seconds at peak times). There is also a comprehensive but overcrowded bus and tram service. Taxi-drivers are unco-operative unless hard currency, a packet of Marlboro cigarettes or anything else in short supply, is offered. There is a very pleasant river trip (Route 1, frequent departures) which leaves from the Kiev terminal (Kievskaya metro station) and passes the Lenin Hills, Gorky Park going towards the Kremlin and tying up after 1½ hrs at the Novopassky Bridge terminal.

TOURS

The hotel Service Bureau offers a wide range of tours, the best being the Kremlin/Armoury tour (2 hrs, daily (except Thurs) at 09.45, US$18.25); the Kremlin Cathedrals tour (1½hrs, daily (except Thurs) at 11.30, US$9.25) and the Kremlin Diamonds (1½hrs, Mon, Tue, Sat at 13.40, US$15.00 but temporarily closed). There is also a city sightseeing tour by bus daily at 10.00 and 14.30, 2½hrs, US$9.25. Every Friday there is an 8 hr trip to Zagorsk for 20 roubles. There are also tours of Red Square, the city and its housing estates, the metro system, a boat trip on the Moskva as well as tours to many museums. You can do most of these just as well on your own though. Excursions further afield include Zagorsk (which you pass on the Trans-Siberian); Borodino, Tolstoy's estate, Yasnaya Polyana; Gorky (Nizhni Novgorod) and the palace at Arkhangelskoye.

MOSCOW METRO PLAN (ENGLISH)

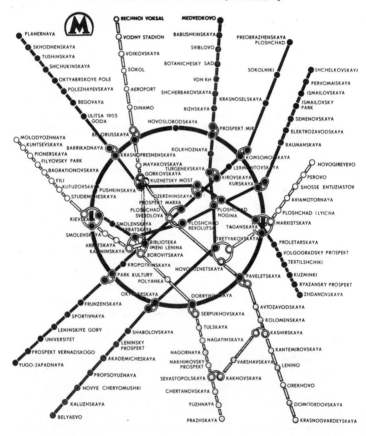

Money

If you need dollars for hard currency restaurants, try offering the hotel bureau de change your travellers' cheques in exchange for cash. If that doesn't work you could purchase a Coke in a Beriozka shop with a travellers' cheque and the change will be in dollars. American Express cheques can be traded in for dollars at the USSR Bank for Foreign & Economic Affairs on Ul. Sadovo Kudrinskaya.

MOSCOW METRO PLAN (RUSSIAN)

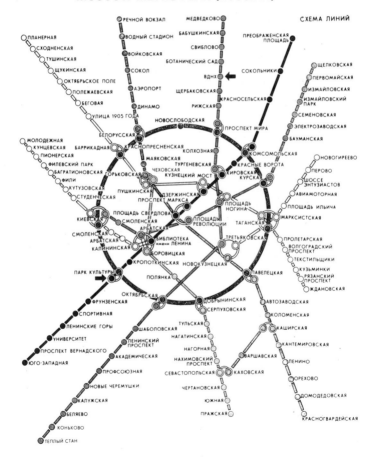

MONGOLIAN EMBASSY

If you need a transit visa these are available on the spot at 7/1 Spasopeskovskij Perelok (Tel 241 15 48) from 09.00-13.00 and 14.00-18.00 Mon to Fri. You need 3 photos and approx US$15. One traveller was given an open-dated transit visa by this embassy, allowing him to spend as long as he liked 'transiting' the country.

WHAT TO SEE

Red Square

This wide cobbled square, *Krasnaya Ploshchad* in Russian, extends across the area beside the north-eastern wall of the Kremlin. The main sights around the square are St Basil's Cathedral, Lenin's Mausoleum, GUM Department Store and the Kremlin.

St Basil's Cathedral

Also known as the Church of the Saviour and nicknamed the Pine-apple Church by Victorian travellers, this whimsical architectural creation is as much a symbol of Moscow as Tower Bridge is of London. Commissioned by Ivan the Terrible, it was completed in 1561 and so pleased with the result was the Tsar that he had the architect's eyes put out (the guides tell you) so that he would never be able to produce anything to equal or surpass it. Apparently the architect went on to produce other buildings so perhaps this is a tall story; but it's a good one fitting the Tsar's character perfectly. St Basil's is indeed a quite incredible building, with its nine brightly-painted, dissimilar domes and the stone-work decorated with the intricate patterns more usually found on the wooden buildings of the time. For many years a museum, it has been returned to the Church.

Lenin's Mausoleum

The low red building that houses the embalmed remains of the Soviet founder is beside the walls of the Kremlin, to one side of the square. A grim pair of sentries guard the entrance. As the clock on nearby Spassky Tower chimes the hour, a **changing of the guard ceremony** takes place and the soldiers being relieved goose-step off to the Kremlin. The pilgrim-queue is always long (not as long as it used to be with communism not held so highly) but moves surprisingly fast. If you're with an Intourist guide (or have got yourself an official slip of paper from the Intourist Main Office located nearby, beside the Intourist Hotel) you'll be ushered to the front. Note that no cameras are allowed, guards check pockets that look suspiciously lumpy and turn away offenders. Slouching and putting your hands in your pockets is also forbidden in the presence of the revered corpse which is laid out in air-conditioned comfort dressed in a suit with blue polka-dot tie. Lenin is certainly well-preserved for someone who's been around for the last 65 years or so. I thought he looked a little pasty, more like a china doll than a wax-work (which the Soviets will assure you he is not). There's even talk of his being removed and given a proper burial. He receives visitors every Tues, Wed, Thurs, Sat, Sun, from 10.00 to 14.00.

Lenin Lives!

On 21 January 1924 Lenin, paralysed since 1923, suffered another severe stroke and died. It was the end of the man but the beginning of the cult which flourishes today, for no Soviet town is without a Lenin statue, no public office lacks a Lenin portrait. After an autopsy had been carried out, a full report was published in all the papers. The public were treated to a ghoulish list of weights and measurements of most of the internal organs of their dead leader (his brain weighed 1340g - far larger than average). Then the embalmers began their work. One wonders if the decision the Central Executive Committee took in 1924 to preserve Lenin's body, had anything to do with Howard Carter's discovery of the Pharaoh Tuthankamun fourteen months earlier. Indeed, Dr Zbarsky, who headed the Russian team of embalmers boasted that Lenin's body would remain unchanged indefinitely.

Meanwhile, the Immortalisation Committee launched a competition to find the best design for a mausoleum. Entries included bizarre designs like a giant screw with a statue of Lenin on the top of it; a working technological display including a turbine, a tractor and a locomotive and, in the best of bad taste, a church. In the end the cubist design of A.V.Shchusev was accepted. He envisaged the cube, like the pyramid, as a symbol of eternity and it was his plan that every Soviet home would have its own little cube to the memory of the dead leader. In spite of pleas from Lenin's wife and several high-ranking officials that it was Lenin's cause, not his corpse, that should be revered and remembered, the mausoleum was built in 1930, of red granite and black labradorite.

GUM Department Store

Built in 1894, this remarkable glass-roofed building houses the largest department store in the Soviet Union. Ten per cent of all the non-food commodities purchased in Moscow are bought over the 1½ miles of counters here. You won't find an awful lot to tempt your pampered Western eyes but it's an interesting place to visit. Here, as in Red Square you are likely to be approached by Russians wanting to buy things off you.

Lenin Museum

Almost every Russian city seems to have a museum devoted to Lenin memorabilia but this is the original. There are photos, paintings, newspaper cuttings, statues and busts as well as his coat and toupée, the chair he used in the Geneva library and a plaque presented by the (former) Greater London Council to mark the London house in which he stayed in 1905. Open daily (except Mon) from 10.00 to 18.30. Entrance free. Nearby, housed in the large red building at the north end of Red Square is the **State History Museum**.

The War Memorial
It has become a tradition for bridal couples to visit this monument on the day of their wedding, posing for photographs beside the eternal flame. Beneath the marble lies the body of one of the soldiers who helped to stop the German advance on Moscow in 1941.

The Kremlin
The heart of Moscow and the seat of the Soviet government, the Kremlin is, in fact, a large walled castle. Although the site has been continuously occupied for at least the last 800 years, the walls and many of the cathedrals date from the fifteenth century. There are 20 towers, the most famous being the **Spassky Tower** above Red Square. The entrance to the Kremlin is over the bridge on the opposite side to Red Square. There's a left luggage office under the bridge. Note that you may not take rucksacks or large bags into the Kremlin and you won't get past the guards in a pair of shorts. If you want to go inside the cathedrals (well worth it) you should buy tickets (20 kopecks per cathedral) at the kiosk in the Aleksandrovsky Gardens (see map) before you go into the Kremlin. In fact there is a ticket machine in the Cathedral Square but it's usually out of order.

Cathedral Square (See map on page 145)
In the centre of the Kremlin is the square around which stand four cathedrals and the **Bell Tower** of Ivan the Great (81m/263ft high), which Napoleon attempted to blow up in 1812. Beneath the tower stands the Tsar Bell, at 200 tons the heaviest in the world. The piece of the bell that stands beside it broke off during the fire of 1737. Nearby is the largest calibre **cannon** in the world (so say Intourist).

The Cathedral of the Dormition/Assumption (Uspenski Sobor), the work of an Italian, was completed in 1479 and was the traditional place of coronation for the tsars of Russia. During the last coronation, of Nicholas II on 26 May 1896, something happened that was taken by those who saw it as a bad omen: as Nicholas walked up the steps to the altar, the chain of the Order of St Anthony fell from the Imperial shoulders to the floor. (The large wooden throne belonged to Ivan the Terrible).

The Cathedral of the Archangel (1505-09) looks classically Russian from the outside but the hand of its Italian architect Alevisio Novi of Milan can be seen in the light interior. Forty-six tsars (including Ivan the Great and Ivan the Terrible) are buried here. The smaller **Cathedral of the Annunciation** (1484-89), the private chapel of the tsars, was the work of Russian architects and contains icons by the great master, Andrei Rublyev. The **Church of the Deposition of the Virgin's Robe** (1484-5) was designed as a private chapel for the clergy. The Patriarch worshipped in the **Church of the Twelve Apostles** (1656) next door to his residence.

Other buildings The **Great Kremlin Palace**, now a government building, is not usually open to visitors. One wall of the Italian-designed **Faceted Palace** (so-called because of its facade of pointed stone blocks) faces Cathedral Square. The **Golden Tsarina Palace** or Terem Palace with its striking red and white tiled roof is one of the oldest parts of the Kremlin and dates from the seventeenth century. The seat of Soviet government is the modern (not unattractive) **Palace of Congresses**. The **Armoury Museum** should not be missed (although admission is usually only possible if you go on a previously arranged tour) and it contains a dazzling display of the jewels of tsars and their regalia, weapons and armour. Of special interest to Trans-Siberian passengers is the ornate **Great Siberian Easter Egg** (probably the finest of the 56 famous Imperial Easter Eggs made by Carl Fabergé). It contained a clockwork model of the great train, complete with golden engine (with a ruby for the headlight), five gold coaches and a church-car (Hall III).

Tretyakov Art Gallery
The best collection in Moscow of Russian paintings, icons and sculpture is housed here. There are icons painted by Andrei Rublyov; *Christ's First Appearance to the People* which took Alexander Ivanov 20 years to complete and two halls devoted to the great Russian masters Ilya Repin and Vasily Surikov. The gallery is at 10 Lavrushinsky Perelok, (Metro: Novokuznetskaya). Opening times 10.00 to 20.00 (except Mon). Now open after extensive renovations.

Pushkin Museum of Fine Arts
Most interesting for its large collection of Impressionist paintings including many famous canvases (Manet's *Déjeuner sur l'Herbe* for example, and Monet's *Boulevard des Capucines*). There are also galleries of Egyptian antiquities and Old Masters. Well worth a visit, the museum is at 12 Ul. Volkhonka, (metro: Kropotkinskaya) open daily (except Mon) 10.00-20.00, early closing Sun at 18.00.

Sandunovskaya Baths
If you've just stepped off the Trans-Siberian, a traditional Russian bath in the oldest public *banya* in the city is an invigorating and

interesting experience. These baths were built 150 years ago and beautifully decorated in the Classical style. There's a sauna, small pool and hot and cold showers. Not very easy to find, they're located on Neglinny Perelok, a side street off Ul. Petrovka, not far from the Bolshoi. Take your own soap and shampoo and note that large bags or rucksacks may not be brought in here.

USSR Economic Achievements Exhibition
Eighty pavilions and open-air displays in this large park show Soviet economic and cultural achievements. Outside the gate is the impressive 295 ft **monument to the Russian space programme** with **museum** beneath it. In the centre of the pavilions are the fountains, gilded hero workers in a rather poor proletarian equivalent of the great golden fountains of Petrodvorets outside Leningrad. Among the more interesting pavilions is the Cosmos hall in which there are replicas of Soviet spacecraft and satellites, including *Vostok* in which Yuri Gagarin made the first flight in space in 1961. Beyond the show-grounds is the eighteenth century **Ostankino Palace**, now a museum of serf art in an enchanting building that is well worth a visit (but closed Tue & Wed), and the Ostankino television broadcasting tower with its revolving restaurant. Located near the Cosmos Hotel (Metro: VDNKh).

Novodevichy Convent
This beautiful sixteenth century walled convent is well worth visiting. Time your visit so you can attend one of the services held in the **Church of the Assumption** here (weekdays: 08.00 & 18.00 daily, Sun: 07.00, 10.00, 17.00). The **Cathedral** is famous for its frescoes and highly-ornate, multi-tiered carved iconostasis. It is at present a museum, open daily (except Tues and the first Mon of each month) from 10.00-17.30 but may soon be reconsecrated. Among those buried in the **cemetery** (entrance around the back of the Convent and interesting for the outlandish headstones - one has a model tank on it!) are Khrushchev, Gogol, Chekhov and Prokofiev. Nearest metro station: Sportivnaya.

Other museums, galleries and churches
There is simply not room in a guide-book of this type to give details of more than a few of Moscow's 150 museums and exhibitions. There are museums devoted to Gorky, Tolstoy, Dostoyevsky, Pushkin, Chekhov, Gogol, Glinka, Lermontov and the icon painter Andrei Rublyev; museums of science, folk art, anthropology, the theatre and famous battles (the Battle of Borodino Museum). Further information from the Service Bureau in your hotel.

RESTAURANTS

The whole restaurant scene has changed over the last few years with co-operatives and foreign joint ventures challenging the former monopoly of the Moscow City Council. With more and more places demanding hard currency (some only in the evening) a visit to a good restaurant may cost about as much as in the West, from about £8-20/US$15-35 per person, tips are expected and bookings usually required (get the Service Bureau to help with a phone-call). If you're short on time and money, see 'Cheap places to eat' below.

Council-run & hotel restaurants There are some good places to be found along Ul. Gorkogo/Tverskaya, which stretches north from Red Square. The **Aragvi** (6 Ul.Gorkogo/Tverskaya, tel 229-3762) serves good Georgian food (shashlik, chicken tabaka, grilled sturgeon); the **Baku** (24 Ul. Gorkogo/Tverskaya, tel 299-8506) specialises in Caucasian cuisine (one of the specialities being Scotch eggs!); For a good view while you eat try **Seventh Heaven**, the revolving restaurant in the Ostankino television tower, or the top of the **Rossiya Hotel** (Russian specialities). Other hotel restaurants to try include the **Savoy** (expensive), the **Sakura** (expensive *sushi* flown in from Japan) and the **Russkiy** at the Mezhdunarodnaya, and the restaurants at the **Intourist** and the **Tsentralny** (10 Ul. Gorkogo/Tverskaya).

Co-operatives and foreign joint ventures Most famous of these is the expensive **Kropotkinskaya** (36, Ul. Kropotkinskaya, tel 201-7500). Traditional Russian cuisine with live music. Roubles and no reservations needed for lunch but credit cards and reservations only for dinner. **Glazur** (12, Smolensky Boulevard, tel 248-4438) is a Swiss joint venture offering excellent Russian food for hard currency and credit cards only. **Kafe Margarita** (28 Malaya Bronnaya (off Ul. Bolshaya Sadovaya), metro: Mayakovskaya, no reservations needed) ideal for a coffee and pastries or an inexpensive light meal. **Lasagne** (40, Ul. Pyatnitskaya, tel 231-1085) - good Italian cuisine. **Mei-hua** for Chinese(ish) food at Ul. Rusakovskaya 2/1, Stoyenie 1 (under railway bridge by Krasnosyelskaya metro station), tel 264-9574, roubles and credit cards. Then there's always **Pizza Hut** (Ul. Gorkogo/Tverskaya) and **McDonalds** (see below) which is further up Ul. Gorkogo/Tverskaya on Pushkin Square.

Cheap places to eat If you're on a tight budget it will probably be better to eat at buffets, *stolovaya* (self-service 'dining-rooms'), cafés and kebab and hamburger stands. There's a good self-service place

100m from the Intourist Hotel along Ul.Gorkogo/Tverskaya (beside the theatre). Outside the Intourist there's a 'Pepsi and Hamburger' stand. The railway stations are often good places for cheap snacks. By the upstairs waiting-room in the Belorusskaya station you can get excellent *pelmeni* (Siberian meat-filled ravioli) and there's a good restaurant in Kievskiy Station. There's a self-service canteen on the ground-floor of the Moskva Hotel (blue sign above side door). More expensive, but still payable in roubles, are take-aways from Pizza Hut, and meals at McDonald's (Pushkin Square).

McDonald's in Moscow

The queue for the world's largest branch of McDonald's (and the first of a planned 20 branches in the USSR) often stretches right the way round Pushkin Square but they say it's the only queue in Moscow where you're guaranteed to get something at the end of it. Probably the most famous joint venture, this one was the result of many years of negotiations between the Canadian subsidiary of McDonald's and Moscow City Council. Most of the ingredients come from the USSR, processed by a US$40 million distribution plant specially built outside Moscow. There was tremendous competition for the 600 jobs (over 27,000 applications) and pay is not much more than the average for the city, except for management. The restaurant is decorated inside with Disneyland panoramas of the world 'outside' (models of the Eiffel Tower and Big Ben, a Rio seascape and a Japanese corner). Apparently Russians had to be educated into the art of eating hamburgers. They began by deconstructing them, eating the top of the bun first, followed by the salad, then the burger! Best time to go is 9.30-12.30 weekdays. Follow Ul. Gorkogo/Tverskaya up from the Intourist Hotel to Pushkin Square (15-20mins). Fries rather salty, say the experts.

NIGHTLIFE

Tickets to the **Bolshoi** can be difficult to come by unless you're prepared to pay high prices in hard currency to the Service Bureau in your hotel (around US$40). There's a chance that you could get returns if you go to the theatre before the performance and touts sometimes sell tickets (check they're for the right day before paying) in front of the Bolshoi for US$5-15. Kiosks on street corners sell tickets for the opera, concerts, the circus and puppet shows. The folk dance display at **Slavyansky Bazaar**, 13, 25th October St, (near Red Square) has been recommended (pay in roubles. The best jazz is at the **Bluebird Jazz Club** (23 Ul. Chekhov, which is just off Ul. Gorkogo/Tverskaya). Heavy metal and rock bands play at the **Hard Rock Café** (basement of Zilyony Theatre in Gorky Park) which was started by former rock star Stas Namen and light meals are available (prices can be high). All the hotels have bars (hard currency only, although the Intourist Hotel does have a roubles bar on the 20th floor), some of which stay open very late. The Savoy has a **casino**;

the Intourist, Cosmos and Mezh have slot machines that are very popular with Muscovites.

SHOPPING

As foreign joint venture boutiques infiltrate Moscow, the State Department Store GUM, on Red Square, now looks even more depressing but is an interesting building. There's probably more to buy in the other department store, TSUM, near the Bolshoi. Other shopping areas are Ul.Gorkogo/Tverskaya, the pedestrianised Arbat (off Prospekt Kalinina) with its street artists, antique shops and cafés; and Prospekt Kalinina (a shopping street built in the sixties). The Russian equivalent of Hamleys is Detsky Mir (Children's World) at 2 Prospekt Marxa. For books, go to Dom Knigi (26 Prospekt Kalinina), Druzhba (15 Ulitsa Gorkogo/Tverskaya) or Moskva (8 Ulitsa Gorkogo/Tverskaya). For records try Melodiya (40 Prospekt Kalinina). A more appealing range of goods is available from the Beriozka shops in most Intourist hotels. The largest is in the Rossiya Hotel. See page 63 for general information about shopping.

MOSCOW: THE KREMLIN

1. War Memorial
2. Left luggage
3. Entrance
4. Palace of Congresses
5. Church of the Twelve Apostles
6. Church of the Deposition of the Virgin's Robe
7. Cathedral of the Assumption
8. Cannon
9. Bell Tower of Ivan III
10. Tsar Bell
11. Cathedral of the Archangel
12. Cathedral of the Annunciation
13. Faceted Palace
14. Saviour Cathedral
15. Terem Palace
16. Grand Kremlin Palace
17. Armoury
18. Poteshny Palace
19. Arsenal
20. Govt Building
21. Supreme Soviet
22. Spassky Tower
23. Ticket kiosk

Novosibirsk

With a population of over one and a quarter million people, this is the largest city in Siberia and its industrial centre but, of the three cities east of the Urals that foreigners usually visit (Novosibirsk, Irkutsk and Khabarovsk), Novosibirsk has probably the least to offer the tourist. It is a relatively young city and has few buildings of historic interest. You can visit the enormous **opera house**, the **museums** and the nearby town of **Akademgorodok**, the controversial Scientists' City. Here, over three thousand scientists and research assistants live in a well-designed town, with shops and other facilities that are superior to those to which other Soviet citizens have access. Winters here are particularly harsh, with temperatures falling as low as -50°C.

HISTORY

Novosibirsk didn't exist before the Trans-Siberian was built and its spectacular growth this century is largely due to the railway. In 1891 it was decided that the railway bridge over the Ob should be built here. A small settlement grew up to house the railway workers and it was named Novo Nikolayevsk in honour of the accession of the new Tsar.

By 1900 over 15,000 people lived here and the numbers grew as railway and water-borne trade developed. As far as tourists were concerned, there was only one reason for getting off the Trans-Siberian in Novo-Nikolayevsk as Baedeker's 1914 *Guide to Russia* points out: 'It is a favourite starting point for sportsmen in pursuit of the wapiti, mountain sheep, ibex and other big game on the north slopes of the Altai'. The town suffered badly during the Civil War when 30,000 people lost their lives. During the first four months of 1920 a further 60,000 died of typhus. In 1925 the town was re-christened Novosibirsk, meaning 'New Siberia'.

Between 1926 and 1939 population growth reached its highest rate. The coal-fields of the Kuznetsk Basin were developed and Novosibirsk became the transit base after a rail link was built. The town of Novokuznetsk, in the centre of the Kuznetsk region, grew quickly and iron ore arrived by rail from the mines in the Urals for its blast furnaces. In the early 1930s the nine-hundred mile Turksib Railway was completed linking Novosibirsk with Turkestan in Soviet Central

Asia, via Semipalatinsk and Alma Ata. Grain from the lands around Novosibirsk could then easily be exchanged for cotton which grew best in Central Asia. The building of this railway, which was the jewel in the new government's first five-year plan, was recorded on movie-film and is still shown today as a fascinating early example of documentary film.

During the Second World War large numbers of people and complete factories were evacuated from European Russia to Novosibirsk and the city has continued to grow since then. It is now the busiest river port in the area and the major industrial centre in Siberia with most workers being employed in engineering or metallurgy factories. In spite of the wealth generated by the natural resources in the area, Novosibirsk is no better run than other Soviet cities. On both occasions when I've visited the place there's been no hot water not just in the hotel but in most of the city. The *dezhurnaya* informed me with a shrug of her shoulders that it's been like this on and off since 1917!

The recent pro-democracy movement that has been seen in many parts of the country involved hunger strikes by Novosibirsk students in the large square in front of the Opera House, in 1990. The main street, Vokzalnaya Magistral, was lined with posters, placards and wall-paintings for new political parties.

NOVOSIBIRSK

1. Station
2. Novosibirsk Htl
3. Tsentralnaya H.
4. Sibir Hotel
5. Opera House
6a/b. Folklore
   Museum
7. Dom Museum
8. Art Gallery
9. TSUM
10. Beriozka
11. Circus
12. Korean Rest.
13. Bus to
   Akademgorodok.
14. Market
15. Ocean Rest.
16. Lenin Sq.
17. Cathedral
18. Preserved Loco
19. Kafe Jazz
20. Bakery

METRO STATIONS

A. Pl. G. Mikhailovskogo
B. Sibirsk/Krasny Prospekt
C. Ploshchad Lenina

ORIENTATION AND HOTELS

Novosibirsk is the third largest city (in area) in the USSR and it was designed on a massive scale. Krasny Prospekt (Red Street) extends across it from north to south for over ten kilometres. The wide Ob River flows through the middle of the city although the centre, with the railway station, the main hotels, Lenin Square (Ploshchad Lenina) and the Opera House is on the east bank. Hotels used for foreigners include the **Novosibirsk** (conveniently located across the square in front of the station), the **Sibir** (opened 1991, claiming to be the most luxurious hotel in Siberia, with several restaurants, bars, hairdresser, shops, sauna and an independent hot water supply) is a 10 min walk from the station at 21 Ul. Lenina; the **Tsentralnaya II**, is just off Lenin Square, at 3 Ul. Lenina and has an older annexe (where they tend to put independent travellers) on the Square itself. Facilities include two restaurants, shops, sauna and a service bureau. The hotel has seen better days but the staff is friendly.

TRANSPORT

On foot, Lenin Square is about twenty minutes from the railway station, straight down Vokzalnaya (Station) Magistral. A **metro** system is being built, its stations lined with solid Siberian marble. The main stations are now open. To get to Lenin Square (metro: Ploshchad Lenina) from the station (metro: Ploshchad Garina Mikhailovskogo), go one stop to Sibirskaya/Krasny Prospekt, change to the 'Studentskaya' line and it's one stop to Ploshchad Lenina. **Taxis** are metered and unlike in Moscow you may be able to find one that doesn't demand hard currency (but not if you try to get it from your hotel). There is an extensive **bus** service which you can also use for Akademgorodok (about 15 miles south of the city). Bus no.8 covers this route and there is a bus-stop on Dimitrova Prospekt. Tickets can be bought in booklets of six from the bus driver and then it is your responsibility to stamp them using the machines in the bus. Taxis to Akademgorodok cost about 7-10 roubles and can be flagged down along Vokzalnaya Magistral. You can also get a **train** to Obskoye More (the station for Akademgorodok) but it's easier to go out by taxi or bus and then back by train.

TOURS

The service bureaux in the hotels offer a morning tour of the city as well as tours to the sights and museums described below. Tours to Akademgorodok usually include a visit to the geological museum there and a boat-trip on the Ob Dam in summer. They will also arrange tickets for the circus (closed in summer) and for opera and ballet at the Opera House. You can organise your own boat trip from the landing stage near Retsnoy Vokzal metro station to Korablik Island, which is popular with Novosibirskians for swimming and sunbathing from May to Sep.

WHAT TO SEE

Lenin Square and the Opera House
This is the centre of the city and the square is dominated by the vast **Opera House**, one of the largest in the world, with its silver dome. It was completed in 1943, when most of the builders had been sent off to join the war effort. Its completion is seen as all the more heroic in that it was to some extent due to the women and children, who helped the few remaining builders. In the middle of the square is a **statue of Lenin**, his coat blowing behind him in the cold Siberian wind, a rather more artistic representation of the man than the many others you will by now have seen. He is flanked by three soldiers on his right and by two 'Peace' figures on his left, who look as if they are directing the traffic that flows around the great square. In the winter there are *troika* rides around the square, and people build ice-sculptures. The low building above the metro station is the oldest stone structure in the city and houses part of the local **folklore museum**.

The Folklore Museum
The bulk of this collection is housed in the ground floor (entrance at the side) of the block right behind TSUM but eventually displays will be moved to the Lenin Square building; a most interesting museum, although you will need a guide to explain the significance of some of the historical exhibits. There are displays showing life before the Revolution, including a rusty British Norton motor-bike (built in 1909), a Singer sewing machine and an early piece of rail (stamped Birmingham 1899). There's a Lenin corner with the usual memorabilia, and a gallery recording the troubled times during the civil war when the city was occupied by White Russian and Bolshevik troops and then devastated by the outbreak of typhus that followed in 1920. There is also a very extensive and interesting display of Siberian flora and fauna, including stuffed mammals (bears, elk, beavers and wolves etc), birds, fish and snakes. (Fifty species of mammal, thirty species of fish and the same number of birds are found only in the Novosibirsk *oblast*.) There's a collection of Siberian grasses and trees, a geological display and the skeleton of a mammoth. The

labels on the natural history exhibits are in Latin as well as Russian. For a translation of some of them refer to Appendix C. Open daily 10.00-18.00.

Other things to see
The **Cathedral** (far end of Krasny Prospekt, near the river) has been given back to the church and is no longer a museum. Restoration is well underway and may now be complete. The **Dom Museum Kirov** is devoted to Kirov, the Party leader that everyone had assumed would succeed Stalin but who was assassinated in 1934. It is housed, close to the new Sibir Hotel, in an attractive log cabin, one of the few that have survived. Outside there is a statue of Kirov and in the neighbouring apartment block there is a small exhibition of local handicrafts, mainly wood-carvings. There is a good **Art Gallery**, along Krasny Prospekt, on Sverdlovsk Square.

RESTAURANTS

The best restaurant in town will probably be in the new **Sibir** Hotel, to which the chef from the **Novosibirsk** has absconded. It is likely to take hard currency only. Also good (and also hard currency only but you may be able to persuade them otherwise) is the **Druzhba** in the Tsentralnaya II (fried fish US$7.00, steak and mushroom sauce US$8.00) which often has a (loud) band playing. The Korean restaurant, **Sobek** (a joint venture), has been recommended. The **Ocean** on Krasny Prospekt specialises in fish dishes. You could try **Kafé Jazz Forum** (35 Ordzhonikidze, see map) which has live jazz at the weekends (19.30hrs). For budget dining there are self-service cafés on Vokzalnaya Magistral, a restaurant in the **station**, while snacks are also available at the **bakery** opposite the Tsentralnaya Hotel.

SHOPPING

There are the usual souvenir shops in the hotels and a Beriozka shop on Cheluskintser Street near the circus. The main streets for shopping are Vokzalnaya Magistral but you'll do better in Akademgorodok. There is a large department store (TSUM) next door to the Folklore Museum and a very good bakery opposite the Tsentralnaya Hotel. The market is one block east of Krasny Prospekt.

AKADEMGORODOK

The trip to Akademgorodok takes about 45 minutes by bus or train (see 'Transport' above), 25 minutes by taxi, following the river south. It makes a good excursion if only to get out into the countryside and walk through the forests around the dam. Built in the late 1950s to house the scientists of the Siberian branch of the USSR Academy of Sciences, the town now comprises 26 special research institutes and a staff of over 12,000 people. They live in pleasant apartment blocks along tree-lined avenues on the edge of the Ob Dam. Akademgorodok was built as an experiment which must be regarded as successful since similar 'Scientist Cities' are planned for Leningrad and Vladivostok. Some of the scientists may have been sent to the town as children to the famous boarding school which takes those children (from all parts of the USSR) who excel in scientific subjects.

AKADEMGORODOK

1. Bus Station
2. Bus to Novosibirsk
3. Supermarket & bookshop
4. Bakery
5. Cafe
6. Geological Museum
7. Market
8. Zolotaya Dolina Hotel
9. Obskoye More Station

The **Geological Museum** in the Institute of Geology & Geophysics is open to tours only. You could follow one in or just say 'Moozay-oh' to the doorman and the museum is straight ahead, up the short flight of stairs. The overpowering mineral wealth of Siberia is displayed here, including the purple mineral charoyit found only in this part of the world. It's interesting to wander round the shops here and note the wider selection of goods available, just one of the incentives provided for the privileged scientists and their families. The well-stocked **bookshop** has maps, posters and books in English. There's a good restaurant at the **Zolotaya Dolina** Hotel but you'll probably need to book.

When you've looked round Akademgorodok you can walk through the birch forest (inhabited by dozens of red squirrels) and over the railway-track (hourly **trains back to Novosibirsk**, 06.02-23.17, from Obskoye More station, tickets from the *kassa*) to the beaches of the **Ob Dam**. It was created by the building of the Novosibirskaya power station, the first large hydro-electric power station in Siberia. This is a good place for swimming as the water is surprisingly warm. If you want to have a picnic on the beach, the bakery sells bread and pastries and sometimes has delicious fish stew in take-away plastic bags.

Irkutsk

If you can afford only one stop on the Trans-Siberian, you should make it in Irkutsk. In this city that was once known as 'The Paris of Siberia', you will find the people far more friendly and relaxed than in European Russia. You can take an excursion to **Lake Baikal** (allow two nights in Irkutsk for this), visit the old churches and museums or simply wander around the streets, a very pleasant way of passing the time. Along some streets you can still find the cozy-looking log cabins (eaves and windows decorated with intricate fretwork) which are typical of the Siberian style of domestic architecture.

History

Military outpost

Irkutsk was founded as a military out-post in 1652 by Ivan Pakhobov, a tax-collector who had come to encourage the local Buryat tribesmen to pay their fur tribute. By 1686 a church had been built and a small town established on the banks of the Angara. The tea caravans from China passed through Irkutsk, fur-traders sold their pelts here and the town developed into a centre for trade in Siberia. By the beginning of the nineteenth century, it was recognised as the administrative capital of Siberia. The Governor, who lived in the elegant white building that still stands by the river (opposite the obelisk), presided over an area twenty times that of France. At the time when prisoners were being sent to Siberia, political exiles often chose to live out their lives in Irkutsk. The most celebrated exiles were the Decembrists, the men who attempted the coup in St Petersburg, in 1825. The houses in which some of them lived can now be visited. With the discovery of gold in the area in the early 1800s, 'Gold Fever' hit Irkutsk. Fortunes were made in a day and lost overnight in the gambling dens.

Boom town

By the end of the century, in spite of a great fire in 1879 which destroyed 75 per cent of the houses, the city had become the financial and cultural centre of Siberia. Its cosmopolitan population included fur traders, tea merchants, gold prospectors, exiles and ex-convicts. Irkutsk had become 'a city of striking contrasts, with the magnificent mansions of the rich at one end of the pole and the dilap-idated shanties of the poor at the other' as an Intourist brochure pointedly remarks. Those prospectors who were lucky became exceedingly rich, some amassing personal fortunes that would be equivalent to £70 or £80 million today. Often no more than illiterate adventurers or ex-convicts, they spent their money on lavish houses, French tutors for their children and clothes from the Paris fashion houses for their wives.

By far the most exciting occasion in the Irkutskian social calendar for 1891 was the visit of the Tsarevich (later Nicholas II) who only stayed a day but still had time to visit the museum, the gold-smelting laboratory and the monastery, to consecrate and open the new pon-toon bridge over the Angara (replaced only in 1936), to review the troops and to attend a ball at the public club. On 16 August 1898 Irkutsk was linked by rail to Europe with the arrival of the first Trans-Siberian Express.

The first rail travellers arrive

The train brought more European tourists than had dared venture into Siberia in the days when travelling meant weeks of discomfort bumping along the *Trakt* (the Post Road) in a wooden *tarantass* (carriage). Their guide books warned them of the dangers that await-ed them in Irkutsk. Bradshaw's *Through Routes to the Capitals of the World* (1903) had this to say about the town: 'The streets are not paved or lighted; the sidewalks are merely boards on crosspieces over the open sewers. In summer it is almost impassable owing to the mud, or unbearable owing to the dust. The police are few, es-caped criminals and ticket-of-leave criminals many. In Irkutsk and all towns east of it, the stranger should not walk after dark; if a carriage cannot be got as is often the case, the only way is to walk noisily along the planked walk; be careful in making crossings, and do not stop, or the immense mongrel mastiffs turned loose into the streets as guards will attack. To walk in the middle of the road is to court attack from the garrotters with which Siberian towns abound.'

The dangers that Bradshaw warned his travellers against were no exaggeration, for at the time, the average number of reported mur-ders per year in Irkutsk was over four hundred, out of a population of barely 50,000. There were also reports of criminals who roamed the streets in sledges, lassoing their victims and dragging them off to murder and rob them in the quieter back-streets.

Irkutsk today

Today's Siberians are rather better behaved, indeed among the most friendly and hospitable Soviet citizens you will meet. A city of over half a million, Irkutsk is still one of the largest suppliers of furs to the world markets, although engineering is now the main industry.

For too long Irkutskians have had to allow Moscow to make all their political, economic and environmental decisions for them. Control is slowly being decentralised and there have been a number of victories recently. The wood pulp mill built on the edge of Lake Baikal is still an eyesore but complex filtration systems now ensure that waste water is purified before being returned to the lake. The city now needs to have direct access to the hard currency earned by the export of furs and minerals from the *oblast*, so that the money can be spent improving the lot of the people of Irkutsk rather than disappearing into the bottomless coffers of Moscow.

ORIENTATION

When you arrive at Irkutsk station, you will be on the west bank of the river and your hotel (the imaginatively named Intourist) is directly opposite on the east bank along with the main part of the city. The tourist bus will take you over the bridge. The 290 room **Intourist Hotel** is the best in town (although reading the notice by the lift:'No interfering with the passenger entering' one wonders about the type of people who put up here; perhaps this is why it is now the only hotel used for foreign tourists. It has two restaurants (slow service and food not as good as it was) and all the usual tourist services, including sauna (14.00-22.00). As far as the local people are concerned, this is the liveliest spot in town and many wedding receptions are held here. Traveller John Webb reported that the reception that was going on while he was here ended in a fight in the hotel foyer. After a certain amount of blood-letting the contestants were driven off in a police-van. Other hotels occasionally used for foreigners include the **Sibir** (Ul.Lenina) and the **Angara** (Ul.Sukhe Bator), both near the main square.

TRANSPORT

Since most of the sights, restaurants and shops are within walking distance of the hotel, this is the most pleasant and interesting way to get around. Taxi-drivers will try to charge in dollars if you get in outside the hotel. There is no metro but the usual cheap bus service operates. Bus No. 20 runs between the station and the airport down Lenin Street. Trams 1 & 2 go from the station over the bridge and into the centre of town. Tram No 4 goes out to the airport (25 mins) from outside the Sibir Hotel and back.

● **To Listvyanka** You can get local buses to Listvyanka (for Lake

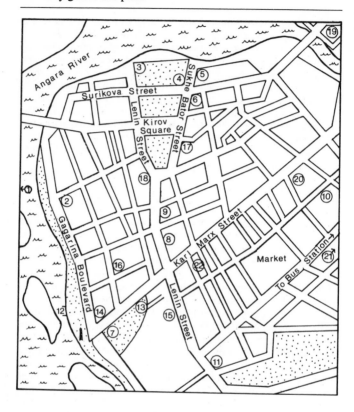

IRKUTSK

1. Station
2. Intourist Hotel
3. War Memorial
4. Church of our Saviour
5. Cathedral of the Epiphany
6. Catholic Church
7. Museum of Regional History
8. Natural History Museum
9. Art Gallery
10. Decembrists' Museum
11. Church of the Holy Cross

12. Boat trips
13. Opera House
14. Governor's House
15. Fikhtelberg Restaurant
16. Chinese Restaurant
17. Angara Hotel
18. Sibir Hotel
19. Znamensky Convent
20. Synagogue
21. Maria Volkonsky's House
22. Mongolian Embassy

Baikal) from the bus station at 7.30, 9.00, 11.30, 13.00, 14.30, 15.30, 17.00 & 19.00 plus additional services on Fri, Sat, Sun at 10.00 & 16.30. It takes about 1½hrs. Taxi from bus station 40 roubles (1hr). Most tourists get together and rent a taxi for the day. In the summer you can also get to the lake by jet-boat.

TOURS

The hotel service bureau offers guided tours to all the sights described below as well as trips to Lake Baikal (US$24 for day trip including excursion on the lake), picnics in the *taiga* and visits to schools and factories. If you need their services, organise your sightseeing as soon as you arrive at the hotel.

WHAT TO SEE

Cathedrals and War Memorial

In Irkutsk in 1900 there were two cathedrals. The splendid Cathedral of Our Lady of Kazan, which was bigger than Kazan Cathedral in Leningrad, was damaged during the civil war. It was demolished and now the ugly bulk of the **Palace of Pioneers** (the Central Government Building) stands in its place, opposite the war memorial. Here you can witness the strange spectacle of children dressed in army uniforms, wielding rifles and guarding the memorial. Only children who get good marks at school are allowed the privilege of goose-stepping round the Eternal Flame. The changing of the guard ceremony takes place every 15 minutes. The second cathedral, the **Cathedral of the Epiphany** (1724), is across the road, beside the river. In the great fire of 1879 it was badly damaged and the heat was so intense that it melted one of its 12-ton bells. It has recently been repainted inside and is now an icon museum and art gallery (look for the painting by Dobrovolsky of the old pontoon bridge (which was replaced in 1936) on a chilly Irkutskian evening). It is also used as a concert hall; the acoustics are particularly good and the concerts are worth going to. The door needs a hard push as it sticks and is unlikely to have been repaired by the time you read this. Open 11.00-18.00.

The Church of Our Saviour

This boat-shaped church, which once stood in the shadow of the cathedral, is now a museum but may be converted back to a church. There are some interesting frescoes on the exterior which depict, from left to right, Buryats being baptised, Christ being baptised and the local bishop, Innocenti, being canonised. The museum inside contains a small display of stuffed local animals (see Appendix C) and some live reptiles and insects from around the world (downstairs). Upstairs there is an interesting religious history display including the robes, rattle of human bones and feathered head-dress of a *shaman* (see below); masks and robes used in Tibetan Buddhist mystery plays; prayer wheels and Buddhist texts from the monasteries south of Irkutsk. One part of the gallery is used for visiting exhibitions. Open 10.00-18.00.

Shamanism
This is a primitive form of religion centred around the *shaman*, who was a kind of medium and healer. Wearing spectacular robes, the *shaman* would go into a trance by beating his drum (the most important of his ritual objects) in order to communicate with the spirits. Thus he would discover the cause of an illness, the reason for the failure of the crops, or he would be warned of some disaster that was approaching. The spirits were thought to select their *shamans* before they were born and then brand them with distinguishing features: an extra finger or toe or a large birthmark. During their adolescence they would be 'tortured' by the spirits with an illness of some kind until they agreed to act as *shaman*. Often such people were epileptic, mentally disordered or physically weak. Through their spiritual power they gained authority and often large amounts of money for performing rituals. 'Shamanism played an extremely negative role in the history of the Siberian peoples... In status, activity and interests, the *shamans* were hand in glove with the ruling cliques of the indigenous populations', wrote the Marxist anthropologists M.G.Levin and L.P.Potapov, in *The Peoples of Siberia*. Other anthropologists have been less severe noting that shamanism gave those with mental and physical disorders a place in society at a time when most other societies shunned the handicapped.

The Catholic Church
Opposite the Church of Our Saviour is a church with a tall steeple: the **Catholic church**. It is the only (mock) Gothic church in Siberia and was built in 1883 by exiled Poles and is now used for organ concerts.

Museum of Regional History
This museum, situated south of the Intourist Hotel beside the river, has some interesting exhibits. Upstairs is a local achievements' gallery including a model of part of the BAM (see p111). Above the stairs is a panorama showing the Great Fire of 1879. The ethnographic galleries are downstairs and exhibits include flints and bones from the archaeological site of Malta, just outside Irkutsk where evidence of human habitation has been found dating back 24,000 years; the inside of a settler's house earlier this century with carved wooden side-board and HMV gramophone and 78s; a set of robes worn by a *shaman*, together with his antlers and drum; photographs

showing what life was like for past inhabitants and the convicts; and also a most peculiar article of clothing: a suit made completely of fish skins, the standard summer costume of the Goldi tribe who lived in the Far Eastern Territories.

Natural History Museum

The Natural History Museum is closed for refurbishment until 1992 when it may be relocated. Check with the service bureau. The collection used to contain examples of local animals that are trapped for their fur and a large collection of stuffed animals including wild boar, Siberian roe deer, musk deer (with protruding fangs), elk, wolves, eagles and also the skeleton of a mammoth.

Places of worship

At the turn of the century, Irkutsk boasted fifty-eight places of worship. This fell to only three or four after the Revolution but with *glasnost* has risen to ten today.

The **Church of the Holy Saviour** at Znamensky Convent lies to the north-east of the city, over the bridge. The church is beautifully decorated and still under restoration. Services are held regularly (usually at 08.00 and 17.00 but check with the Service Bureau). Beside it are the graves of Yekaterine Trubetskoi (see page 160) and also Gregory Shelekhov, who founded the colony of Alaska in 1784 (sold to the USA in 1868). His grave is marked by an obelisk decorated with cartographic instruments.

Orthodox services are also held at the **Church of the Holy Cross** which is reputed to have the best choir in the city.

It's also interesting to visit the **synagogue**, a large blue building, the lower storey of which has been converted into a factory. Enter through door on left with the three stars above it. You may need to knock loudly to get the care-taker's attention and he'll then shuffle down in shirtsleeves and braces to open up. He'll check that you have some kind of head covering (there are a few caps you can borrow) and give you a photocopy of the Ten Commandments.

Art Gallery

This is the most impressive art gallery east of the Urals and includes works by eighteenth and nineteenth century Russian, German, Flemish, French, Italian and English painters. The collection was begun by Vladimir Sukachev in the 1870s and 'donated' to the city after the Revolution. There are, however, the inevitable modern Soviet galleries where you can see such socialist masterpieces as A.A.Plastov's *Supper of Tractor Operators* and A.V.Moravov's *Calculating of Working Days*. The gallery devoted to nineteenth century local scenes is particularly interesting and in the gallery of the Western Art (XV-XIX centuries) you will find a small canvas with the label 'Landsir 1802-73' which is *The Family of Dogs* by Sir Edwin Landseer, the man who designed the lions in Trafalgar Square. The gallery is open daily (except Tue) from 11.00 to 19.00; 1.50 roubles.

Decembrists' 'Dom' Museum (Trubetskoi house)

This cozy wooden house that was occupied by Sergei and Yekaterine Trubetskoi (who is buried in the graveyard of the Church of the Holy Saviour) and other nobles involved in the unsuccessful coup in 1825 is preserved as a museum, kept as it was when the exiles lived there. The beautiful white porcelain fireplace in the drawing-room came from the old Grand Hotel. In the cellar there is an interesting display of old photographs showing life in the Nerchinsk silver mines and a prison cell in Chita. There is also a picture of Maria Volkonsky (see below) and her child. Open daily (except Tue) from 10.00-18.00 (40kop). 'With thermopane windows it would be a great place' Louis Wozniak (USA) - Visitors' Book in this museum.

Maria Volkonsky's House

The large and attractive blue and white house of this famous Decembrist who followed her husband into Siberian exile is open to the public. If you've read Caroline Sutherland's *The Princess of Siberia* then you must visit Maria Volkonsky's house. It is a grand old building but rather a pity it's so sparsely furnished as it doesn't have the lived-in feel of the other 'Dom' museum. Displays include Maria's clothes, letters, furniture, and church robes of 18th and 19th centuries. In the yard there are several wooden buildings and a well. Open daily (except Mon) 10.00-18.00 (80kop).

Other sights

In the **Fur Distribution Centre** (on the southern outskirts of the city) you will be shown some of the 18 varieties of mink and also the most valuable pelts, those of the Barguzinsk sable, which sell for £500 each. The Centre and also the **Mineral Museum** in the Geological Institute across the river can be visited only as part of a tour. In the summer, touring companies perform in the imposing **Opera House**, built at the turn of the century, in Karl Marx Street. There

---

(Opposite) Top: In spite of considerable rehousing programmes, there are still many traditional wooden buildings in Irkutsk. **Bottom:** The Khamar Daban mountains seen from across Lake Baikal (photo: Jim Malcomson).

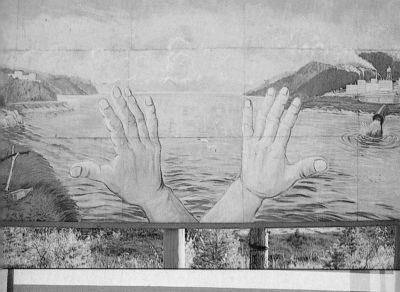

СОХРАНИМ ПРИРОДУ Байкала

Стивен Спилберг

РЕТРОСПЕКТИВНЫЙ ПОКАЗ
ФИЛЬМОВ САМОГО
ПОПУЛЯРНОГО
КИНОРЕЖИССЕРА

ИНДИАНА ДЖОНС:

- В ПОИСКАХ НОЕВА
КОВЧЕГА

- ХРАМ СУДЬБЫ

- ПОСЛЕДНИЙ КРЕСТО-
ВЫЙ ПОХОД

- Е.Т. ИНОПЛАНЕТЯНИН

- ЦВЕТЫ ЛИЛОВЫЕ
ПОЛЕЙ

are also **boat trips** (1-2hrs) along the river to the Dam and power station. They leave daily at 9.00 from the landing-stage near the **Explorers' Obelisk** (Yermak, Count Muravyev-Amursky on its sides and the double-headed Imperial eagle on the railings surrounding it) and cost 40 kopecks. If you're wondering what the building beside the obelisk is (the one that looks like a mini Sydney Opera House), its main use is for dog shows.

MONGOLIAN EMBASSY

Located at 11, Ulitsa Lapina (tel 42370/42260), it's possible to get visas here. Some travellers report that they're issued on the spot, others have had to wait a few days. If you need one go as soon as you arrive in Irkutsk. Open 09.00-18.00 for visas (US$ required).

RESTAURANTS

The best place in town is the **Chinese Restaurant** (joint venture) at 67, Fifth Army St, a ten-minute walk from the Intourist Hotel and open 11.00-16.00, 18.00-23.00. You will need to book for dinner and will probably have to pay hard currency. The other successful co-operative was the **Fikhtelberg** (run by East Germans and changing hands following the demise of the DDR and the special concessions that allowed the proprietors to run the place). Apart from these two restaurants the **Intourist Hotel** is the other premier eating spot, according to the locals who go there for special occasions. A sign outside the door invites you to 'make a journey to the world of Siberian cuisine with its secrets of national dishes and peculiar drinks'. The national dishes can be good and they often serve the delicious Baikal *omul* here.

For cheap places to eat there are self-service **cafés** on Karl Marx Street and a reasonable one (good ice-cream) opposite the bus station. **Cafe Blinniya** (Ul.Lenina) serves pastries and hot chocolate.

SHOPPING

The main street for shopping is the one that runs north-east from the obelisk: Karl Marx Street. There are several department stores here, some good **bakeries**, a **liquor store** that sometimes has vodka and in

(Opposite) Top: The concerns of local environmentalists over pollution in Lake Baikal are evident from this lake-side billboard. **Bottom:** Now showing in Siberia: Spielberg's 'ET'.

the **photographic shop** you can buy either Lenin's *Speeches* or *The Battleship Potemkin* as 8mm home movies. The **central market** is one block south of Karl Marx Street. One stall was selling imitation USSR passports, so that if you couldn't get the real thing you could still impress your friends. There's a good **bookshop** with a wide selection of posters opposite the square (with the statue of Lenin hailing a taxi) at the west end of Karl Marx Street.

The main area for **black market** transactions is in the park by the river opposite the Intourist Hotel, where there's even a special black market kiosk which is where anything you've sold tends to land up. The Poles dominate the scene and have made themselves so unpopular with local people that one was recently found floating face-down in the Angara River. Artists sell their work in the same park and will try to get you to pay in dollars.

Excursions from Irkutsk

LAKE BAIKAL

The world's deepest lake is 64 km (40 miles) south of Irkutsk. Known as the 'Blue Eye of Siberia' it is also the world's oldest lake, formed almost 50 million years ago. It is over 1500 metres (5000 feet) deep and is estimated to contain more than 20,000 cubic kilometres of water - roughly 20% of the world's freshwater supplies. If all the world's drinking water ran out tomorrow, Lake Baikal could supply the entire population of the planet for the next 40 years.

It is also one of the largest lakes, being about 400 miles long by between 20 and 40 miles wide. The water is incredibly clear and completely safe to drink owing to the filtering action of the numerous types of sponge which live in its depths, along with hundreds of other species found nowhere else.

Russian colonists called Baikal the 'Holy Sea' since there were so many local myths and legends surrounding it. The Buryats believed that the evil spirit Begdozi lived on Olkhon Island in the middle, though the Evenki *shaman*s held that this was the home of the sea god, Dianda. It is hardly surprising that these primitive tribes were impressed by the strange power of the lake for at times sudden violent storms spring up, lashing the coast with waves up to seven feet high. It freezes to a depth of about ten feet for four months of the year, from late December. The Angara is the only river that flows out of the lake and since the dam and hydro-electric power station were built on the Angara in 1959, the water-level of the lake has been slowly rising.

The remoteness of the lake kept it safe from the threat of environmental damage until the building of the Trans-Siberian at the end of the last century. Damage to the environment is increasing following the building of the new towns on the northern shores for the construction of the BAM line, and also owing to industrial waste from Ulan Ude (the Selenga River flows past the city into the lake via one of the world's last large wetlands, the Selenga Delta). The most famous campaigner for the protection of the lake is author, Valentin Rasputin. Demonstrations in Irkutsk in 1987 resulted in proper filtration equipment being installed in the wood pulp mill on the edge of the lake. Campaigners bemoan the fact that the government's anti-pollution laws have no teeth and believe that the lake should be placed under the independent protection of UNESCO.

Excursions to Lake Baikal

The road from Irkutsk takes you through *taiga* forests to the lakeside village of Listvyanka. Intourist offer tours for US$24 (English-speaking guide, lunch, visit to the Limnological Institute, short boat-trip on the lake) leaving from the Intourist Hotel daily at 10.30 and returning around 17.00hrs. Book as soon as you arrive at the hotel. There are cheaper alternatives. Local buses (see page 155) go from Irkutsk bus station but you should go as early as possible as they get very crowded. If you can't get on the bus, get together with some other travellers and rent a taxi from opposite the bus. You might even be able to negotiate a day-rate but ensure your driver understands how long you want to spend at the lake. It is much easier to get a bus back from Listvyanka: just stand at the stops by the port or by the Limnological Institute and flag the bus down. It leaves Listvyanka at 07.00, 11.50, 14.40, 18.00, plus an extra bus at 15.50 (Fri, Sat, Sun) and there may be an additional bus at 09.45 daily in the summer but check. A further alternative might be to get a group of travellers together and approach the touts hanging around outside the Intourist Hotel. Given enough hard currency they will arrange anything you want. Don't hand over any money until the transaction is complete.

The Open-Air Museum of Wooden Architecture

Beside the road between Irkutsk and Listvyanka is the **Museum of Wooden Architecture**, an interesting collection of reconstructed, traditional wooden houses. It is located at the km47 marker from Irkutsk, the km23 marker from Listvyanka - ask the bus driver for the 'Moozeyoh'. There is a large farmhouse, a bathroom with a vast wooden tub and, a short way along a path, a water-mill and a post-house, complete with the Imperial crest on its roof-top. When the only way to cross Siberia was by road and river, fresh horses and extremely basic accommodation were available from post-houses. The museum is open only in the summer but you can wander round outside in spring and autumn.

The Legend of Shaman Rock
The Old Man Baikal had three hundred and thirty-six sons (the number of rivers which flow into the lake) and one daughter, the beautiful but headstrong Angara. As fast as her brothers collected water for their father, she gave it away. She further enraged him by refusing to marry the weak and feeble Irkut, preferring the mighty Yenisei (the longest river in the USSR). Papa chained her up but one stormy night she slipped her bonds and fled north to her lover. As she ran her furious father hurled a huge boulder after her. She got away but the rock re-mained to this day, a small point showing above the water. The level of the lake has since risen and very little of Shaman Rock is now visible. It lies in the stretch of water between the hotel and Port Baikal.

The Limnological Institute and Museum
This was set up for the study of the unique marine life and animals in the Baikal area. Over 80 per cent of the species here cannot be found anywhere else in the world. The very high oxygen levels in the lake created the ideal environment for many creatures which have long since become extinct elsewhere. They include the freshwater seals, found only here and until recently threatened with extinction by the Buryats who turned them into overcoats. They are now a protected species, listed in the 'Red Book' and currently number about 60,000. A unique Baikal fish is the *golomyanka* which is tiny, composed almost entirely of transparent fat and lives at extreme depths. The most surprising thing about it is that, like a mammal, it gives birth to its young alive and fully formed. There's also a model of the ship, the Angara, there are some examples of the tasty *omul* (which ap-pears on local menus) and a collection of the sponges which keep the water so clean. The colonists' wives discovered that they were also very useful for polishing the samovar. Turn to Appendix C for a translation of the Latin labels on the stuffed local fauna in the museum. There are ambitious plans for a new ecology centre to be built here and a model is on display.

Baikal Hotel
Above the road and just before the village is the pleasant Intourist hotel where most tours stop for lunch and it's also possible to stay here. ('At Lake Baikal our bath actually had a plug! - Yes we left it!'

Keith Fothergill, Guernsey). The hotel restaurant is good and there's a Japanese restaurant 'Baikal Tokyo' (hard-currency only) in the grounds, open 12.-15.00 and 18.00-21.00, where Siberian girls in kimono serve *teppanyaki*, *sukiyaki* set, fried crab set, and take-away lunch-boxes are also available. Behind the hotel is a hill that gives a good view over the water to the Khamar Daban mountains. The half-hour hike up is well worth it. At the top there's a little shelter and a tree decorated with paper ribbons that people have tied to it for good luck, a very old Siberian superstition. Intourist guides never fail to recount another superstition, concerning the power of Baikal water. Dip your hands in, they say, and you will live a year longer than you otherwise would. Dip your feet in too and this will be extended to five years. Brave the icy waters and go for a swim and you'll be around for twenty-five extra years.

Listvyanka

This attractive village of wooden houses lies at the end of the road. A pleasant ten-minute walk through the village takes you to a tiny church in which an old woman sells cheap-looking icons. Although the village is worth seeing, one feels that this church has been part of the Intourist 'milk-run' for a long time. 'No smoking on the territory of the Church' warns a sign in English on the gate. Concessions to tourists have their advantages: five-star lavatories are thoughtfully located behind the church.

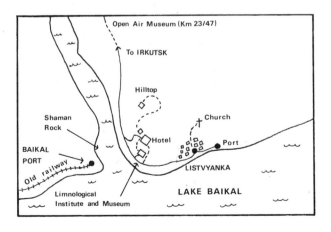

Excursions to Port Baikal

Across the water the dilapidated old station and warehouses of old Port Baikal lie rotting. Until the railway line round the south of the lake was completed in 1904, passengers crossed by steamer to Mysovaya. The largest ship was a 290 foot ice-breaker, the *Baikal*, which transported the carriages from the train on her deck. She was built by the English firm of Sir W.G.Armstrong, Whitworth and Co. in Newcastle, delivered by train in kit-form and she sank in 1919 during the Civil War. Her sister ship, the smaller *Angara*, supplied by the same firm, survived and is being turned into a museum.

It's possible to visit Port Baikal, and *Babushkin* makes the half hour crossing (May-Dec) from Listvyanka at 07.35, 9.10, 11.45, 16.10, 18.10, 19.40, 20.45 and back from Port Baikal at 06.25, 8.05, 10.00, 14.00, 17.05, 18.40, 20.05. Tickets available on the quay.

Intourist organise an all-day excursion to see the old railway line by boat, landing for lunch on a beach. Tunnels and viaducts are still in perfect condition and a train is reputed to run at night along the track from Port Baikal to Kultuk on the main Trans-Siberian line. It would be difficult to try to ride this railway as there seem to be numerous guards in the area.

Other excursions in the area

Other excursions include a 25km hike through the *taiga* to the settlement of **Bolshoi Koty**, then by boat to **Kadilnaya Pad**, where tourists stay in hunters' lodges and can have authentic Siberian Baths (see below). You could do part of this trip without the services of Intourist as there is a boat that makes the trip to Bolshoi Koty from Listvyanka at 12.30, returning at 16.30.

Special helicopter trips can occasionally be arranged to **Olkon Island**, with an overnight stay in tents, walking, fishing and a get-together with local fishermen. A 40min helicopter ride over Lake Baikal would be cheaper but would have to be specially laid on by Intourist.

Siberian bath rituals with birchen besoms

In the words of an Intourist brochure: 'Siberian bath is an incomparable experience. Its heat is milder than in sauna, it is lighter and not scorching. A birchen besom exuding forest fragrance is its traditional accessory. In the steam room bath lovers lightly lash each other with birchen besom for hours on end, and then plunge into a snow-drift or into a cold stream, depending on the season. This makes the ritual complete'.

BRATSK

An hour's flight north of Irkutsk lies one of the largest dams in the world. The enormous hydro-electric power station at Bratsk, second largest in the USSR after the one at Krasnoyarsk (also in Siberia), is the chief attraction of this town. Originally founded in 1631 it was never more than a tiny village until construction started on the dam in 1955. It reputedly produces 4.5 million kW of electricity and until recently Intourist guides enjoyed informing Westerners that this was almost twice the output of the largest power station in the USA and ten times the best British figures. With the Grand Coulee, in Washington State, USA, pumping out 9.7 million kW, and the new Soviet power station on the Tungusku River estimated at 20 million kW, Bratsk is losing out in the field of superlatives.

Orientation and hotels

Most people come by 'plane but it would also be possible to get here by jet-boat (Meteor) from Irkutsk (leaving 08.30, arriving in Bratsk at 20.55. On the return journey it leaves at 07.50 arriving at 20.45 in Irkutsk. Theoretically you could come by train, along the line that branches off the Trans-Siberian at Tayshet (650km west of Irkutsk) to join the Baikal Amur Mainline.

The town of Bratsk is actually four separate communities arranged around the vast dam and connected by a road which runs right over the five-kilometre-long dam wall. Tourists stay at the bleak **Taiga Hotel**, the best of the three in the town, located in the centre of Bratsk, or else in the **Bratsk**.

Sightseeing

Once tourists have seen the **power station** and been taken to the plush demonstration hall for a lecture about the great achievement, they can go for a swim in the chilly waters of the dam, or visit the **open-air museum** (which has some interesting reconstructions of traditional houses, a Cossack watchtower and an abundance of azaleas in spring) and the wooden **puppet theatre**. Guided tours often include a visit to a nursery school where the children go through the motions of entertaining the tourists. That just leaves the **aluminium smelter**, the **timber complex** and the **toboggan slide**.

TRAILBLAZER feedback 'The dam is a dam. You can go down into the bowels of the Hoover Dam and be over-awed. This one just has a posh reception centre with a huge mural of Lénin. It's really not worth the effort to visit the dam or even to go to Bratsk at all'. Bob Helling (UK).

ABAKAN

Founded at the end of the 18th century as Ust Abakanskoye, the town became Abakan in 1931 and has now developed into an industrial city of 150,000 people, and the administrative centre of the Khakass Autonomous Region. Its main attraction is its pleasant location among rolling hills, and hiking trips can be organised from here.

Orientation and hotels
There are flights from several cities including Moscow and Irkutsk. To come by train you leave the main Trans-Siberian line at Krasnoyarsk (Train Nos 23/24 & 657/658) or Achinsk (Nos 193/194 & 659/660) and it's about 12hrs from both stations. The main tourist accommodation is in the **Khakasia Hotel**, at 88 Prospekt Lenina.

Sightseeing and excursions
Sights include the **Local Lore Museum** with its unique collection of outlandish stone sculptures, many just rough-hewn heads on huge long necks. Found along the banks of the Abakan and Yenisei Rivers, they are reminiscent of the Easter Island statues. There is also a zoo with Siberian and Far Eastern Territories fauna.

Several excursions can be organised from Abakan. **Sushenskoye**, on the banks of the Yenisei, is where Lenin began his married life. Exiled in 1897, he was joined by Krupskaya and they stayed in the village until 1900. The Soviets are good at open-air museums and whole streets are recreated here: houses of rich traders, poor peasants, shop, tavern and bathhouse. **Minusinsk** is a small town 20km from Abakan, with a well-preserved central part, a museum and the Cathedral of Our Saviour. You may also be taken to the **Sayano-Sushenskoye Dam and Hydro-electric Station** (claimed to be the world's largest when completed), the old mining settlement at **Maina** and the tourist centre on the banks of the Yenisei.

YAKUTSK

The capital of the vast Yakut Autonomous Region (see page 234), Yakutsk was recently opened to tourists. Lying only 600km south of the Arctic Circle, this is one of the world's coldest cities (average temperature in January is minus 32°C) although summers are pleasantly warm (plus 19°C in July). It is also one of Siberia's oldest settlements, founded in 1632 on the banks of the mighty Lena River as a base for exploration and a trading centre for gold and furs. There is little left of historic interest in this polluted city but it is worth visiting for the excursions on the Lena and to see the effects of permafrost. All the buildings have to be built on massive stilts or they would sink into the ground as the heat from them would melt the permafrost.

Only about 30% of the people are Yakut, the majority of the rest being Russians and Ukrainians. Like other minority groups in the USSR the Yakuts are starting to make themselves heard in Moscow. They have been exploited since the region was first colonised 350 years ago and even now most of the foreign exchange earned from their fabulously rich region stays in Moscow.

Orientation and hotels

Until the rail link is finished (which will be many years from now as there are still 800km to cover) the only way in is by plane from Irkutsk, Moscow and several other cities. Direct flights are being established with Yakutsk's twin city, Fairbanks in Alaska. The smartest hotel (although visitors complain about the shortage of lavatory seats) is the **Yakutsk**, reputed to have the best restaurant in the city. The other hotels used for foreigners are the **Taiga** and the **Lena**.

Sightseeing and excursions

Possibly the most interesting place to visit in Yakutsk is the **Permafrost Institute**. You are taken 12 metres underground to see part of the old river bed, where the temperature never varies from -5°C. Permafrost is said to affect 25% of the earth and 50% of the USSR. Outside the Institute is a model of the baby mammoth (now in Leningrad Natural History Museum) that was found preserved in permafrost. Other sights include the **Geological Museum** - crammed full of all the geological wealth of Yakutia; the **Yakutian State History and Culture Museum**; the **Literature Museum** which has a *yurt* outside it and the **Natural History Museum** housed in what was formerly the Bishop's Palace. Outside is an *ostrog* (wooden fort). Tours can be arranged to Yakut and Evenk reindeer breeding farms. So far only two churches are open: the Russian Orthodox (5, Ul. Ushakov) and Baptist (40, Ul. Pilodor). The church that can be seen from the Taiga Hotel has been converted into the Communist Party Archives but will be reconsecrated soon.

Excursions on the Lena River The geological formations known as the **Lena Pillars** have fascinated travellers since the 17th century. About 140km upriver from Yakutsk, the rock of the cliffs alongside the river has been eroded away into delicate shapes of a reddish brown colour. The excursions (by jet-boat) leave around 08.00, with breakfast (followed by vodka and cognac) on board. You reach the landing spot about four hours later and it takes about an hour's strenuous climb to reach the top for a great view of the river and the cliffs. A picnic (with delicious fish soup) is usually organised. Be very careful disembarking, one of our party (who'd overdone the vodka at breakfast), toppled off the flimsy gang-plank into the chilly waters. On the way to the Lena Pillars you pass the archaeological site of Dering Yuryakh, where in 1982, evidence was discovered of man dating back 1-2 million years, putting the site on a par with Professor Leakey's excavations in Africa. There's not much to see but there are plans for a museum, in which case a stop would be made on the day-trip to the Lena Pillars.

There are cruise ships *M/S Demyan Bedny* and also *M/S Mikhail Svetlov* which do 7-10 day trips along the Lena River starting from Yakutsk, passing the Lena Pillars and continuing to the river port of Lensk before returning.

Intourist in Yakutsk are very helpful and keen to develop tourism in their region. Possible future excursions may include trips to the Arctic and even the North Pole.

Ulan Ude

Recently opened to foreigners, Ulan Ude is well worth a stop if only to visit the **Datsan** (25km outside the city), which until recently was the only operating Buddhist monastery in the USSR. Rail enthusiasts may be interested to visit the **locomotive repair workshops**. Quite apart from these two attractions, the people of Ulan Ude are very friendly and hospitable, the place has a relaxed atmosphere to it with quite a few traditional Siberian wooden buildings still standing. Tourist facilities are rudimentary but the people in the Intourist office are charming and helpful. Hotel facilities will be basic, unless the 'new' hotel, which has been under construction for more than 10 years, has at last been finished. Ulan Ude is a 45min flight or 7½hr train journey from Irkutsk.

HISTORY

Military outpost
Once known as Verkhneudinsk, this city of almost 400,000 people is the capital of the Buryat Republic (although only 21% of the people are Buryats, the others Russians (70%), Tartars and Ukrainians). In 1668 a military outpost was set up here in the valley between the Khamar Daban and Tsaga Daban ranges, beside the Selenga and Uda Rivers. A cathedral was built in 1745 and the town became an important trading centre on the route of the tea caravans from China. The railway reached the town in 1900 and in 1949 the branch line to Mongolia was opened. There are now large railway repair workshops here and a locomotive assembly plant which until 1956 produced steam engines. Other industries include food-processing, helicopter assembly and glass-making.

Ulan Ude opens to foreign tourists
The military bases in the area kept Ulan Ude definitely off-limits to foreigners until the recent thaw in East-West relations.

Princess Anne led the tourists in in 1990 with the first royal visit to Siberia since the Tsar's execution in Sverlovsk in 1917. A local official declared that her visit was probably the most exciting thing that had happened in Ulan Ude since Genghis Khan swept through on his way to Moscow in 1238.

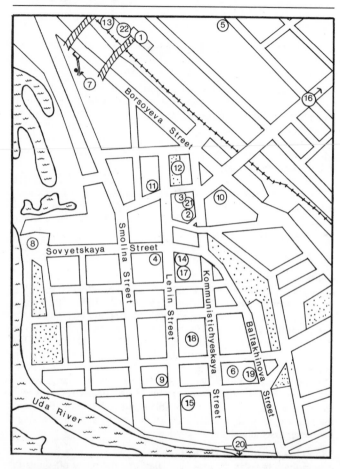

ULAN UDE

1. Railway station
2. Ulan Ude Hotel
3. Baikal Hotel
4. Barguzine Hotel
5. Odon Hotel
6. Zolotoy Kolos Hotel
7. Intourist Bureau
8. Main bus station
9. Bus park
10. Book/poster shop
11. Opera House
12. Main Square
13. Locomotive Works
14. Natural Hist. Museum
15. Historical Museum
16. Open Air Museum
17. Bookshop
18. Department store
19. Market
20. Church
21. Coffee shop
22. Preserved loco

ORIENTATION AND HOTELS

To walk into the town (15min) from the station you will need to cross over the railway tracks on the pedestrian bridge. The new **Ulan Ude Intourist Hotel**, located just off the main square, may now be completed and should be the classiest place to stay in town. There have been problems constructing such a high building (13 storeys) in an earthquake zone and the concrete has been flowing for the last 10 years or so. The **Baikal Hotel** on the main square is next best and perfectly adequate. The third hotel used by Intourist is the **Barguzine** with a stuffed menagerie (birds dangling by their legs from the ceiling and an elderly grizzly) in the foyer. There is also the **Odon**, near the station on the northern side of the track and the **Zolotoy Kolos** by the market. The **Intourist Service Bureau** is down a side street near the station (see map) but will move to the new Ulan Ude Intourist Hotel when it opens.

TRANSPORT

Most places (except the Datsan and the Open-air museum) are within walking distance but there's also a tram and bus service that operates as in any other Soviet city. Taxi-drivers are less likely to demand payment in dollars since not too many western tourists have been this way yet. They congregate in the usual places: outside the hotels and by the railway and bus stations but are not in great supply. To get to the **Datsan** either get a taxi or take local bus No 104 (Kolonova) from the main bus station. It leaves at 07.10, 12.00 & 16.00 taking about 45 mins. It's best to take the early morning bus but you'll need to get to the bus station by 06.45 to get a seat. Buy a ticket from the bus driver (65kop). Alternatively bus No 130 (every 30 mins) goes as far as the village of Yevolga from which it's a 4½ mile/7½km walk across the plain to the Datsan (walk straight ahead out of the village, then turn right after about 2 miles/3km. You can see the Datsan from there). To reach the *Open-air museum* (20mins) take bus No 8 from the bus park near the old church (see map).

TOURS

Until tourism gets going here tours are organised on an individual basis which means that they are expensive. A fully guided tour to the Datsan by car could be as much as US$80 for an individual and you'll need to make arrangements as soon as you arrive. Tours to any of the sights described here, including visits to the Locomotive Works, can be arranged through the service bureau (see above).

WHAT TO SEE

Datsan (Yevolga Monastery)

The centre of Buddhism in the USSR and until recently the only operating monastery in the country stands on a wide plain 25km outside the city and it's a fascinating place to visit. (See 'transport' above for how to get there.) Before the revolution there were hundreds of similar monasteries in the area with the largest and most important at Selenginsk (see p247). All were closed and the monks sent to the *gulags* but when Stalin allowed more religious tolerance in the 1940s, astrologers selected this site for a new monastery, built in 1946. There are now 30 lamas, some of them very elderly but novices still join each year and most spend up to five years studying in Ulan Bator. Tibetan Buddhism is practised here and the Dalai Lama has visited the Datsan several times, most recently in September 1990 when the crowds that came to see him filled the whole of the monastery enclosure.

Visiting the Datsan As you walk around the Datsan don't forget that you should pass objects of Buddhist veneration (prayer wheels, temples and stupas) on their left (ie in a clockwise direction) and hats must be taken off inside the buildings. The largest temple, a three-storey pagoda, was built in 1971, burnt down 4 months later (with the loss of numerous valuable *thangkas* (paintings)) and rebuilt in 7 months. Inside, its joyous technicolour decoration seems rather out of place in the grey USSR: golden dragons sliding down the 16 wooden columns supporting the upper galleries (where there is a library of tantric texts), and hundreds of incarnations of Buddha lining one wall. Easy to recognise is *Manla*, with dark blue face, the Buddha of Tibetan medicine. The largest *thangka* hanging above the incarnations is of the founder of this 'yellow hat' (Gelukpa) sect. Juniper wood is burnt and food and money offered to the incarnations. Visitors are shown round by a smiling monk and you should make a donation of some kind, bearing in mind the tremendous rebuilding projects that are now being carried out on old monasteries in the area.

Beside this is a smaller pagoda, and the **green temple** behind it is the oldest building in the complex, constructed in 1946. The octagonal white building houses a model of **Buddhist paradise** (*Devashin*) and a library of several hundred Tibetan and old Mongolian texts, each wrapped in silk. In the big **white stupa** nearby are the ashes of the most famous former head lama of the Datsan, Sherapov, who died in 1961. There is even a **Bo tree** growing very successfully from seeds brought in 1956 from Delhi, in its own greenhouse. Visiting Buddhists stay in the 'hotel' and Soviet visitors now come from as far away as Estonia to spend time studying Buddhism on a retreat here.

Snacks are available at the kiosk outside the Datsan, which is where the buses go from. You could also try hitching a ride back in a tour-bus. There is another monastery at Aginskoye near Chita and several others are reopening now.

Natural History Museum

Some of the interesting displays here include a Lake Baikal panorama with flora and fauna, and a model of the mini-submarine Pisces XI which reached a depth in the lake of 1410m in 1977; a comprehensive gallery of local birds (one of the world's few remaining wetlands is the Selenga Delta on the edge of Lake Baikal, and it is suffering badly from the pollution from the factories of Ulan Ude); two large galleries of local wildlife: eagles, wolves, bears and reindeer etc. Labels are in Cyrillic and Latin (see Appendix C for a translation). Various local arts and crafts are sold, mainly to tour groups, in the room just inside the entrance (horse-hair weavings: 120 roubles, paintings: 30-60 roubles, cedar carvings: 30 roubles). Open 11.00 - 19.00; 80 kopecks.

Cultural/Historical Museum

By the time you read this a new building should have been found for this collection devoted to lamaism (Tibetan Buddhism) and the spiritual culture of the Buryat people from the eighteenth century. It was assembled mainly from the numerous Buddhist monasteries that were closed after the Revolution. In late 1990 it was stored in the old church by the river and visits were only possible by special arrangement through the Intourist office (say you wish to visit the *fond*, (museum warehouse). Packed into the dilapidated building there are numerous Buddha figures; the robes of a Buryat *shaman* (see p158); musical instruments (conches and horns and a beautiful guitar with a carved horse's head); a large collection of masks used in Buddhist mystery plays; icons dating back to the 17th century; a display of day-to-day objects from the houses of the rich traders of Kyakta (see p247) including a Roger & Gallet shaving-cream mug; a large and valuable collection of Tibetan *thangkas* including healing *thangkas* used by those monks practising Tibetan medicine. There is also a unique *Atlas of Tibetan Medicine*.

Open-air/Ethnographic Museum

One of the best of the numerous open-air museums in the country, this collection of reconstructed buildings lies on the northern out-skirts of the city (see Transport above for how to get there). Exhibits include a Bronze Age stone circle; Evenki camp with birchwood wig-wam, implements including a sable trap, skis and sledges, and the *shaman's* hut with wooden carvings outside it: birds on poles, animals and fish. There is a dreadful zoo with camels standing in the mud, bears in tiny cages and disconsolate reindeer (the more people that complain to the guides about this the better). The Buryat area contains *ghers* (yurts) or tents of felt and wood and also a log cabin in which there are silk robes, saddles and day-to-day items. There are houses of Kazakh Russians and also 17th century orthodox Christians, built around large brick ovens with sleeping platforms on the top of them. Except in mid-summer it gets very cold walking round here so bring warm clothing.

Locomotive Works

Otherwise known as 'The Order of Lenin Locomotive and Railway Car Repair Plant', this is situated at the northwest end of the station. Between 1938 and 1956 steam locomotives were built here and there is a preserved example of one (Co17u) mounted on the right-hand side of the road to the open-air museum, not far after the railway bridge. Tours may be arranged through Intourist.

Other sights

Check with the Service Bureau to find out if there is anything on at the impressive **opera house**, which stands on the square dominated by the sinister bulk of **Lenin's head** (said to be the biggest in the USSR). It's worth spending some time wandering around the town and there are still quite a few wooden buildings to be seen, some of them really very ornate (see map for location). Over the bridge at the south end of town is the **Russian Orthodox church** where services are held regularly. Marriages take place at the **Wedding House** next door to the Baikal Hotel.

(**Opposite**) **Top:** The library at Yevolga Monastery (Datsan), 25km outside Ulan Ude contains priceless Buddhist texts and a colourful model of the Buddhist paradise. **Bottom:** This reconstructed *shaman's* hut is part of a large ethnographic display at the Open-air Museum (see above).

RESTAURANTS

There is a convenient bakery/coffee shop around the corner from the
Baikal and Ulan Ude Intourist Hotels. The coffee-shop in the Barguzine hotel is not bad. There is also a buffet/coffee shop on the 2nd
floor of the Baikal Hotel. As in most Soviet cities the locals go to the
restaurants in the hotels (no doubt the Intourist/Ulan Ude will be top
of the list when it opens) and they also recommend the Kirdir Restaurant (Shushkovka district in the north of the city).

SHOPPING

Fresh fruit and vegetables are available in the market. Inaccurate
maps and post-cards are available from kiosks. There is a good
bookshop with a wide selection of posters, books in English and also
sheet music near the main square, and another down Ul. Lenina,
which is the main shopping street.

(Opposite) Top: The mounted statue of Mongolia's Sukhe Bator in heroic pose
stands opposite his mausoleum in the square named after him, in the centre of
Ulan Bator. Bottom: Lost in a time-warp, the Bogdo Khan Palace in Ulan Bator
is a fascinating place to visit.

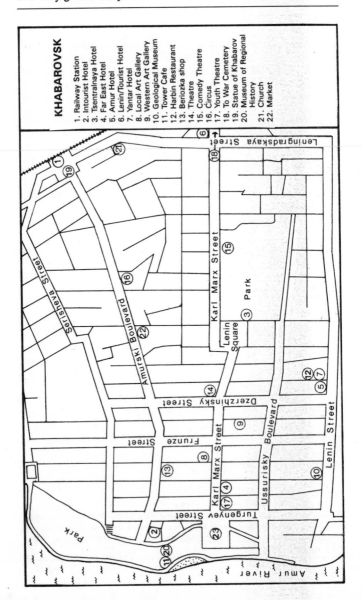

KHABAROVSK

1. Railway Station
2. Intourist Hotel
3. Tsentralnaya Hotel
4. Far East Hotel
5. Amur Hotel
6. Lenin/Tourist Hotel
7. Yantar Hotel
8. Local Art Gallery
9. Western Art Gallery
10. Geological Museum
11. Tower Cafe
12. Harbin Restaurant
13. Beriozka shop
14. Theatre
15. Comedy Theatre
16. Circus
17. Youth Theatre
18. To War Cemetery
19. Statue of Khabarov
20. Museum of Regional History
21. Church
22. Market

Khabarovsk

Until recently, travellers bound for Nakhodka and Japan were required to spend a night in Khabarovsk before catching the overnight train to the coast. Now trains from the west are timetabled to arrive in the morning, which gives you the day to spend sightseeing in this sleepy capital of the Far Eastern Territories. However, if you can stay a little longer, it's worth it. Khabarovsk is a pleasant, relaxed place though it's bitterly cold in winter. In the summer the big attraction is swimming in the **Amur River** and holiday crowds flock to its sandy banks, giving the place the atmosphere of a friendly English seaside resort; for some reason sunbathing in the USSR is often done standing up. In winter, when the river freezes, people drive their cars onto it and fish through holes chopped through the two foot thick ice. Apart from the river, the other sights include an interesting **regional history museum**, an **art gallery** and the **arboretum**, which was founded over 100 years ago to supply the numerous parks and gardens in the city.

HISTORY

In 1858, Count Muravyev-Amurski, the governor general of East Siberia who did much to advance Russia's interests in the Far East, founded a military settlement here. It was named Khabarovka, in honour of the Cossack explorer who conquered the Amur region in the seventeenth century, and whose statue now stands in the square in front of the railway station. By 1883 the town was known as Khabarovsk and the following year, when the Far Eastern Territories were made a region separate from Eastern Siberia, it became the administrative centre and the home of the governor general of the area.

Until the railway arrived, the town was just a trading and military post picturesquely situated on three hills on the banks of the Amur River, at the point where it is joined by its tributary the Ussuri. It was a junction point for passengers who arrived by steamer from East Siberia, along the Shilka and Amur rivers. Here they would transfer to another ship for the voyage down the Amur and Ussuri to Vladivostok. From 1875 onwards several plans were submitted for the building of the Ussuri Railway, which now runs along the great river between Khabarovsk and Vladivostok. Work began in 1893 and on 3rd September 1897 a train completed the first journey between these two towns. A railway technical school was opened in the following year in the street that is now called Karl Marx Street.

Early visitors

As more of the sections of the Trans-Siberian Railway were built, greater numbers of foreign travellers arrived in Khabarovsk. The *1900 Guide to the Great Siberian Railway* did not encourage them to stay long, reporting that: 'The conditions of life in Khabarovsk are not attractive, on account of the absence of comfortable dwellings, and the expensiveness of some products and of most necessary articles..... Imported colonial goods are sold at a high price and only fish is very cheap.' Tourists at the time were also advised against trying Mr Khlebnikov's locally produced wine, made from the wild vines that grow in the area because: 'it is of inferior quality and without any flavour'. Recommended sights included the wooden triumphal arch (now demolished) erected in commemoration of the visit of the Tsarevitch Nicholas in 1891 and the bronze statue of Count Muravyev-Amurski on the promontory above the river. Unfortunately, this has been replaced by one from the Lenin Statue Factory.

The city today

The railway brought more trade than tourists and though it suffered during the Civil War, the town quickly grew into the modern city it is today. Few of the old wooden cabins remain but there are some attractive stone buildings from imperial times. It is the capital of Khabarovsk *kray* (territory), one of the regions with the richest mineral deposits in the USSR, although the land is little more than a gigantic swampy forest. With its population of about half a million people, the city is a major industrial centre involved in engineering, petroleum refining and timber-working.

ORIENTATION AND HOTELS

The railway station and the **Intourist Hotel** (the main hotel for foreigners) are quite far apart, being at opposite ends of Amurski Boulevard. The hotel, which describes itself in its brochure as: 'a twelve-storey modern-style building with a clear-cut architectural silhouette', is set in a park near the river. In winter the park is filled with decorative ice-sculptures (pagodas and various animals) some of them illuminated. The Museum of Regional History is conveniently located nearby. The ugly **Tsentralnaya Hotel** is nearer the station, on Lenin Square at the east end of Karl Marx Street. Other hotels include the **Amur**, the **Hotel Lenin/Tourist** (not to be confused with the Intourist above) and the **Far East Hotel**. See map for locations.

One block south of Amurski Boulevard and parallel to it, is Karl Marx Street which runs from Komsomolskaya Square out to the airport. The impressive building on Komsomolskaya Square housed the offices of the Amur Steam Navigation Company.

TRANSPORT

Many of the tourist sights are within walking distance of the Intourist Hotel but it's a forty minute walk from the station to this hotel. There is no metro but there are regular bus and trolley-car services. Bus No.1 goes from the station to Komsomolskaya Square. Bus No.3 and trolley-bus No.1 run the length of Karl Marx Street to the airport. Taxis are available from hotels, the airport and the station. Boat trips go from the jetty below Amurski Cliff.

TOURS

The tourist service bureaux in the hotels will organise tours to the sights mentioned below as well as visits to factories, kindergartens and schools. They will also arrange tickets for the Drama Theatre, the Musical Comedy Theatre and the circus . Note that they are all closed on Mondays and that tickets must be booked before 13.00 on the day you wish to go to a performance. Additional entertainments that can be organised are boat trips (with a folk group performing on deck) and traditional Russian tea parties (at which you will be served the local delicacy, the *booblick*, which is a kind of dough-nut).

WHAT TO SEE

Museum of Regional History

The museum was opened in 1894 and based on the extensive collection of Baron Korff, a former Governor General of the Amur region. In 1897 it was moved into the three-storey building in which it is now housed. With donations made by hunters and explorers over the last ninety years, the collection has grown into an impressive display of local history, flora and fauna. The labels on the natural history exhibits are, as usual, in Russian and Latin. Refer to Appendix C for a translation.

Among the animals on the galleries on the ground floor are two **Amur tigers**. Also known as the Siberian or Manchurian tiger (*Felis/Panthera tigris altaica*), this is the largest member of the cat family and can weigh up to 350 kg or about twice the average weight of an African lion. In the same gallery are various fur-bearing animals including the large sea-otter or Kamchatka beaver (*Enhydra lutris*) from which comes the highest-priced pelts in the world. Before protection of the animal began in the early 1900s single pelts were selling for over US$2,000.

The upper galleries are devoted to local history and ethnography. The area was inhabited by several tribes at the time of the Revolution. The Goldis and Orochis lived near the mouth of the Ussuri; the Olchis and the Giliaks beside the Amur. All tribes had their *shamans* and some of their robes and equipment are on display as well as a suit made entirely from fish-skins. The skin of a common fish, the *keta*, was not used only for clothing but also for tents, sails and boots. There's also a display of early settlers' furniture, samovars and other utensils, including some bread baked by the original colonists.

Other sights and things to do

The **Geological Museum**, which has been closed for renovations for some time, is on Lenin Street, two blocks from the Amur Hotel. The **Art Gallery** is divided into local and West European sections and is also being reorganised. It was established in 1931 and includes eighteenth and nineteenth century Flemish, Italian and French paintings, Soviet works and, by far the most interesting, arts and crafts of the 'national minorities', modern Goldis, Orochis, Olchis and Giliaks who now live in 'community units'.

Founded long before the railway arrived in Khabarovsk, the **Arboretum** is an interesting place to visit. Originally set up to provide trees and shrubs for the new town's parks, it now claims to have specimens of all the plant species found in the Far Eastern Territories, well over a thousand of them. It's usually possible to go only with a tour group.

The **Amur River** is a focus of interest in both winter and summer. In the winter when it freezes local fishermen drill holes through the ice and set up little tents to sit in while they fish. In the summer the beaches along the banks become crowded with swimmers. The water is certainly not crystal clear but refreshing on a hot summer's day. You should watch out for the strong current though. There are also boat trips on the river.

There are regular services at the **church** on Leningradskaya Street.

RESTAURANTS

Tour guides will tell you that the best restaurant in town is the **Harbin**, a Chinese joint venture which even managed an accolade from the *Washington Post* ('You have to go all the way across the USSR for good *mu-shu* pork'). The food is good by Khabarovsk standards but that's not saying much. They may refuse to let you in unless you pay in hard currency and then it will be expensive (US$20+ for three-course meal). The clientèle is certainly not dull: 'We spent an evening in this excellent Chinese restaurant in the company of the local mafia' (Robert Bray, UK). Other recommended places to eat include the **Intourist Hotel**, and the **Ussuri Restaurant** near the Sovkino cinema on Karl Marx Street. For good ice-cream sundaes and meringues and a great view across the river, try the **Tower Café** in the tower on Amurski Cliff. There are also numerous cafés along Karl Marx Street.

SHOPPING

Interesting local products include ginseng and a special blend of vodka and herbs known as *Aralievaya Vodka*. The attractive, tree-lined Karl Marx Street is the place to go shopping, although the shops close from 14.00 to 15.00 for lunch. There are also the usual tourist shops in the hotels and also a Beriozka shop two blocks east of the Intourist Hotel on Amurski Boulevard.

Excursions from Khabarovsk

BIROBIDZHAN

Excursions are now possible to the capital of the Jewish Autonomous region, 170km from Khabarovsk, although most of the Jewish people have now emigrated to Israel. Located between the Biro and Bidzhan Rivers on a sheltered fertile plain, the town grew up around the railway after it was decreed that all spare lands in the Amur River basin should be given over to working people of Jewish nationality. Birobidzhan was declared the capital of the autonomous region in 1937. There's not much to see apart from the farming combinats.

NAKHODKA

Passengers on their way to Japan pass through Nakhodka but it's also an open city and so possible to stay here, in the **Nakhodka Hotel**. There are excursions to the docks, a fishing base and Vostochny port. See also page 242 for further information.

VLADIVOSTOK

Recently opened to foreign visitors after years on the 'off-limits' list. 'My tour traveled from Khabarovsk to Vladivostok on the 'Ocean' train, which like the 'Vostok' train to Nakhodka, travels almost the entire route at night. Vladivostok was a delightful city to tour (quite reminiscent of San Francisco - believe it or not) and our group had a very nice meal at the new Korean Restaurant located a few blocks from the Hotel Amursky Zaliv. We then took a two-hour hovercraft ride from Vladivostok to Nakhodka before taking the Vostok train back to Khabarovsk.' Jack Carter (USA). See page 242 for further information.

Ulan Bator

The world's coldest capital city is a fascinating place to visit even if it does, at first sight, look like just another Soviet city (links with the USSR are weakening now) with its polluted industrial suburbs and dreary concrete buildings. Amongst all this there are vibrant splurges of colour in the temples and old palaces. The Mongolian people are charming and cheerful (Luigi Barzini, driving across the country in 1907, was amazed at their high spirits; the nomads he encountered galloped alongside his car roaring with laughter). Against all this it is a very expensive place to stay (minimum US$100-160 per night depending on season. There are few hotel beds and large numbers of people who would like to sleep in them. The country desperately needs foreign cash and there is talk of opening up the country to tourism as China did in the early 1980s. Check on the current situation with the Mongolian Embassy.

As well as rail connections from Moscow and Beijing, there are flights from these two cities and also from Irkutsk.

HISTORY

Home of the Living Buddha

Until 1911 Ulan Bator was known as Da Khure to the Mongolians and by its Russian name, Urga, to foreigners. Although nomadic herdsmen had been erecting their *yurts* here for a few months each year for many preceding centuries, a permanent settlement did not materialise until 1639, when the Da Khure Lamasery was built. Until the Revolution this was the abode of the 'Living Buddha' or Dalai Lama, one of three mortal incarnations of the Buddha, the other two being in Tibet and Beijing. The Dalai Lama in Urga was usually a child, who died (or rather was murdered) shortly before reaching maturity, since it was believed that the soul of a god could dwell only in the body of a child.

Independence

When Mongolia declared herself independent of China in 1911, the city was renamed Niisled Khurehe. By this time it had become a large trading centre on the route between China and Russia. There were, in fact, three separate cities here: the Chinese, the Russian and the Mongolian. This last city was concerned not with trading tea and

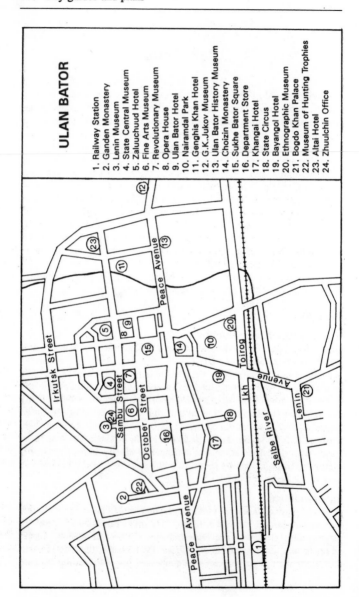

ULAN BATOR

1. Railway Station
2. Ganden Monastery
3. Lenin Museum
4. State Central Museum
5. Zaluuchuud Hotel
6. Fine Arts Museum
7. Revolutionary Museum
8. Opera House
9. Ulan Bator Hotel
10. Genghis Khan Hotel
11. Nairamdal Park
12. G.K.Jukov Museum
13. Ulan Bator History Museum
14. Choizin Monastery
15. Sukhe Bator Square
16. Department Store
17. Khangai Hotel
18. State Circus
19. Bayangol Hotel
20. Ethnographic Museum
21. Bogdo Khan Palace
22. Museum of Hunting Trophies
23. Altai Hotel
24. Zhuulchin Office

selling silks (as the other two were) but with the salvation (or rather the liberation) of souls. There was a population of 30,000 Buddhist monks in the many lamaseries here.

Ulan Bator today

After the communist party came to power in 1921, the capital was renamed Ulan Bator, meaning 'Red Hero'. With considerable help from the USSR, the city was redesigned and you will recognise the Soviet influence in the austere architecture of the tower blocks and municipal buildings. With a population of almost half a million people, Ulan Bator is the industrial centre of the country. The two lignite burning power stations here cause severe pollution problems, especially bad in winter, and respiratory ailments are common amongst the youthful inhabitants - more than 70% of the people are under the age of 35. There is a chronic shortage of housing which is why many people still live in *yurts*, in large groups around the out-skirts of the city.

ORIENTATION AND HOTELS

A bus from Zhuulchin (the national tourist organisation) meets the train each day and even if you've opted for their cheapest 'bed only, no tour' package ask the Zhuulchin representative by the bus (parked beside the station) which hotel you've been assigned to and they'll probably give you a lift. In any case they usually have to take you to the Zhuulchin office to relieve you of your dollars in payment for your stay after you've checked into the hotel. Onward bookings are confirmed at the same time. The top hotel, the **Genghis Khan** should be completed soon and promises to be 'international' stand-ard. Until it is, the best hotel is the **Ulan Bator**, which is more centrally located, near Sukhe Bator Square. The other hotel used by Zhuulchin is the **Bayangol**, opposite Nairamdal Park and entirely adequate. The three lower class hotels which tourists occasionally find themselves in are the **Zaluuchuud**, the **Altai** and the **Khangai**. 'For safety reasons, the hotel reception counter will retain your passport during your stay'. Since you will have already have paid it's easy to forget to collect it as you leave.

BANKS AND CURRENCY

You can exchange only US$, UK£, German DM, Swiss and French francs, and Japanese Yen for Mongolian tugriks (1 tugrik = 100 mungos) and there are bureaux de change in all hotels (open 10.00-15.00). Don't change too much as there's little to buy and ensure you keep your exchange receipts in the unlikely case that you need to prove that you haven't been dabbling on the black market. Black marketeers hang round the statue of Lenin in the park outside the Ulan Bator hotel, as well as in the entrances to the hotels themselves. Credit cards will probably be introduced soon.

TOURS AND TRANSPORT

If you've picked the independent traveller's package that includes tours, you'll be provided with a guide, car and driver for the day. It's up to you say what you'd like to do, although the guide will offer suggestions. If you're on the 'bed only, no tour' package you could enquire at the reception desk to find out if there's a tour bus you could tag along with. Most of the main sights are within walking distance but there are also trolley buses.

WHAT TO SEE

Sukhe Bator Square
The mounted statue of Sukhe Bator in heroic pose stands in the centre of this large square, opposite his mausoleum (modelled on Lenin's in Red Square). His preserved body does not receive visitors but newly-weds queue up to have their photos taken at the foot of his statue. In 1990 the square was the scene of the pro-democracy demonstrations that led to the first free elections.

Ganden Monastery
Mongolia once had 700 monasteries, virtually all of them destroyed in the communist crackdown at the end of the 1930s, following Stalin's lead in the USSR. More than 14,000 monks were killed and tens of thousands forced to give up their vows. With the pro-democracy movement in 1990 restrictions have been eased allowing some monasteries to reopen and Ganden to operate less as a show-piece for tourists. The first group of buildings here was put up in 1938 and as well as the main temple there are stupas, a library and the accommodation for the monks. Powdered juniper (which is thrown into the big burner outside the temple, for good luck) is dispensed in a side building. It's best to go in the morning (09.00-12.00) when services are being performed.

Bogdo Khan Palace & Museum
This is a wonderful old place, full of ghosts and rather like Beijing's Forbidden City on a human scale. Seems as if the owners walked out a few years ago leaving it in the hands of rather relaxed caretakers who've forgotten to mow the lawn. Entered through a gateway

guarded by four fierce-looking incarnations, the palace comprises two courtyards with small pavilions on each side. There are exhibits of *thangkas* (Buddhist paintings), musical instruments and Buddha figures, as well as the day-to-day furnishings of the buildings. The museum is beside the palace complex and exhibits include Bogdo Khan's throne, fur-lined robes and crown, and his luxurious *yurt* (covered with the skins of 150 snow leopard and containing stove and portable altar). His collection of stuffed animals is also displayed somewhat haphazardly: a moth-eaten lion sharing the same quarters as a grubby polar bear. Outside is an interesting display of conveyances (palanquins and carriages). Open 10.00-17.00 (3 tugrik).

State Central Museum

Mongolia is well known for its dinosaur graveyards and some of the discoveries are on display here, including several fossilised nests of dinosaur's eggs. These come in a fascinating range of shapes: cannon balls, ostrich-eggs, even Cornish pasties. Also worth seeing are the displays of stuffed animals arranged in quite imaginative panoramas of the Gobi and the mountains in the west. Here are many of the animals in the Red Data Book (Mongolian equivalent of the Soviet Red Book of endangered species) including snow leopard (*panthera uncia*), wild Bactrian camel, Gobi bear, hulan (wild ass), red wolf, northern otter, snow griffon and Przhevalsky's horse. On the top floor are displays of national dress (smelling strongly of moth-balls) and a number of *yurts*. Housed in a large building with creaky floor boards, a notice on the door warns: 'Closed last Monday of the month for cleaning'. Hardly surprising that the displays are rather dusty. Open Mon 10.00-16.00 (but not last Mon of the month); closed Tue; other days open 10.00-18.00.

Choizhin Monastery/Religious Museum

Preserved for many years as a museum of religion, this temple complex is being handed back to the monks in the new spirit of religious freedom. The temple is brightly decorated and houses a large collection of ornate masks for Buddhist mystery plays. Take a close look at the golden seated Buddha figure, no statue but the mummified body of a lama, encased in gold. Open daily (except Thurs) 10.00-17.00, early closing Wed: 15.00, (3 tugrik).

Fine Arts Museum

Includes a comprehensive display of *thangkas*, one more than 15m long. There are copies of prehistoric cave paintings, robes and masks from Buddhist mystery plays and a gallery of modern paper-cutting art. Open 10.00-17.00 (4 tugrik).

Other museums and sights

The small **Ulan Bator History Museum** (open 09.00-17.00) is housed in Sukhe Bator's bungalow and concentrates on the revolutionary history of the city. You may be even less interested in the **Revolutionary Museum**; the **Jukov Memorial Museum** and the **Lenin Museum**. The **Hunting Trophy Museum** near Ganden Monastery focuses on a highly controversial issue: the lucrative industry the Mongolians have set up selling hunting packages to foreign tourists (see 'Hunting trips' below). There are some good panoramas of the Gobi here, showing the animals (camels and gazelles) you may see from the train. (Open daily (except Mon) 09.00-13.00, 14.00-18.00, early closing Sun 15.00). It would be worth inquiring in the hotel to see if the **Janraisag Temple** is open yet. Built in 1911 at a reputed cost of 45 tons of silver in order to commemorate the formation of the sovereign Mongolian state, this temple has been undergoing extensive restoration since 1989. **Nairamdal Park** (opposite Bayangol Hotel is where Ulan Batons go to relax and it has a boating lake, ferris wheel, camel rides, model dinosaurs and a small ethnographic museum. **Evening activities** may include a visit to a ballet or opera in the State Theatre on Sukhe Bator Square (enquire at reception in your hotel for tickets and times). There is also a circus. A disco is occasionally held in the bar (1st floor) of the Bayangol Hotel.

FOOD AND RESTAURANTS

Breakfast at the hotels is usually good (fried eggs, bread, butter, jam, coffee). Lunch and dinner tend to include mutton or lamb in some guise or another. The national drink is *koumiss* (fermented mares' milk). *Mongolia Magazine* gives the following tip: 'Before drinking shake *koumiss* well. Keep it in a skin suspended on the wall of your yurt and periodically shake it with a special beater'. Every year 22 million litres are produced in late summer and early autumn - it's a seasonal drink. Mongolian beer is rather weak and gassy, 'Arkhi' vodka expensive at about 50 tugrik for a litre.

SHOPPING

Things to buy include leather goods, cashmere shawls and sweaters, sheepskin, astrakhan and fur coats, carpets, jewellery, dinosaur cards and models. The country is also noted for its wonderfully bizarre, oversize **postage stamps** with naive representations of cars and trains etc. So many are needed for air-mail postage that there is little room left on the postcard for a message. The **State Department**

Store is interesting to visit and claims to satisfy the retail needs of 25,000 people a day. There are plaster casts of Marx and Sukhe Bator or you could buy yourself some of the black riding boots (110.00 tugrik - sizes up to 42) which the men wear with their *del*, the national costume. These are also available here (fur-lined in winter, cotton in summer) as well as knitted Mongolian hats (14 tugrik). For stocking up on food there's a bakery selling loaves, buns and cakes. The usual Russian system of payment prevails: choose, then pay taking your receipt to exchange for the goods. There's a bookshop opposite the department store. The 'duty-free' shops in hotels sell some Western products and liquor. (Open 10.00-15.00, longer in some hotels).

Excursions from Ulan Bator

ULAN BATOR AREA

For those staying more than one night there are numerous possibilities for excursions. Overnight stays can be arranged to **Terelj** in the hills, 85km from the capital, where visitors stay in *yurts* and sample mare's milk for breakfast. A British-Mongolian joint venture is now constructing a hotel there.

From Ulan Bator it's possible to visit **Manzshir Monastery** on a day-trip.

FURTHER AFIELD

Excursions requiring more time (and only possible between 01 May and 01 Oct) include a visit to the **South Gobi** for game viewing (camels, gazelles, Gobi bears etc); the hot springs of **Khangai**; **Khuzhirt** where tourists stay in a *yurt* camp and visit the ruins of the 14th century capital **Karakorum** (450km west of Ulan Bator), the 400 year old monastery at **Erdene-dzu** and the **Orkhon Falls**. **Hunting trips** may also be organised and they are big foreign-currency earners for the Mongolians. In their tourist brochure Zhuulchin see nothing amiss with the following statements four paragraphs apart: 'The South Gobi, the habitat of rare animals entered in the Red Data Book, such as....the snow leopard', and 'Most foreigners are attracted by the chance to get rare hunting trophies: the skin of a snow leopard, the horns of argali sheep ibex, gazelle or maral'. This seems slightly out of key with the 17th century law called Halkh

192 City guides and plans

Juram which was passed enforcing a caring attitude to nature in Mongolia. The country may need hard currency but there are many ways to attract tourists other than by inviting them to contribute to the extinction of rare species.

Genghis Khan

For many decades the name of this famous Mongolian conqueror has been taboo in his home country. With Russian influence in Mongolia waning (the Soviets saw Genghis Khan as brutal invader to be erased from the history books) there has been a sudden rise in Mongolian nationalism. Genghis Khan, the founder of the thirteenth century Mongolian Empire, is a hero once more, lending his name to the newest (and most luxurious) hotel in town and also to a brand of vodka. Even the prestigious Mongolian pop group with the wonderful name of 'Honk' have produced a record entitled 'Genghis Khan'.

PART 5: ROUTE GUIDE AND MAPS

Using this guide

Introduction

This route guide has been set out to draw your attention to points of interest and to enable you to locate your position along the Trans-Siberian line. On the maps, stations are indicated in Russian and English and their distance from Moscow is given in the text. Note that on the maps there is an orientation symbol (M), indicating the direction towards Moscow. Stations and points of interest are identified in the text by a kilometre number. Note that in some cases these are approximate so be ready for a particular point a few kilometres before the stated position. Where something of interest is on only one side of the track, it is identified by the letters N (north or left-hand side of the train, going from Moscow east) or S (south or right-hand side) after the kilometre number. The altitude of major towns and cities is given in metres and feet beside the station name. Time zones are indicated through the text (MT = Moscow Time). See inside back cover for **key map**.

Kilometre posts

These are located on the southern side of the track. They are sometimes placed so close to the train that they're difficult to see. The technique is either to hang out of the window (dangerous) or press your face close to the glass and look along the train until a kilometre post flashes by. Note that there is a difference of one kilometre between one side of the sign and the other.

Station name boards

These are almost as difficult to catch sight of as the kilometre posts since they are usually posted once only (on the station building) and not also along the platforms as in most other countries. Rail traffic on the line is heavy and even if your carriage does pull up opposite the station building you may have your view of it obscured by another train. For the station name in Cyrillic script see the strip-maps.

Stops

Where the train stops at a station the length of the stop is indicated by ● (short stop: 1-5mins), ●● (medium stop: 6-10 mins) or ●●● (long stop: 11-15 mins). The carriage attendant will tell you the precise amount of time as this may be reduced if the train is running late. Don't stray too far from the train as it moves off without a signal or whistle (except in China) and passengers are occasionally left behind. Three of us, our carriage attendant included, were once almost left in sub-zero temperatures on the platform of some tiny Siberian station, when the train left five minutes ahead of schedule.

Speed calculations

Using the kilometre posts and a stop-watch (or the second hand of your watch), it's possible to calculate how fast, or more usually how slowly, the train is going. Note the time that elapses between one post and the next and consult the table below. Since the average speed of the train over the seven day journey between Moscow and Nakhodka is only 69 kph (43 mph), you are unlikely to use the higher figures on this table.

Seconds	kph	mph	Seconds	kph	mph
24	150	93	52	69	43
26	138	86	54	66	41
28	129	80	56	64	40
30	120	75	60	60	37
32	113	70	64	56	35
34	106	66	68	53	33
36	100	62	72	50	31
38	95	59	78	46	28
40	90	56	84	43	27
42	86	53	92	39	24
44	82	51	100	36	22
46	78	49	120	30	18
48	75	47	150	24	15
50	72	45	180	20	12

Precautions against invaders

In 1940s' Britain with the fear of German invasion, road signs were removed to make orientation difficult for the invader. Until very recently Soviet cartographers attempted a similar sort of deception with deliberate errors and misspellings. Russian maps are notorious for their inaccuracies. On the Trans-Mongolian route, just before reaching the border I noticed an inconsistency between the name of a small station whose signboard read 'Azhida' and the name as it appeared on my Russian map, 'Dzhida'. The reason for this misspelling became obvious as the train reached the southern part of the town and a large military airfield came into view. Note that the distances sometimes given on train timetables are also unreliable, usually out by 5-8km. If you notice any inaccuracies in the distances given in this book please write to the author - address on page 2.

Trans-Siberian route

Km0: Moscow: Yaroslavl Station

Most Trans-Siberian trains arrive and depart in the afternoon. If you're arriving from Siberia and continuing immediately to Poland and Western Europe, you need to take a taxi or the metro to Belorusskaya Vokzal (see page 131). If your journey begins here make sure you get to the station early as trains invariably leave on time. The station (see photo on p81 so that you will recognise it) is one of the three at Komsomol Square (Metro: the palatial **Komsomolskaya Ploshchad** with its marble pillars and mosaic ceilings). Yaroslavl station was built in 1902 as a stylised reproduction of an old Russian *terem* (fort), its walls decorated with coloured tiles. The Trans-Siberian, known to the Russians as the *Rossiya*, usually leaves from platform two and any railway official will point you in the right direction if you show them your ticket.

In about twenty minutes, the smoking factories and suburban blocks of flats will have been left behind and you'll be rolling through forests of pine, birch and oak. Amongst the trees there are picturesque wooden *dacha* (holiday homes where many of Moscow's residents spend their weekends). You pass through little stations with long, white-washed wicket fences and empty platforms. About an hour out of Moscow you come to Zagorsk.

Km73 (N): Zagorsk
Have your cameras ready for the stunning sight of the blue and gold domes of the cathedrals of Zagorsk. Look north back to the city just after you leave the station. For many years Zagorsk was the seat of the Russian Orthodox Church (until it was moved back to Moscow in 1990) and

one of the most important seminaries in the country is here. The beautiful buildings of the seminary are much visited by tourists.

Until 1930, the city was known as Sergievo, after St Sergius of Radonezh who founded the *lavra* (monastery) here in 1340. The fortified monastery complex now comprises nine cathedrals and churches. The most striking is the **Cathedral of the Assumption** (Uspenski Sobor) with its four blue cupolas dotted with golden stars and, in the centre, a larger gold cupola. It was built between 1559 and 1585. The **Cathedral of the Holy Trinity** (1422) stands beside it and in spite of its gilded roof, seems quite plain in comparison. The 285ft **bell-tower** was designed by Rastrelli, the principal architect of the Winter Palace and many other buildings in Leningrad.

Until the time of the Revolution, literally millions of people made the pilgrimage to this sacred city. After the Revolution, the monks were disbanded and sent out into the fields and the churches became museums. With the slightly more relaxed religious climate that came after Stalin's time, the monastery was re-established and is now reported to be taking in record numbers of novices.

Km112: Aleksandrov (●) There is usually a one minute stop here which just gives you time to see the six old steam locomotives that lie rotting in the station yard.

Km121-1266: Time zone MT + 1 After Aleksandrov you cross into the next time zone. Local time is now Moscow time + 1 hour.

The train now enters Yaroslavlskaya oblast (administrative district), an area of 36,000 square kilometres in the upper Volga basin, famous for its cheeses. Apart from dairy farming, oats, flax and vegetables are grown in this region.

Km240 (N): Amidst the fields and quite close to the track is a sadly neglected but **picturesque church** with five dilapidated domes and a tower.

Km280 (N): Another rotting church, this one with a soaring steeple (like a more humble version of the Cathedral of St Peter and St Paul in Leningrad) and a clock with no hands.

Km284: Yaroslavl (●) Passing through factories that look as if they've been deserted with piles of rusting machinery left outside them, you come to the large industrial city of Yaroslavl, population 620,000. It is said to have been founded in 1010 by the Christian King Yaroslavl the Wise. It grew quickly into an important trading centre on the Volga shipping route. Many of the ancient cathedrals still stand in spite of the heavy fighting that went on here during the Civil War. The **Spassky Monastery**, badly damaged in the fighting, dates from the thirteenth century. Most of the other large religious buildings, including the **Cathedral of St Elias** with its five large green domes, were built in the seventeenth century. The theatre, founded in 1750, is the oldest in the USSR. Since the early eighteenth century, Yaroslavl has been a major textile centre. The production of petroleum products is the other important industry in the city today.

Km289: Volga River In times gone by Russians regarded this river with such high respect that they would stand and take off their hats to Mother Volga, as the train rattled onto the first spans of the long bridge. Rising in the Valdai hills, Europe's longest river meanders 3,700km down to the Caspian Sea. It is to Russia what the Nile is to Egypt: a source of life and a thoroughfare. You get a good view of the city of Yaroslavl and its cathedrals looking back south as you go over the bridge.

Km357: Danilov (●●●) There's usually a fifteen minute halt here for an engine change. The platform is crowded with little fat women wearing overcoats and scarves, selling bunches of gladioli, buckets of purple onions and small paper bags of potatoes, freshly boiled with herbs. Waddling up and down the train with their produce, they look like animated *matrioshka* dolls.

Km370-378 Some quite good views on both sides of the train in the breaks between the trees. The train soon enters Kostromskaya *oblast*, a 60,000 sq km plain in the middle Volga basin. Most of the northern part of the oblast is covered with *taiga* (swampy forest). There is some cultivation (flax and oats) in the south. Main industries are linen-making and timber-processing.

Km447: Over the Kostroma River and into **Buy (●)** (pronounced B'wee) station. The two minute stop here will give you more than enough time to view the gold-painted statue of Lenin on the platform, although by the time you read this he might have gone the way of most other gold-painted statues of Lenin.

Km501: Galich A large town beside the equally large Lake Galichskoye.

MAP 2

Монаково
MONAKOVO
Антролово
ANTROLOVO
Николо-Угол
NIKOLO-UGOL
Николо-Полома
NIKOLO-POLOMA
Номжа
NOMZHA
Еленский
YELENSKIY
Нея
NEYA
Нельша
NELSHA
Брантовка
BRANTOVKA
Петрушино
PETRUSHINO
Кострика
KOSTRIKHA
Мантурово
MANTUROVO
Вочерово
VOCHEROVO
Шекшема
SHEKSHEMA
Варакинский
VARAKINSKIY
Шарья Vetluga R.
SHARYA
Зебляки
ZEBLYAKI
Якшанга
YAKSHANGA
Бурундучиха
BURUNDUCHIKHA
Супротивный
SUPROTIVNIY
Метил
METIL
Гостовская
GOSTOVSKAYA
Шабалино
SHABALINO
Свеча
SVECHA
Юма
YUMA
Капиданцы
KAPIDANTSI
Ацвеж
ATSVEZH
Даровица
DAROVITSA
Котельнич
KOTELNICH
Быстряги
BISTRYAGI
Оричи
ORICHI
Стрижи
STRIZHI
Лянгасово
LYANGASOVO
Чухломинский
CHUKHLOMINSKIY
КИРОВ(KIROV)
Поздино
POZDINO
Полой (POLOY)
Бумкомбинат
BUMKOMBINAT
Просница
PROSNITSA

Km701: Shariya (●●) There is usually an eight to ten minute stop at this station where some steam locos are stored (L & Er classes).

Km818: Svetcha Roughly mid-way between Shariya and Svetcha, you enter Kirovskaya *oblast*. Most of the 120,000 square kilometres of this region are within the basin of the Vyatka River. Since the greater part of the *oblast* is made up of *taiga* (swampy forest), the main industry here is logging.

Km870: Kotelnich Junction with the line down to Gorky. A few kilometres east of the town you cross the Vyatka River, which rises in the foothills of the Urals and flows 1,300km down to the Kama River

Km957: Kirov (●●●) Standing on the banks of the Vyatka River, the city was founded in 1181 and named Klynov. It developed into a fur-trading centre entirely dependent on the river for transport and communication with the rest of the country. In the eighteenth century it fell under the rule of Moscow and was renamed Vyatka, soon gaining a reputation as a place of exile. In 1934 its name was changed once more and it became Kirov, in honour of the communist leader assassinated earlier in the same year. Kirov was, at one time, so close to Stalin that most people assumed that he would eventually succeed him as General Secretary of the Party. However, in the 1930s he broke away and it is more than likely that Stalin had a hand in his murder. His death served as the excuse for Stalin's Great Purge in the mid-1930s during which time several million people died in labour camps.

Modern Kirov is a large industrial and administrative centre with a population of over 400,000. There are saw-mills, chemical plants, tanneries and a tyre-making factory.

For the next 300km after Kirov the line follows the Vyatka River (for a short distance) then the Cheptsa, climbing into the foothills of the Urals.

Km1128: Yar About twenty kilometres before this station you leave the Russian Republic (RSFSR) and Kirovskaya *oblast* and cross the administrative frontier into the Udmurt ASSR (Autonomous Soviet Socialist Republic). This region was settled by the Udmurts, a people of Finno-Ugric extraction, and was established as an autonomous republic in 1920. It is now a heavily industrialised area.

Km1190(N): Note the large number of well-preserved steam locomotives (strategic reserve?), just before Balyezino station (W).

Km1191: Balyezino Between Yar and Balyezino there are many co-operative farms specialising in market-gardening in this rolling, open countryside. You pass vast fields of grey-green cabbages, and long rows of greenhouses covered in plastic sheeting line the track in some places. There are tiny villages of *izbas* (log cabins) with brightly painted front doors.

Km1216: Cheptsa A few kilometres before this station, the line crosses the Cheptsa River which the train has been following for the last 250kms. The train begins to wind its way up towards the Urals.

Km1267-2510: Time zone MT + 2
About 40kms east of Cheptsa you enter another time zone (Moscow Time + 2).

Km1317 (S): Vereshagino There's a preserved tender loco, high up on embankment plinth just west of the station. Between Cheptsa and this station is the frontier between the Udmurt ASSR and the Russian SFSR. From here towards the east lies Permskaya *oblast*.

MAP 3

Permskaya's 160,000 square kilometres are, like those of Kirovskaya *oblast*, lost in the swampy forests of the *taiga*. However, Permskaya has greater prizes than its millions of pine and birch trees, for the region includes the mineral-rich Ural Mountains. Main industries therefore include mining, logging and paper-making. Agriculture is confined to market-gardening. There are some quite good views south, a few kilometres after Vereshagino. Other views at km1365 (S); km1375 (N) and kms1397-1402 but nothing really spectacular.

Km1431: Kama River This mighty river flows over 2,000kms from the Urals into the Volga and is one of the great waterways of the Soviet Union. Its power has been harnessed by the Perm hydro-electric power station. Near the bridge, the banks of the Kama are lined with cranes and warehouses. A short distance before you reach Perm station (to the north of the line) there is a turntable and beside it an ancient green **'O' Class locomotive** (0B 14). Engines of this type were hauling the Trans-Siberian at the turn of the century.

Km1433: Perm (●●●) This city of more than one million inhabitants was founded in 1723 when the copper smelting works were established here. From its important position on the Kama River, the Great Siberian Post Road and later the Trans-Siberian Railway, Perm quickly grew into a major trading and industrial centre.

Before the railway reached Perm most travellers would arrive by steamer from Nizhny Novgorod (now Gorky) and Kazan. R.L.Jefferson (see Part 3) cycled here from London in 1896 on his Siberian ride and was entertained by Gospodin Kuznetsoff, the 60 year old president of the Perm Cycling Club and fifty enthusiasts. On 20 July 1907, the cyclists came out to escort an equally sensational visitor, the Italian Prince Borghese who had just driven across Siberia from Peking in his Itala and was on his way to Paris, where he would win the Peking to Paris Motor Rally. One of the wheels of the car was damaged and, when the Prince's chauffeur had replaced some of the wooden spokes, he declared that the wheel needed to be soaked to make the wood expand. A local official advised them to send it to one of the bathing establishments along the Kama River. A bathing-machine (of the type used by Victorian swimmers at English sea-side resorts) was hired and the wheel spent the night taking the waters.

Between 1940 and 1957 the city was called Molotov, after the communist official who fell from favour after the Stalin era. Modern Perm is a vast industrial metropolis (the suburbs extend east to the oil refineries at km1452) and its population is engaged in producing heavy machinery, petroleum products and chemicals.

Kms1460-1777: The train winds its way up to the highest point in the Urals. One would expect the range of mountains that divides Europe from Asia to be rather more impressive than these hills but they're not much more than 500 metres in this area. R.L.Jefferson wrote in 1896: 'The Urals certainly are not so high or majestic as the Alps or the Balkans but their wild picturesqueness is something to be seen to be appreciated.' Their wild picturesqueness is somewhat marred and scarred today by open-cast mines (km1507 (N) and km1509 (N)). There is a large timber-mill at km1523 (N).

Km1530: Khungur Founded in the mid-seventeenth century as a military outpost, this large town lies away from the track to the north. Of less importance now than in the past, Khungur has six large churches, each built in a different style, and a large cathedral with a gold dome.

Km1537(N): A picturesque church stands alone on the hill across the Sylva River. The line follows this river up the valley to km1556 where it cuts across a wide plain. The trees close in again from about km1584 but there are occasional clearings with villages and timber-mills (km1650 (N)).

Km1672: Shalya Fifty kilometres west of here, you enter Sverd-lovskaya *oblast*. It covers 195,000 square kilometres taking in parts of the Urals and extending east onto the Siberian plain. Like most of the other *oblasts* you have passed though, this one is composed almost entirely of *taiga* forests. From the rich deposits in the Urals are mined iron ore, copper, platinum, gold, tungsten, cobalt, asbestos and bauxite as well as many varieties of gemstones. The soil is poor and consequently there is very little agriculture in the region.

Km1727-9: Kuzino East of the large marshalling yard here the line rises once more, passing a little town built around a freshly whitewashed church with a green dome.

Km1748: A large factory, with rows of apartment blocks for its workers, looks a little out of place up here in the Urals. There are several more factories and mining complexes around the town of Pervoralsk, about 15km east of Kuzino. From km1764 east the area becomes quite built up.

MAP 4

СВЕРДЛОВСК
SVERDLOVSK
Шарташ
SHARTASH
Путевка
PUTEVKA
Косулино
KOSOLINO
Гагарский
GAGARSKIY
Баженово
BAZHENOVO
Грязновская
GRYAZNOVSKAYA
Богданович
BOGDANOVICH
Пышминская
PISHMINSKAYA
Еланский
YELANSKIY
Камышлов
KAMISHLOV
Аксариха
AKSARIKHA
Ошепково
OSHCHEPKOVO
Проселок
PROSELOK
Талица
TALITSA
Юшала
YUSHALA
Бахметское
BAHKMETSKOYE
Тугулым
TUGULYM
Кармак
KARMAK
ТЮМЕНЬ
TYUMEN
Войновка
VOYNOVKA
О-Андреевское
OZERO ANDREYEVSKOYE
Винзили
VINZILI
Богандинская
BOGANDINSKAYA
Ялуторовск
YALUTOROVSK
Tobol R
Заводоуковская
ZAVODOUKOVSKAYA
Новая Заимка
NOVAYA ZAIMKA
Вагай
VAGAY

SVERDLOVSKAYA OBLAST
TYUMENSKAYA OBLAST

Km1777 (S) Europe/Asia Obelisk

People begin collecting in the corridor long before you reach this white stone obelisk which marks the continental division at this point in the Urals. Just before you get to it, when travelling east, there is a large brick tower beside the track at km1776(S). One kilometre east you reach the obelisk which has 'Europe' written on the west-facing side, 'Asia' on the east side and 'Asia Europe' on the side facing the train. It stands on the south side of the line.

When R.L.Jefferson reached the point near here where the road crosses the Urals (also marked with an obelisk) he wrote enthusiastically of the view: 'Hills piled upon hills, shaggy mountains and gaunt fir trees, and beyond them dwindling away into the mist of the horizon the great steppe lands of Siberia.' George Kennan wrote in 1887: 'The scenery of the Urals where the railroad crosses the range resembles in general outline that of West Virginia where the Baltimore and Ohio railroad crosses the Alleghenies; but it differs somewhat from the latter in colouring, owing to the greater preponderance in the Urals of evergreen trees.'Unfortunately you won't get much of a view from the train today.

Km1813: Sverdlovsk (●●●) After a large lake (kms1807-9) the Trans-Siberian halts in this, the largest of cities in the Urals, for a change of engine. In 1721 the town was founded and named Yekaterinburg in honour of Empress Catherine II. The ironworks and garrison were established in the following year and the town grew quickly as the centre of a rich mining region. The railway reached the town in 1878 bringing foreign travellers on their way to Siberia. Kate Marsden (see Part 3), who was on her way to the Siberian leper colonies, visited the local jail in 1895 which she found 'badly run, badly ventilated

and badly kept'. R.L.Jefferson, on his epic bicycle journey, was well entertained by the members of the Yekaterinburg Cycling Club, whom he described as 'jolly good fellows all'.

The murder of the Romanovs

There is a blacker side to Yekaterinburg's history, for it was in the cellar of a house here, on the night of July 16th 1918, that the brutal murder of the last Tsar of Russia and his family took place. The Romanovs were moved from Tobolsk to Yekaterinburg in May 1918 and imprisoned in a house that belonged to a rich merchant, in the centre of the city. Here the family spent the last two months of their lives, being tormented by their guards, who openly referred to Nicholas as 'The Blood Drinker' and scrawled lewd pictures on the bathroom walls, showing the Tsaritsa with Rasputin.

Several attempts were made to save the royal family and soon the Bolshevik government decided that the Tsar was too great a threat to their security. The order for the massacre was given. Shortly before midnight Nicholas, Alexandra, their four daughters Olga, Tatiana, Marie and Anastasia, and their haemophiliac son, Alexis, were taken down into the cellar where they were shot and bayonetted to death. The bodies were then driven 20km out of the city to the Four Brothers Mine where Red Guards spent three days destroying all the evidence. The corpses were dismembered with axes, doused with petrol and burnt. Sulphuric acid was used to destroy the charred remains before the ashes were thrown down a disused mine shaft in the outskirts of the city.

A week later the White army took Yekaterinburg and their suspicions were immediately aroused by the sight of the blood-spattered walls of the cellar. In the garden they found the Tsarevich's spaniel Joy, neglected and half-starved. However, it was not until the following January that the investigators were led to the mine shaft, where they found fragments of bone and pieces of jewellery that had once belonged to members of the Imperial family. They also found the well-manicured finger of a lady and the body of Jimmy, Anastasia's dog, that the murderers had carelessly flung down the mine shaft without bothering to destroy. All the evidence was identified by the Tsarevich's tutor, Pierre Gilliard.

At first the Bolshevik government would not admit to more than the 'execution' of Nicholas. They accused a group of counter-revolutionaries of the murders of his family. Five of them were tried, 'found guilty' and executed. However, in 1919, after the death of the prominent party official Yacob Sverdlov (once an important Yekaterinburg revolutionary) it was acknowledged that it was in fact

Sverdlov who had arranged the massacre of the Imperial family. In his 'honour' the town was renamed. (There is now talk of it reverting to the old name of Yekaterinburg.)

Anastasia: the real Grand Duchess?

Many people refused to believe that the whole of the Imperial family perished in the cellar of the house in Yekaterinburg. George V did not attend the memorial service in London for his beloved Russian cousins. Rumours abounded, some credible, others more than a little far-fetched. Some believed that only the servants had been killed, that the Tsar and his family had escaped down a secret tunnel to the British Consulate in Yekaterinburg and were living in secret exile in Tibet.

As well as the rumours there emerged a whole string of pretenders, people claiming to be members of the Imperial family. It is almost certain that the Tsar and several members of his family were killed, but there is a very slight possibility that one or two of the children might have escaped although this seems highly unlikely. The Polish spy who defected to the West in 1960 and claimed to be Alexis, the Tsarevich, was surely an impostor for he did not suffer from haemophilia. However, the girl found in the Berlin canal in 1920 could possibly have been Anastasia, the youngest daughter.

Anastasia Anderson (as she came to be known after marrying an American) spent her life trying to prove her identity. She claimed that she had been wounded in the massacre and left for dead. Two guards had taken pity on her, finding her alive, and had smuggled her out of the country. Her aunt Princess Irene of Prussia, her cousin Grand Duke Andrew, and several other family members were convinced she was not lying. Hospital tests showed she had a fractured skull, an injury that could have been caused by the butt of a gun. A scar on her shoulder and bunions on her feet were in exactly the same place as those known to afflict the Russian Grand Duchess.

Many more, however, believed she was an impostor trying to claim the vast family fortunes in Europe. Some were not entirely pure in their motives for disbelieving her. Grand Duke Cyril, the Tsar's cousin and the surviving head of the Romanovs, refused even to meet her: if she were Anastasia, he would lose his claim to the Romanov fortunes. There were several protracted court cases concerning the claim but in 1968 a Hamburg court decided that there was insufficient evidence for a verdict to be reached. Anna Anderson died in the USA in 1984.

American spy?

The next time Sverdlovsk became the focus of world attention was in May 1960, when the American U-2 pilot, Gary Powers, was shot down in this area. U.S. Central Intelligence were probably unhappy to hear that he had parachuted into the arms of the Soviets and had informed them that his mission had been to fly across the USSR from Pakistan to Norway, taking a series of photographs. He obviously hadn't read the section on photography in the Intourist booklet. All this was, of course, strongly denied by the Americans but the ensuing confrontation between the two powers led to the collapse of the summit conference in Paris. The pilot was sentenced to ten years imprisonment but exchanged in 1962 for a Russian spy held in the West.

Modern Sverdlovsk

Sverdlovsk is now one of the most important industrial cities in the USSR and has a population of one and a quarter million. Industries here include heavy engineering, the production of chemicals and the cutting and setting of gemstones.

The city's most famous son is Boris Yeltsin, President of the Russian Federation, now well known for his clashes with Gorbachev. His was the only city in Russia to vote 'no' in the recent referendum on a renewed Soviet Union.

After years of being a 'closed' city for foreigners (on account of the armaments factories here) Sverdlovsk was opened to tourists in late 1990. Visitors are taken to see the spot where the house where the Tsar and his family were murdered once stood. It was demolished in 1990 on Yeltsin's orders and the place is now marked with a wooden cross.

If you've managed to arrange a stop here you may be staying in the **Hotel Sverdlovsk** which is conveniently located across the square outside the station.

For about 70km east of Sverdlovsk, the train winds down and out of the Urals to the Great Siberian plain. You are now in Asia (not quite in Siberia yet) but the scenery and houses look no different from those on the European flank of the mountains.

Km1917: Bogdanovich The *1900 Guide to the Great Siberian Railway* drew its readers' attention to the Kurinsk mineral springs 'situated 15 *versts* (a *verst* is slightly longer than a kilometre) from the station.....They are efficacious for rheumatism, paralysis, scrofula and anaemia. Furnished houses and an hotel with good rooms are situated near the baths. There is a garden and a promenade with band; theatricals and concerts take place in the casino'. Such frivolous capitalist jollities are hard to imagine in this rather gloomy region today.

Km2078: Siberia begins here (ends here, for those going west). This is the frontier between Sverdlovskaya and Tyumenskaya *oblasts*. Tyumenskaya comprises 430,000 square kilometres of flat land, *tundra* in the north, *táiga* in the south. Until oil was discovered in the region twenty years ago, the inhabitants were engaged in reindeer-herding in the north and farming in the south. Many people have been brought into the *oblast* recently to work in the petroleum and construction industries.

South of the line, the point where the Great Post Road crossed Siberia's frontier was marked by 'a square pillar ten or twelve feet in height, of stuccoed or plastered brick', wrote George Kennan on his way to research *Siberia and the Exile System* in 1887. He added: 'No other spot between St Petersburg and the Pacific is more full of painful suggestions, and none has for the traveller a more melancholy interest than the little opening in the forest where stands this grief-consecrated pillar. Here hundreds of thousands of exiled human beings - men, women and children; princes, nobles and peasants - have bidden good-by (sic) forever to friends, country , and home.....The Russian peasant even when a criminal is deeply attached to his native land; and heart-rending scenes have been witnessed around the boundary pillar.....Some gave way to unrestrained grief; some comforted the weeping; some knelt and pressed their faces to the loved soil of their native country and collected a little earth to take with them into exile.....Until recently the Siberian boundary post was covered with brief inscriptions, good-bys and the names of exiles.....In one place, in a man's hand, had been written the words "Prashchai Marya" (Goodby Mary!) Who the writer was, who Mary was, there is nothing now left to show.....' (see page 76).

Km2141: Tyumen (●●) The oldest town in Siberia, founded in 1586. It was built on the banks of the Tura River, the site of the former Tatar town of Chingi Tura, said to date back to the fourteenth century. The Russian town was named by Tsar Feodor Ivanovich after Tyumen Khan, who formerly ruled this region. It grew quickly as a trading centre with goods arriving and being shipped on from the large port on the Tura River.

At least one million of the people who passed through this town before 1900 were convicts and exiles. Many were lodged, under the most appalling conditions, in the Tyumen Forwarding Prison (See Part 3: 'The Exile System'). When George Kennan visited the prison in 1887, he was horrified by the overcrowded cells, the dirt and the terrible smell. He wrote: 'The air in the corridors and cells.....was laden with fever germs from the unventilated hospital wards, fetid [sic] odors from diseased human bodies and the stench arising from unemptied excrement buckets.....' After a miserable two-week stay here, convicts were sent on prison barges to Tomsk. Things were not much better for the 500,000 emigrants who flooded through the town between 1883 and 1900, but they at least had their freedom.

When the new railway reached Tyumen in 1888 prisoners from Russia were no longer herded over the Urals in marching parties but travelled in relative luxury in box-cars used also for the transport of cattle and horses.

Tyumen is growing again now, in population (at present about 400,000) and in importance because of oil and gas discoveries in the *oblast*. Other industries include ship-building and timber-processing.

Watch out for working steam engines, used for shunting in the station.

Km2433: Ishim (●●) The town lies beside the Ishim River, which is a tributary of the Irtysh. This is the centre of the fertile agricultural region known as the **Ishim Steppe**. George Kennan recounts an amusing incident that occurred here in 1829, when Baron von Humboldt was conducting a geological survey for the Tsar. The famous explorer (who gave his name to the Humboldt Current off the west coast of South America) had by then become more than a little annoyed by the petty Siberian officials who kept him from his studies. He must have been rather short with the police prefect in this little town for the man took great offence and despatched an urgent letter to his governor-general in which he wrote:

'A few days ago there arrived here a German of shortish stature, insignificant appearance, fussy and bearing a letter of introduction from your Excellency to me. I accordingly received him politely; but I must say I find him suspicious and even dangerous. I disliked him from the first. He talks too much..... despises my hospitality .....and associates with Poles and other political criminals.....On one occasion he proceeded with them to a hill overlooking the town. They took a box with them and got out of it a long tube which we all took for a gun. After fastening it to three feet they pointed it down on the town.....This was evidently

MAP 5

Вагай
VAGAY

Омутинская
OMUTINSKAYA

Ламенская
LAMYENSKAYA

Голышманово
GOLISHMANOVO

Карасульская
KARASULSKAYA

TYUMENSKAYA OBLAST

Ⓜ

Ишим
ISHIM

Vetluga R.

Маслянская
MASLYANSKAYA

Ново-Андреевский
NOVO-ANDREYEVSKIY

Мангут
MANGUT

OMSKAYA OBLAST

Называевская
NAZEVAYEVSKAYA

Драгунская
DRAGUNSKAYA

Любинская
LYUBINSKAYA

Irtysh R.

ОМСК
OMSK

Ob R.

a great danger for the town which is built entirely of wood; so I sent a detachment of troops with loaded rifles to watch the German on the hill. If the treacherous machinations of this man justify my suspicions, we shall be ready to give our lives for the Tsar and Holy Russia.' Kennan adds: 'The civilised world is to be thanked that the brilliant career of the great von Humboldt was not cut short by a Cossack bullet.....while he was taking sights with a theodolite in that little Siberian town of Ishim.'

North of Ishim, up the Ishim and Irtysh Rivers, lies the city of **Tobolsk**, one of the oldest settlements in Siberia. Yermak (see page 71) reached the area in 1581 and established a fort here. The Tsar hoped to develop the region by encouraging colonisation but as far as the Russian peasant was concerned, Siberia was as far away as the moon and no voluntary mass exodus over the Urals occurred. The policy of forced exile was rather more successful. The first exiles that arrived in Tobolsk were former inhabitants of the town of Uglich where they had been witnesses to the murder of Tsarevich Dimitri. With them was banished the **Uglich church bell** which rang the signal for the insurrection following the assassination. The bell was reconsecrated in Tobolsk church but in the 1880s the Uglich Town Council decided it would like its bell back. Tobolsk Council refused and the case eventually went to court. The judge ruled that as the bell had been exiled for life, and it was still calling the people to prayers, it had not yet completed its sentence and must therefore remain in Tobolsk.

Km2520: Administrative frontier between Tyumenskaya and Omskaya *oblasts*. **Omskaya** is on a plain in the Irtysh River basin, occupying 140,000 square kilometres. The thick forests of the *taiga* cover the northern part of the *oblast*. In the south there is considerable agricultural development, the main crops being spring wheat, flax and sunflowers. As well as sheep and cattle farms, there are many dairy-farming co-operatives. This has been an important butter-producing region since the nineteenth century, when butter was exported to as far away as Turkey and Germany. It is said that butter-making was introduced to the region by the English wife of a Russian landowner. There are many swamps and lakes in the *oblast* which provide the habitat for a multitude of water birds, including duck, coot, grey goose, swan and crake.

Km2521-2870: Time zone MT + 3 Local time is now Moscow Time + 3 hours.

Km2567: Nazevayevskaya (●●●) This area is famous as much for its insects as for its dairy produce. In 1887, Kennan found that travelling through this marshy region was a singularly unpleasant experience. He wrote: 'We were so tormented by huge gray mosquitoes that we were obliged to put on thick gloves, cover our heads with calico hoods and horse hair netting and defend ourselves constantly with leafy branches.' You, however, should be quite safe in your compartment.

Km2707: Irtysh River which is joined here by the Om. The Irtysh rises in China and flows almost 3,000km into the Ob River (not to be confused with the River Om).

Km2712: Omsk (●●●) (87m/285ft) Founded in 1719 when a small fortress was set up on the west bank of the Om. At the centre of a fertile region, Omsk soon developed into an important agricultural market town. By the beginning of the nineteenth century it had become a regional administrative centre and had been accorded city status.

Omsk was the military headquarters of the Cossack regiments in Siberia. The fortress had been considerably enlarged and included a large *ostrog* (prison). It was here that Dostoyevsky did four years hard labour for political crimes in 1849. His unenviable experiences were recorded in *Buried Alive in Siberia*. He was twice flogged, first for complaining about a lump of dirt in his soup. The second time he saved the life of a drowning prisoner, ignoring a guard who ordered that the man be left to drown. Dostoyevsky received so severe a flogging for this charitable act that he almost died and had to spend six weeks in the hospital.

Annette Meakin and her mother had a more amusing time in Omsk in 1900. Visiting the German pastor and his wife they asked what the strange crying sounds were that they heard each morning, to be told that they were made by the camels. 'So you have camels in Omsk!' was the excited Mrs Meakin's response to this news. 'I have always wished to mount a camel.' The German lady replied frostily: 'Intelligent people do not mount camels. They are beasts of burden.'

The vast **Cathedral of the Ascension** was completed in 1898 and the 1900 Guide to the Great Siberian Railway advised its travellers to see the banner of Yermak (the sixteenth century conqueror of Siberia) which was kept in the cathedral: 'This banner was brought from the town of Beriozov and is two *arshins* and six *vershoks* long (66ins/1.7m; 1 *arshin* = 28ins, 1 *vershok* = 1.75ins). On one side is represented the Archangel Michael on a red winged horse, striking the Devil with his spear and precipitating houses and towers into the water; on the other, is seen St Demetrius on a dark horse thrusting Kuchum, mounted on a white horse, into an abyss.'

During the Civil War, Omsk was the capital of the White Russian government of Admiral Kolchak, until November 1919 when the Red Army entered and took the city. The population grew fast after the war and now more than a million people live here. Textiles, food, agricultural machinery and timber-products are the main industries. There is also an important petro-chemical industry here, supplied by a pipeline from the Ural-Volga oil region. There are often good snacks to buy from the *babushkas* on the platform (doughnuts stuffed with egg and chives, four for a rouble).

Km2761(S): About **50 locos** in strategic reserve beside the line.

The West Siberian Railway (kms2716-3343)
The original line started in Chelyabinsk, south of Sverdlovsk, and ran through Kurgan and Petropavlovsk (both south of the modern route) to Omsk. Work began in July 1892 under the direction of chief civil engineer, Mikhailovski. His task was beset by problems that were to be experienced along other sections of the line: a shortage of labour and animals, a complete lack of suitable trees for sleepers and inhospitable working conditions (swamps that swarmed with insects). However, the first section (Chelyabinsk to Omsk) was completed in 1894 and the Omsk-Novo Nikolayevsk (now Novosibirsk) section opened in October 1895. The total cost of the line was 46 million roubles, one million roubles fewer than the original estimate.

Baraba region
Between Omsk and the Ob River (which flows through Novosibirsk) you cross a vast area of swampy land known as the Baraba region (sometimes wrongly referred to as the Barabinsk Steppe, according to the *1900 Guide to the Great Siberian Railway*). The scenery is monotonous: wide grassy plains interspersed with groves of birch trees. There are numerous shallow lakes and ponds which form a perfect breeding ground for the gnats and mosquitoes which terrorise the local population during the summer months. Before the Russian settlers arrived in the eighteenth century, the region was occupied by a few Tartar and Kirghiz tribes (see page 212).

Km2870: The administrative frontier between Omskaya and Novosibirskaya *oblasts*. The 178,000 square kilometres of **Novosibirskaya** *oblast* extend across the Baraba region of swamps and lakes. Some of the land has been drained and is now extremely fertile. Crops include spring wheat, flax, rye, barley and sun-flowers with dairy farming in many parts of the Baraba region. You may see cow-herds rounding up their cows on horseback.

Km2871-4475 Time zone MT + 4 Local time is now Moscow Time + 4hrs.

MAP 6

Km2880: Tatarskaya A rather uninteresting small town of apartment blocks and log cabins. The *1900 Guide to the Great Siberian Railway* was not enthusiastic about the place. 'The country is swampy and infested with fever. The water is bad, supplied by a pond formed by spring and bog water.' There was a church, a centre for emigrants, a school and 'the butter manufactures of Mariupolsky, Padin, Soshovsky, Popel and Weiss, producing annually about 15,000 *puds* (250,000 kg) of cream butter'.

Km2883(N): Attractive group of brightly painted log cabins. About fifty kilometres south of the line between Chany and Barabinsk lies Lake Chany, the centre of a fishing industry. Catches are smaller now but in the nineteenth century it was famous for its abundant stock of large pike (weighing up to 14kg/30lbs) and carp.

Km3035: Barabinsk (●) There is a short stop by this ugly station building and fish (from the surrounding lakes) are often sold (uncooked) on the platform. Other possible purchases might include Bruce Lee or Iron Maiden badges from the kiosks. At the centre of the swampy **Baraba region**, Barabinsk was founded in 1722 when a field fortress was built here and the town which grew up around it was, until after the Revolution, called Kainsk. Cossacks were stationed here to try to encourage the nomadic Tatars, Kirghiz and Kalmyks to pay their taxes. For the 300km east of Barabinsk to Novosibirsk the scenery continues the same: fields of sunflowers or pastures dotted with cows and sheep, small clumps of birch trees or swamps and ponds.

Km3204: Chulimskaya This is a large junction.

Km3319: Ob station The city of Novosibirsk can be seen to the northeast of here.

Km3332: Bridge over the Ob River The original bridge, built at the end of the nineteenth century, still stands. The writers of the **Guide to the Great Siberian Railway** were clearly very proud of this tremendous feat of engineering, which at the time had only just been completed. They devote almost a whole page of their book to a detailed description of the bridge, beginning: 'At the 1,328 *verst*, the line crosses the Ob by a bridge 327.50 *sazhens* long, having 7 spans, the I and VII openings are 46.325 *sazhens*, the II, IV and VI, 53.65 *sazhens*, and III and V, 53.15 *sazhens*. The upper girders of the bridge are on the Herber's system.' If you are unfamiliar with the Russian Imperial units of measurement, a *verst* is 1.06Km or 3500ft and a *sazhen* is 2.1m or 7ft. For those interested, the bridge is therefore about 690m in length.

The Ob River is one of the world's longest rivers, flowing more than 4000km north across Siberia from the Altai Mountains to the Gulf of Ob, below the Arctic Ocean.

After you cross the bridge there is a preserved steam loco mounted on a plinth at km3333(S)

Km3335: Novosibirsk (●●●) (183m/600ft) is the capital of Western Siberia. See page 146 for further information.

The Kirghiz
South of Omsk and the Baraba region lie the **Kirghiz Steppes**, the true home of the Kirghiz people. The area extends from the Urals in the west to the mineral-rich Altai Mountains in the south. The Kirghiz are direct descendants of the Turco-Mongol hordes that joined Ghengis Khan's armies and invaded Europe in the thirteenth century A.D. When S.S. Hill paid them a visit in 1854, they were nomadic herders who professed a mixture of Shamanism and Mohammedanism and survived on a diet of boiled mutton and *koumis* (fermented mare's milk). They lived in *kibitkas* (felt tents or yurts), the doors of which were arranged to face in the direction of Mecca. Fortunately this alignment also kept out the southern winds that blew across the Steppe. Of these people Hill wrote: 'The Kirgeeze have the high cheek bones.....of the Mongol Tatars, with an expression of countenance that seemed at least to us the very reverse of agreeable.' However he warmed to his 'new half-wild friends' when they shared their 'brave mess of *stchee*' (soup) with him.

George Kennan found them equally hospitable in 1887. Inside the tent he was offered a large container filled with about a litre and a half of *koumis*. For fear of causing offence he swallowed the lot and to his horror, his host quickly re-filled the container. Kennan wrote 'When I suggested that he reserve the second bowlful for my comrade, Mr Frost, he looked so pained and grieved that in order to restore his serenity I had to go to the *tarantas*, get my banjo and sing "There is a Tavern in the Town"'. This did not have quite the desired effect and they left shortly after.

The suburbs of Novosibirsk stretch out east to about km3348. Travelling east you pass through flat land of fields and swamps with the *dacha* of Novosibirskians in little groups amongst the trees. Some are particularly photogenic (km3409 (S)). The line traverses an area of thin *taiga* to Oyash (km3424)

Km3485: This is the **administrative frontier** between Novosibirskaya and Kemerovskaya oblasts.

Km3498: Yurga A few kilometres east of here, the train crosses the River Tom, which flows an unimpressive (by Siberian standards) 700km (or twice the length of the Thames) from the Kuznetsk basin into the Ob.

Km3565: Taiga (●●) Junction of the branch line to Tomsk. During the stop here you can visit the kiosks on the platform, which offer only four items for sale: bread, cheese, eggs and suitcases. R.L.Jefferson was here in 1897 and wrote later: 'This little station was bang in the midst of the most impenetrable forest I had ever set eyes on.....in the centre of a pit it seemed, for the great black trunks of pines went up all around and left only a circular space of blue sky visible.' Annette Meakin wrote a few years later: 'We thought Taiga one of the prettiest stations in Siberia. It is only a few years old, built something after the style of a Swiss chalet.' Unfortunately it has since been replaced by a building that is rather more substantial but less aesthetically pleasing.

If you were to take the other line from Taiga, you would come after about 80km, to the ancient city of **Tomsk**, once the most important place in Siberia, and recently opened to foreigners. It was founded in 1604 on the River Tom and developed into a large administrative, trading and gold-smelting centre on the Great Siberian Post Road. When

MAP 7

it was bypassed by the railway (although later connected by a branch-line) Tomsk began to lose out to the stations along the main line. However, it is still a sizeable city of almost half a million people, the administrative capital of Tomskaya *oblast* and a large centre of industrial engineering.

Tomsk was visited by almost every nineteenth century traveller who came to Siberia. The city was an important exile centre and had a large forwarding prison. Having almost succumbed to the stench from the overcrowded cells in 1887, Kennan wrote: 'If you visit the prison my advice to you is to breakfast heartily before starting, and to keep out of the hospital wards.' By the time Annette Meakin visited it fourteen years later, the railways had removed the need for forwarding prisons and she could write: 'It was not unlike a group of alms houses. We found very few prisoners.'

Between Taiga and Mariinsk there are deposits of coal. The USSR has no shortage of this fossil fuel: 25 per cent of world supplies lie within her borders. It has been mined around the town of Yar since the nineteenth century. However the centre of the coal-mining district lies 300km south of here, around the city of **Novokuznetsk**, in the Kuznetsk (or Kuzbass) Basin. In the early 1900s a plan had been put forward to link these coal-fields with the Ural region where iron-ore was mined and coal was needed for the blast furnaces. This plan was not put into action until the 1930s when the so-called Ural-Kuzbass Kombinat was developed. Trains bring iron-ore to the Kuzbass furnaces and return to the iron foundries of the Urals with coal. You will have met (or will meet if you're going west) a good deal of this traffic on the line between Novosibirsk and the Urals. According to Eric Newby this stretch of the line has more freight traffic than any other in the world, with a train every couple of minutes.

Kms3613-3623: Several long views south across the fields. The line climbs slowly through birch forests and small fields to Mariinsk (km3717).

Km3717: Mariinsk (●●) Just west of the station there are large engine repair yards (S). Two kilometres east of the town you cross the Kiya River, a tributary of the Chulim. East of the river the line rises to cross the watershed at km3760, where there are good views south. The line descends through the market town of **Tiazhin** (km3779) to the river of the same name and then climbs over the next watershed descending to **Itat**, another agricultural town.

Km3820: This is the administrative frontier between Kemerovskaya *oblast* and Krasnoyarskiy *kray*. A *kray* is a large *oblast*, usually found in less developed areas like Siberia. This is also the border between West and East Siberia. **Krasnoyarskiy** is large, covering 2½ million square kilometres (an area the size of Saudi Arabia) between the Arctic Ocean in the north and the Sayan Mountains in the south. Most of the *kray* is covered with *taiga*, though there is *tundra* in the region within the Arctic Circle and some agricultural land in the south. The economy is based on timber processing but there are also important mineral reserves.

Km3852: Bogotol (●●) Market town. About 30km east of here the line begins to descend, crossing the **Chulim River** at km3917. R.L.Jefferson arrived here in the winter of 1897 and described the river as 'rather a small stream when compared to the Obi, Tom or Irtish but still broad enough to make two of the River Thames at London Bridge'. The bridge had not been completed but engineers had had the brilliant idea of freezing the rails to the thick ice, thus enabling the train to cross the river.

Km3920: Achinsk (●) (214m/700ft) Founded in 1642 when a stockaded outpost was built here, on the banks of the Chulim. It was burnt down by the Kirghiz forty years later but was soon rebuilt. In the eighteenth and nineteenth centuries Achinsk was an important trading centre, linked by the Chulim to Tyumen and Tomsk. Tea arrived by caravan from China and was forwarded in barges. To the north, in the valleys around the Chulim basin, lay the gold mines. However, the most valuable and productive mines today are those producing lignite (brown coal). Achinsk is also an agricultural centre.

MAP 8

Kms3932-33(S): The half-way point on the line from Moscow to Beijing (via Mongolia). There is a **white obelisk** to mark it on the south side of the line but it is difficult to see. The line continues through a hilly region of *taiga* winding round sharp curves (kms4006-12) and past picturesque groups of log cabins (km4016). There are occasional good views at km4058(N) and after the village of Minino (km4072) at 4078(N).

The Mid-Siberian Railway (kms3343-5191)
Work began on the line at the River Ob in the summer of 1893. Since Tomsk was to be bypassed, part of the route had to be hacked through the thick forests of the *taiga* regions around the station aptly named Taiga. It would have been far easier to have followed the route of the Great Siberian Post Road through Tomsk but some of the city's administrators wanted nothing to do with the railway, since it would break their trade monopolies and bring down prices, damaging the economy as far as they were concerned. By the time they realised that the effect was quite the opposite it was too late to change the route of the line. Besides, the engineers had discovered that the bypass would save 90km. The tiny village of Novo Nikolayevsk (now Novosibirsk) situated where the railway crosses the Ob, grew quickly and soon eclipsed Tomsk as an industrial and cultural centre.

This was difficult territory to build a railway across. The swampy *taiga* is frozen until mid-July, so the building season was barely three months long. There was the usual labour shortage and 1,500 convicts had to be brought in to help. In 1895 a branch line from Taiga reached Tomsk. Although only about 80km long, it had taken a year to build, owing to the virtually impenetrable *taiga* and the terrible swamps. In 1896 the line reached Krasnoyarsk and work began on the eastern section to Irkutsk. Numerous bridges were needed in this hilly country but by the beginning of 1898 the mid-Siberian was complete and the first trains rolled into Irkutsk. Total cost was about 110 million roubles.

Km4099: Krasnoyarsk (●●●) (159m/520ft) A major industrial city of 850,000 people. It was founded in 1628 beside the Yenisei River. (*Yenisei* is also the name of the Moscow-Krasnoyarsk Express which you may see standing in the station). A fort was built and named Krasny Yar. As an important trading centre on the Great Siberian Post Road and the great Yenisei waterway, the town grew fast in the eighteenth century. The railway reached Krasnoyarsk in 1896, some of the rails for this section of the line having been brought from England by ship via the Kara Sea (within the Arctic Circle) and the Yenisei. By 1900, the population was 27,000 and the town boasted 20 churches and two cathedrals, a synagogue, 26 schools, a railway technical college and a botanical garden reputed to be the finest in Siberia.

Murray would not recognise the town he described as 'pleasantly situated and sheltered by hills of moderate elevation', in the 1865 edition of his *Handbook for Russia, Poland and Finland*. R.L.Jefferson wrote in 1897: 'Its situation cannot fail to elicit admiration - the tall mountains rear up around it.' Most of the townsfolk he met here were ex-convicts. So used were they to their own kind, that they were particularly suspicious of anyone who lacked a criminal record. He was told of a certain merchant in the city who found it difficult to do business, never having been behind bars. To remedy the situation he travelled all the way to St Petersburg and deliberately committed a crime that was punishable by exile to Siberia. After a short sentence in Irkutsk he returned to his business in Krasnoyarsk and 'got on famously' thereafter.

Travelling intellectuals were advised to visit the library of the Krasnoyarsk merchant, Yudin. This bibliophile assembled a collection of 100,000 volumes, including almost every publication ever issued in Siberia. At the end of the nineteenth century, while sentenced to exile in Krasnoyarsk, Lenin spent several months working in this library. In 1906 Yudin sold his valuable collection to the Library of Congress, for less than half of its true worth. By this act of generosity he said that he hoped closer relations between the United States and Russia would be established.

During the Second World War, many factories were evacuated from European Russia and rebuilt here. Industrial growth has continued since then and the long list of things the city now produces includes aluminium, chemicals, ships, televisions, fridges and large quantities of heavy machinery.

Km4100-2: Yenisei River Good views (N) & (S). Leaving Krasnoyarsk, travelling east, the train crosses the great river that bisects Siberia. The Yenisei (meaning 'wide water' in the language of the local Evenki people) rises in Mongolia and flows into the Arctic Ocean, 5,200km north of its source. This bridge, which is almost a kilometre in length, dates from the 1890s and had to be built on heavy granite piers to withstand the huge icebergs which steamroller their way down the river for a few weeks each year. The cement was shipped from St Petersburg, the steel bearings from Warsaw.

The lumber mills and factories blight the countryside for several kilometres after you've crossed the river. Open-cast mining has slashed ugly gashes into the hills around km4127(N). Between Krasnoyarsk and Nizhneudinsk the line crosses hilly, picturesque countryside, and the train climbs out of one valley and descends into the next. There are numerous bridges on this section. There are some good places for photographs along the train as it curves round bends at km4165-7 and km4176-7, then the scenery becomes flatter.

MAP 9

КРАСНОЯРСК
KRASNOYARSK
Злобино
ZLOBINO
Зыково
ZIKOVO
Сорокино
SOROKINO
Камарчага
KAMARCHAGA
Балай
BALAY
Уяр
UYAR
Заозерная
ZAOZERNAYA
Камала
KAMALA
Солянка
SOLYANKA
Бошняково
BOSHNYAKOVO
Канск
KANSK
Иланская
ILANSKAYA
Ингашская
INGASHSKAYA
Тинская
TINSKAYA
Решоты
RESHOTI
Ключи
KLYUCHI
Юрты
YURTI
Бирюсинск
BIRYUSINSK
Тайшет
TAYSHET
→BRATSK
Разгон
RAZGON
Алзамай
ALZAMAY
Камышет
KAMISHET
Ук
UK
Нижнеудинск
NIZHNEUDINSK

KRASNOYARSKIY KRAY · 131
IRKUTSKAYA OBLAST · 163 · 224 · 63

Km4228: Uyar Large strategic reserve of working **steam locos** at west end of station (N) where there is also a dump of about ten engines rusting away amongst the weeds. This town's full name is something of a tongue-twister. Try saying 'Ular-Spasopreo-brazhen-skoye' after a few glasses of vodka. Before the Revolution the station was called Olgin-skaya in honour of Grand Duchess Olga Nikolaevna.

Km4344: Kansk Another ancient Siberian settlement. A fort was built here in 1604 beside the River Kan. By 1900 it was an important station on the railway and a stop-ping point on the Great Siberian Post Road. The original station building has been replaced by a modern concrete eyesore. Leaving Kansk you cross the River Kan at km4346.

Km4375: Ilanskaya (●●) Several rusting **steam locos** in this station: one at the west end (S) and a further three quite ancient types at the east end (N). This agricultural town was founded in the early nineteenth century beside the Ilanka River. Between here and Tayshet, there are large deposits of lignite (brown coal). Our *provodnitsa* was well aware of this last bit of information and issued four of us with buckets to collect coal (for the carriage boiler) from the piles that were lying about the platform.

Km4459: Reshoti Junction for the line south to Abakan, an industrial centre in the foothills of the Sayan Mountains. Abakan is open to tourists (see page 168) and there is good hiking in the area.

About nine hundred kilometres due north of here lies the town of Tura, the capital of the **Evenki National Okrug**, 745,000 square kilometres of permanently frozen land, spe-cially reserved for the indigenous population. The **Evenkis** belong to the Tungu group of people (the names are often used interchangeably) and they were originally nomadic herders and hunters. After the Buryats and the Yakuts, they form the next largest ethnic group in Siberia but they are scattered into small groups, right across the northern regions. They used to live in wig-wams or tents and survived off berries and reindeer-meat (a great delicacy being the raw marrow sucked straight from the bone preferably while it was still warm). They discovered that Christianity fitted in well with their own Shamanistic religion and worshipped St Nicholas as deputy to the Master Spirit of the Underworld. After the revolution they were organised into collective farms and although most of the population is now settled, there are still some reindeer-herders in the extreme north of the region.

Km4475: This is the administrative frontier between Krasnoyarskaya and Irkutskaya oblasts.

Km4476-5755: Time zone MT + 5 Local time is now Moscow Time + 5hrs.

Kms4500-01: The river here conveniently marks the **half-way point** for the Moscow to Beijing (via Manchuria) run.

Km4516: Tayshet (●) (317m/1040ft) Junction for the line to Bratsk and the Baikal Amur Magistral Railway (BAM).

Km4555(S): Razgon A small, poor-looking community of log cabins. About a kilometre east of here, the line rises and there are views across the *taiga* at km4563(S), km4569(N) and km4570.

Between Razgon and Nizhneudinsk, the line passes through Kamyshet, which was where George Kennan stopped in 1887 for repairs to his *tarantass*. While the wheel was being replaced, he watched the amazing spectacle of a Siberian blacksmith shoeing a horse. 'The poor beast had been hoisted by means of two broad belly-bands and suspended from a stout frame so that he could not touch the ground', he wrote. Three of the horse's legs had been secured to the frame and 'the daring blacksmith was fearlessly putting a shoe on the only hoof that the wretched and humiliated animal could move.'

Kms4640-4680: The train snakes its way through the foothills of the Eastern Sayan Mountains. The Sayan Range forms a natural frontier between Siberia and Mongolia. There are some good views and a number of chances to take photographs of the whole length of the train as it winds around the valleys. The best spots are around km4657(S), km4660(S), kms4662-5 and km4667. The line descends to Nizhneudinsk.

MAP 10

Km4680: Nizhneudinsk (●●)

(415m/1360ft) There's not much more than saw-mills, swamps and insects in this area. Of the mosquitoes, Kennan complained 'I found myself blotted from head to foot as if I were suffering from some eruptive disease.'

About 800km due north of here, on 30 June 1908, one of the largest (pre-atomic era) explosions took place, in the Tunguska River region. Two thousand square kilometres of forest were instantly destroyed in what came to be known as the **Tunguska Event**. The sound of the explosion was heard up to 350kms away; the shock waves were registered on seismic equipment right around the world, and the light from the blast was seen throughout Europe. Newspapers of the time proposed all kinds of theories to explain its cause - from the testing of new explosives to crash-landing Martian space-ships. Scientists now believe that the explosion was caused by a fragment of Encke's Comet, which disintegrated as it entered the Earth's atmosphere, creating a vast fireball.

Between Nizhneudinsk and Irkutsk the country becomes flatter and the *taiga* not so thick. The train passes through numerous timber-yards.

Kms4720-21: The **half-way point** on the line from Moscow to Nakhodka (for Japan).

Km4789(S): Large **graveyard** with a blue fence around it, standing close to the line. Some of the graves are topped with red stars, some with red crosses. Kennan wrote in 1887: 'The graveyards belonging to the Siberian settlements sometimes seemed to me much more remarkable and noteworthy than the settlements themselves.....Many graves (are) marked by three armed wooden crosses and covered with narrow A-shaped roofs.'

Km4794: Tulun An agricultural and wood-processing centre on the Uya River. The line follows the river, crossing it at km4800 and passing a large saw-mill at km4804(S) which might make a good photo with the town behind it. For once there are no wires to get in the way. At km4809(S) there is a large open-cast mine. You pass through an area of large cultivated fields.

Km4875: Kuytun The town's name means 'cold' in the language of the local Buryat tribe (see below). There are cold springs in the area.

Km4940: Zima (●●●) (460m/1500ft) Founded by exiles in the early nineteenth century. When the Tsarevich Nicholas visited Zima on 8 July 1891, the Buryats presented him with a model of one of their *yurts* (tents) cast in silver. Three kilometres east of the town, the line crosses the River Oka, a tributary of the Angara. As the line rises out of one valley, crosses the watershed and drops down to the next river you get several reasonable views: km4958(S), km4972(N), km4977(S) and km4990(S).

Kms5000-40 You pass through the Ust-Ordinsky Autonomous Okrug. There's another graveyard close to the track at km5010(S).

Km5061: Cheremkhovo The centre of the coal-mining district of the same name.

Km5100: Near here is the village of **Malta**, on the banks of the Belaya River. It was in a house in Malta, in February 1928, that farmer Platon Brilin was helping a comrade to build a cellar. While he was digging, his spade struck a white object which turned out to be a mammoth tusk carved into a female form. Excavations revealed dwellings with walls made from mammoth bones and roofs of antlers. He had discovered the remains one of an ancient settlement, dating from the thirteenth millenium B.C. A grave yielded the body of a child, still wearing a necklace and headband of bones. He may have been a young *shaman* (see page 158) for the gods were thought to select their earthly representatives by branding them with some kind of deformity - the boy has two sets of teeth. Numerous ivory figurines have been found at Malta and also at the site in **Buret**, eight kilometres from here. Many of the excavated artifacts may be seen in the museums in Irkutsk. The oldest settlement in the USSR that has so far been discovered is at Dering Yuryakh (1-2.5 million years old) in northern Siberia near Yakutsk (see page 168).

Between km5100 and Irkutsk (km5185) there are fields interspersed with large industrial areas. In the distance, at km5130(N) there is a large oil refinery.

MAP 11

Km5160: Angarsk (●) Known as Sukhovskaya before the Revolution, the town is on the banks of the Angara River, the only river which flows out of Lake Baikal. Travellers have reported a large strategic reserve of L and Ye 2-10-0s held at this station (N).

Km5179: Irkutsk Sort. (Irkutsk marshalling yard) The station used to be called Innokentievskaya, in honour of St Innocent, Archbishop of Irkutsk, who was said to have been the first miracle-worker in Siberia. The **St Innocent Monastery of the Ascension** near here was founded in 1672. The Tsarevich looked in on his tour of Siberia in 1891. The visit was thus described: 'After having listened to the singing, the Tsesarevich (sic) knelt at the shrine of the Siberian Saint, kissed the relics and received the image of Innocent, presented to him by Agathangelius, Vicar of Irkutsk. At the same time a deputation from Shaman Buryats expressed the desire of 250 men to adopt the orthodox religion and to receive the name of Nicholas in commemoration of the Tsesarevich's visit to Siberia, which was thus to be preserved in the memory of their descendants. The Imperial traveller graciously acceded to this request.'

Km5185: Irkutsk (●●●) (440m/1450ft) See Part 4 for information and a description of this city, once known as the 'Paris of Siberia'.

Leaving Irkutsk, travelling in the direction of Khabarovsk and Nakhodka, the line climbs up into the hills before giving magnificent views over the lake. It then winds down through a series of tunnels and a Swiss-style horseshoe bend to follow the mountainous shore of Lake Baikal. At many points the rails lie right beside the lake and some of the best views of the whole trip are along this section of the line, over this immense stretch of water. (See Part 4 for information on Irkutsk/Lake Baikal)

The Circumbaikal Line (kms5191-5483)

Until 1904, passengers crossed Lake Baikal on ferries which took them from Port Baikal to Mysovaya. In 1893 it had been decided that this short section of line along the mountainous southern shore of the lake would be impossibly expensive to build, and the plan was shelved in favour of the ferry link. A specially designed combined ice-breaker and train-ferry was ordered from the English company of Armstrong and Mitchell. The 4,200 ton ship, christened the *Baikal*, had three pairs of rails laid across her decks for the carriages and could smash through ice up to four feet thick. A sister ship, the *Angara*, was soon brought into service.

However, the ferry system was not a great success. In mid-winter the ships were unable to break through the ice and in summer the wild storms for which the lake is notorious, often delayed them. Since they could not accommodate more than 300 people between them, many passengers were subjected to a long wait beside the lake. The Trans-Siberian Committee realised that, however expensive it might prove, a line had to be built to bridge the 260km gap between the Mid-Siberian and the Transbaikal Railways. Further surveys were ordered in 1898 and in 1901 ten thousand labourers started work on the line.

This was the most difficult section to build on the whole railway. The terrain between Port Baikal and Kultuk (near Slyudyanka) was virtually one long cliff. Thirty-three tunnels and more than two hundred bridges and trestles were constructed, the task being made all the more difficult by the fact that in many places the labourers could reach the route only by boat. Work was carried on simultaneously on the Tankhoi to Mysovaya section.

The labour gangs hacked out embankments and excavated seven kilometres of tunnels but the line was not ready at the time it was most needed. On 8 February 1904, Japan attacked the Russian Navy while it lay at anchor in Port Arthur on the Pacific. Troops were rushed by rail from European Russia but when they arrived at Port Baikal, they found the *Baikal* and *Angara* ice-bound by the severe weather. The only way across the lake was a seventeen-hour march over the ice. It was then that the Minister of Ways of Communication, Prince Khilkov, put into action a plan which had been successful on several of Siberia's rivers: rails were laid across the ice. The first train to set off across the frozen lake did not get far along the forty-five kilometre track before the ice gave way with a crack like a cannon and the locomotive sank into the icy water. From then on the engines had to be stripped and their parts put on flat-cars that were pulled over the ice by gangs of men and horses.

Working as fast as possible, in all weathers, the Circumbaikal line was completed in September 1904 at a cost of about 70 million roubles. The first passengers found this section of the line particularly terrifying, not on account of the frequent derailments but because of the tunnels - there were none in European Russia at the time. In the 1950s a short cut was opened between Irkutsk and Slyudyanka, which is the route followed by the train today. The line between Irkutsk and Port Baikal is partly flooded and no longer used but much of the Port Baikal to Kultuk section is still operational and can be visited by boat from Listvyanka.

Winding through valleys of cedar and pine, and crossing numerous small streams, the train passes **Kultuk**, the junction for the old line from Port Baikal. At km5228(N) a giant-size etching of Lenin waves nonchalantly from the hill above. The line climbs steeply to km5254 and then snakes downwards giving you your first glimpses of Lake Baikal from kms5274-8. After the tunnel (km5290) there is a splendid **view** over the lake at km5292(N).

Km5297-8: Tunnel as the line curves sharply round the valley and descends to the water's edge. After the junction and goods yard at Slyudyanka II (km5305) the train crawls slowly along a part of the line that is liable to flooding from the lake, and into the main station.

Km5312: Slyudyanka (●●●) As the station is only about 500m from the lake there is just enough time to run down to the water and dip your hand in for good luck (see page 165). Check with the carriage attendant that the train is stopping for the usual 15mins and hurry down between the log cabins to the lake. You must be quick since people have been left behind. If you're not feeling energetic there's usually lots to buy on the platform - bread-sticks (1 rouble) and bags of *orecha* (cedar seeds, which are the classic Siberian snack). Although there are some photogenic log cabins near the station, Slyudyanka is a rather unattractive mining town and port. Fur-trappers hunt sable and ermine in the forests around this area.

For the next 200km the line is never far from the lake, occasionally running right beside it.

Km5397: This is the **administrative frontier** between Irkutskaya *oblast* and Buryatskaya Autonomous Soviet Socialist Republic. This region, which is also known as **Buryatiya**, comprises an area of 350,000 square kilometres (about the size of Italy). It was set aside for the Buryats (see page 226), an indigenous ethnic group once nomadic but now adapted to an agricultural or urban life. Their republic is composed of mountainous *taiga* and the economy is based on fur-farming, stock-raising, food and timber-processing and the mining of gold, aluminium, manganese, iron, coal, asbestos and mica. In fact almost all the elements can be found here.

When Prince Borghese and his team were motoring through this area in 1907, taking part in the Peking to Paris Rally, they found that since the building of the railway the Great Siberian Post Road had fallen into disrepair. Most of the post-stations were deserted and

(Opposite) Siberian Winter. Top: Exercises on the platform, minus 25°C. **Bottom:** Lake Baikal, the world's deepest lake (see page 162), does not freeze over until the end of December, in spite of the extreme cold.

many of the bridges were rotten and dangerous. The Italians were given special permission by the governor-general to use the railway bridges. In fact they covered a considerable part of the journey here by driving along the railway line. However, their 40 h.p. Itala was not the only unorthodox vehicle to take to the rails. On his cycle-tour through south Siberia in 1896, R.L.Jefferson found it rather easier to pedal his Imperial Rover along the tracks than along the muddy roads.

Km5421(N): The lonely looking collection of ramshackle buildings by the water's edge might make a good photograph.

Km5477: Mysovaya This port was where the *Baikal* and *Angara* delivered their passengers (and their train). Also called Babushkin in honour of an Irkutsk revolutionary, it was the western starting point of the Transbaikal railway (see page 227). When Annette Meakin and her mother disembarked from the *Baikal* in 1900, they were horrified to discover that the awaiting train was composed entirely of fourth class carriages. The brave ladies nabbed places in the corner of one compartment but soon they were hemmed in by emigrating peasants. When two dirty *moujiks* climbed into the luggage rack above them, the ladies got out deciding it would be better to wait at Mysovaya than spend four days in such claustrophobic conditions. However, the station-master allowed them to travel in an empty luggage-van, which gave them privacy but not comfort.

Between Mysovaya and Petrovskiy Zavod the line skirts around the lower reaches of the Khamar Daban mountain range. The train passes through Posolkaya (km5531) where there was once a large walled monastery, set up by an abbot and a monk in 1681. Around km5536, the line enters the wide valley of the River Selenga, which it follows as far as Ulan Ude (km5642).

Km5568: Selenga Founded as a stockaded outpost in the seventeenth century. Unfortunately the wood-pulping factories are rather more in evidence than the sixteenth century monastery which was the centre for missionaries attempting the conversion of the Buryats. From about km5515 east, the line begins to climb, crossing the Selenga River at kms5617-8. At km5633-4(N) there's an army camp with some abandoned tanks.

(Opposite) Siberian Summer Top: Listvyanka, beside Lake Baikal.
Bottom: Lake Baikal - note the ribbons tied to the tree for good luck.

Km5642: Ulan Ude (● ● ●) (544m/1785ft) A city of 400,000 people, this is the capital of the Buryat Republic. Stretch your legs on the platform where there is a *steam train* (Cy205) preserved outside the locomotive workshop (N) at the western end of the station.

See Part 4 for further information about the city and sight-seeing possibilities if you're staying here.

Turn to page 246 for **Trans-Mongolian Route to Beijing**.

The Buryats

The largest ethnic minority group in Siberia, these people are of Mongolian descent. When Russian colonists arrived in the lands around Lake Baikal, the Buryats were nomads who spent their time herding their flocks between the southern shores of the lake and what is now northern Mongolia, in search of pastureland. They lived in felt-covered *yurts* and professed a mixture of Buddhism and Shamanism.

The Buryats lived on fish from Lake Baikal, bear-meat and berries. However, their favourite food was said to be *urme*, the thick dried layer of scum skimmed from the top of boiled milk. They hunted the Baikal seal for its fur and in winter, when the lake was frozen, they would track these animals on the ice by wearing white clothing and pushing a white sledge as a hide. Back in their *yurts* the Buryats were not the cleanest of Siberian tribes, lacking even the most basic of social graces as the anthropologists Levin and Potapov point out in *The Peoples of Siberia*. Describing an after-dinner scene, they wrote: 'The vessels were not washed, as the spoons and cups were licked clean. An unwashed vessel was often passed from one member of the family to another as was the smoking pipe. Customs of this kind promoted the spread of various diseases.' Most of the diseases were probably brought by the Russian colonists.

Although at first hostile to the Russian colonists, the Buryats became involved in the fur-trade with the white men and a certain amount of inter-marriage occurred. Some gave up their nomadic life and felt-covered *yurts* in favour of a log cabin in Verkhneudinsk (now Ulan Ude) or Irkutsk. The Buryats, who number about 350,000, now have their own **Buryataya Autonomous Soviet Socialist Republic**, around the southern part of Lake Baikal. The capital, Ulan Ude, was recently opened to tourists and is an interesting place to visit.

East of the city the line crosses the River Uda and from Onokhoi follows the valley of a river named Brian. From Zaigraevo, the train begins to climb to Ilka, a town on the river of the same name. It continues to ascend the Zagon Dar range, reaching the highest point (882m/2892ft) at Kizha, near the administrative frontier.

Km5676(N): Onokhoy Large number (about 40) of steam locos kept at the west end of this station.

Km5755: This is the **administrative frontier** between the Buryataya ASSR and **Chitinskaya** *oblast*. The 432,000 square kilometres of the Chitinskaya *oblast* comprise a series of mountain ranges interspersed with wide valleys. The dominant range is the Yablonovy (highest peak: Sokhondo, 2,510m/8,200ft) which is crossed by the Trans-Siberian near Amazar. The mountains are covered in a vast forest of conifers and the climate is dry. The economy is based on mining (gold, tungsten, tin, lead, zinc, molybdenum, lithium, lignite), timber-processing and fur-farming.

Km5756-8150: Time zone MT + 6 Local time is Moscow Time + 6hrs.

Km5782: Petrovskiy Zavod (Works) (●●●) The line descends from Kizha to this town which is also known as Petrovsk-Zabaikalskiy. It was named after the Imperial ironworks set up here in 1790 and still going strong today. The town was a place of exile for several of the Decembrists, including the Princes Trubetskoi and Volkonsky. Their wives received special permission from the Tsar to join their husbands in exile. They arrived in 1830 and spent the next ten years imprisoned here. For a very readable account of the life of Maria Volkonsky and the Decembrist Exiles see *The Princess of Siberia* by Christine Sutherland. Maria Volkonsky's house in Irkutsk is now a museum.

The Transbaikal Railway (kms5483-6532)

Work was begun in 1895 to connect Mysovaya (the port on Lake Baikal) with Sretensk, on the Shilka River near Kuenga, where passengers boarded steamers for the voyage to Khabarovsk. Materials were shipped to Vladivostok and thence by boat along the Ussuri, Amur and Shilka Rivers. There was a shortage of labour, for it proved impossible to get the local Buryats to work on the line. Gangs of convicts were brought in and became more interested in the operation after it was decided that they should receive 50 kopecks a day in return for their labour.

The terrain is mountainous and the line meanders up several valleys and over the Yablonovy Range. Owing to the dry climate work could continue throughout the winter, although water was in short supply during these months. Workers were also faced with the problem of permafrost which necessitated the building of bonfires to thaw the ground, or dynamite to break it up. A terrible set-back occurred in July 1887, when 350km of track and several bridges were swept away in a freak flood.

The line was completed in early 1900 by which time it had cost over 60 million roubles.

East of Petrovskiy Zavod, the line turns north-east into the wide, picturesque valley of the River Khilok, which it follows for almost 300kms to Sokhondo, crossing the Yablonovy Range between Mogzon and Chita.

MAP 12

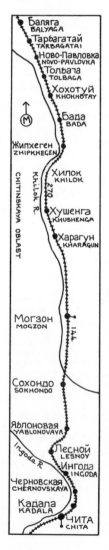

Km5883: Large graveyard of about 40 old **steam locos**.

Km5884: Bada Aerodrome The little town beside the runway is built around a silver, skyward-facing jet-plane.

Km5899(S): Good place for a photo along the train as it travels on higher ground beside the river. Also at km5908(S), when the train winds slowly along the water's edge.

Km5932: Khilok (●) (805m/2,640ft) A small industrial town. East of here you continue to climb gently up the valley beside the Khilok. There are pleasant views over the wide plain all along the river. North of the line are the Khogoy and Shentoy mountains, part of the Tsagan Khuntei Range.

Km6052: Mogzon (●●) (907m/2,975ft) For several kilometres around this town there are what appear to be **prison camps**, heavily guarded (km6055(N) is one example).

Km6093: Sokhondo (944m/3,095ft) Named after the highest peak (2,510m/ 8,230ft) in the Yablonovy Range. The line leaves the river valley and climbs over the Yablonovy. There is a long view at km6097(N). About 7km east of here you reach the highest point on the line (989m/ 3242ft). In the 1914 edition of his *Russia with Teheran, Port Arthur and Peking*, Karl Baedeker drew his readers' attention to the '93 yard tunnel inscribed at its western entrance "To the Great Ocean" and at its eastern entrance "To the Atlantic Ocean" in Russian', that was here. The line has now been re-routed up onto a huge grassy plain. It then descends steeply through Yablonovaya and there are several good views (kms6107-6109).

Km6116(S): There was a vast graveyard of steam locomotives here (I counted fifty-two along the siding in 1986) but now most of the engines have been dismantled. West of the town of Ingoda, the train enters the narrow winding valley of the River Ingoda, which it follows for the next 250km east. The line passes through Chernovskaya, where lignite is mined.

Km6131(S): The line crosses a picturesque meadow with a stream meandering across it. Good for a photograph when the flowers are out in May and June.

Km6199: Chita (●●●) (655m/2150ft) Founded in 1655, the capital of the Chitinskaya *oblast* stands beside the Chita and Ingoda rivers, surrounded by low hills. A stockaded fort was built here by the Cossacks at the end of the seventeenth century and the town became an important centre on the Chinese trade route. In 1827 a large group of exiled Decembrists arrived here and spent the first few months building the prison that was to be their home for the following three years. Many stayed on after they had served their sentence and the development of the town in the nineteenth century into an industrial and cultural centre was largely due to their efforts. George Kennan was here in 1887 and wrote: 'Among the exiles of Chita were some of the brightest, most cultivated, most sympathetic men and women we had met in Eastern Siberia.'

By 1900 more than 11,000 people lived here. There were nine churches, a cathedral, a nunnery, a synagogue, thirteen schools and even a telephone system. The modern city is near the junction for the line to China and there are large repair workshops here. Other industries include light engineering and the production of food and textiles.

Likely to remain off-limits owing to the military centre here. If you do manage to stay it will probably be in the modern Ingoda Hotel, or else in the Dauria Hotel which dates from the 19th century.

East of the city of Chita, the train continues to follow the left bank of the Ingoda River downhill, for the next 250kms. The train passes through Novaya, where the original community and the whole of the town was wiped out in the great flood of 1897.

Km6225(S): Big radio masts and a collection of log cabins (some of them quite photogenic) which look rather vulnerable being built on the edge of the river flood plain.

Km6265: Darasun (●) About one kilometre east of the station there is a good view as the train snakes along the river.

Km6270: Army supply base surrounded by a wooden stockade.

MAP 13

ЧИТА
CHITA
Песчанка
PESCHANKA
Атамановка
ATAMANOVKA
Новая
NOVAYA
Маккавеево
MAKKAVEYEVO
Дарасун
DARASUN
Карымская
KARYMSKAYA
Тарская
TARSKAYA
Урульга
URULGA
Зубарево
ZUBAREVO
Размахнино
RAZMAKHNINO
Солнцевая
SOLNTSEVAYA
Онон
ONON
Шилка-Пасс
SHILKA-PASS
Холбон
KHOLBON
Приисковая
PRYISKOVAYA
Нерчинск
NERCHINSK
Кузнга
KUENGA
Укурей
UKUREY
Чернышевск
Забайкал.
CHERNISHEVSK
Сретенск
SRETENSK
Бушулей
BUSHULEY
Хоктонга
KHOKTONGA
Зилово
ZILOVO
Ульякан
ULYAKAN

CHITINSKAYA OBLAST

TO BEIJING VIA MANCHURIA (MAP 21)

Ingoda R.

Onon R.

Shilka R.

Km6293: Karymskaya (●●●)
(605m/1985ft) Small industrial town first
settled by the Buryats.

Km6312: Tarskaya Formerly known as
Kaidalovo, this is the junction for the **railway
to Beijing via Manchuria** (see Map 21, page
257). A whitewashed church stands on the hill
(S) above the village. Good views along the
river at km6316(S) and across the wide plains
for the next 100km, especially around
km6332(S) and km6369(S). There are large
fields around the river and bare hills to the
north. The best views are all to the south,
across to Mongolia.

Km6417: Onon (515m/1690ft) A few
kilometres east of here the clear waters of the
Ingoda River are joined by those of the muddy
Onon, on whose banks the great Mongol
leader, Genghis Khan, was born in 1162. The
Onon and the Ingoda together form the Shilka
River, a tributary of the mighty Amur. The
railway follows the picturesque valley of the
Shilka for the next 120kms.

Km6446: Shilka Pass (●●●)
(505m/1655ft) There are several interesting-
looking wooden buildings near the platform
and a photogenic bank of propaganda posters.
Crossing the River Kiya, the train traverses a
great wide plain, grazing land for cattle that
you may see being rounded up on horseback.

Km6496: Pryiskovaya Junction with the
line to **Nerchinsk**, which lies 10km north of
here. It was here that the Treaty of Nerchinsk
was signed with the Chinese in 1689, depriv-
ing the Russians of the Amur region. Nerchinsk was the centre of a rich silver, lead and
gold mining district in Tsarist times. The
mines were known to the Buryats long before
the arrival of the Russians in the seventeenth
century. In 1700, a Greek mining engineer
founded the Nerchinski Zavod (Works) and

the first convict gangs arrived in 1722. George Kennan visited the mine in 1887 and was shown round by one of the convict labourers. Not all the mines were the property of the Tsar and some owners became immensely wealthy. In one mansion he visited in Nerchinsk, Kennan could hardly believe that such opulence and luxury (tapestries, chandeliers, Oriental rugs, silk curtains and a vast ball-room) were to be found in one of the wildest parts of Siberia.

Kms6511-2(S): There is a large deserted church with another building beside it, standing on the bank just across the river. In the middle of nowhere and with a thick forest of conifers rising behind them, these two lonely-looking buildings form an eminently photogenic scene.

Km6532: Kuenga Junction for the line to **Sretensk**, which was the eastern end of the Transbaikal Railway. Sretensk was a thriving river-port in the nineteenth and early twentieth centuries (considerably larger than Chita) before the Amur Railway was opened in 1916. Passengers transferred here from the train to the ships of the Amur Steamship and Trade Company. Most of the forty steamers that plied between Sretensk and Khabarovsk were made either in Belgium or the Glasgow yards of Armstrong and Co. Waiting here with her mother in 1900, Annette Meakin caught sight of some Chinese men with their traditional pig-tails. She was not impressed and wrote 'To me their appearance was quite girlish.'

Kuenga was the western starting point for the **Amur Railway**. The line leaves the Shilka River here, turns north, crosses the plain and climbs towards the eastern end of the Yablonovyy range.

Km6593: Chernishevsk (●●) After this stop the train ascends into the foothills of the Yablonovyy mountain range towards Zilovo.

Km6670: Zilovo (●) (Aksenovo Zilovskoye) South of here were the gold mines of the Kara region, also visited by Kennan, who found 2500 convicts working under the most appalling conditions. These mines were the property of the Tsar and from them and the other Imperial mines in Eastern Siberia, he could (according to Kennan) expect an average of 3600 pounds (1630kg) of pure gold each year.

Km6806: Ksyenevskaya The line continues across the forested southern slopes of the Eastern Yablonovy Range for the next 200km. There are occasional good views over the trees.

MAP 14

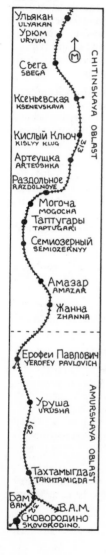

Ульякан
ULYAKAN

Урюм
URYUM

CHITINSKAYA OBLAST

Сбега
SBEGA

Ксеньевская
KSENEVSKAYA

Кислый Ключ
KISLYY KLUG

Артеушка
ARTEUSHKA

Раздольное
RAZDOLNOYE

Могоча
MOGOCHA

Таптугары
TAPTUGARI

Семиозерный
SEMIOZERNYY

Амазар
AMAZAR

Жанна
ZHANNA

Ерофеи Павлович
YEROFEY PAVLOVICH

AMURSKAYA OBLAST

Уруша
URUSHA

Тахтамыгда
TAKHTAMIGDA

Бам
BAM

В.А.М.

Сковородино
SKOVORODINO.

Km6930: Mogocha (●) The town of **Olekminsk** on the River Lena lies about 700km due north of here (this being no more than a short hike to a Siberian for, as Intourist guides love to tell you, 'In Siberia a thousand kilometres is nothing to travel, a hundred roubles is nothing to spend and a litre of vodka is nothing to drink'). As well as holding the world record for greatest temperature range - from -60°C (-87°F) to 45°C (113°F) - Olekminsk was the place of exile in the eighteenth century for a bizarre Christian sect whose followers were known as the Skoptsy. They saw their salvation in sexual abstinence and castrated themselves to be sure of a place in heaven. They lived in mixed communities, which they referred to as 'ships', each having a 'helmsman' and 'crew'. They avoided drink and tobacco and were excellent farmers. Since Olekminsk is experiencing something of a baby-boom at present it must be assumed that the more unconventional practices of the Skoptsy have been abandoned.

Km7010: Amazar (●●) About 100km south of here the Shilka flows into the Amur River. The Amur rises in Mongolia and flows 2,800km along the frontier with China, to the Sea of Okhostk (part of the Pacific Ocean). The river is known as the Heilung Chiang to the Chinese. It is exceptionally rich in fish and navigable for six months of the year. After initial explorations along the Amur by the Russians in the seventeenth century, following the Treaty of Nerchinsk with the Chinese in 1689, they were kept out of the region for the next 150 years. Colonisation began in the mid-nineteenth century and the Cossacks established garrisons along the river. By 1860 there were 60 villages with a population of 11,000 in the Amur Basin. The Amur is still a vital communications link in the area.

Km 7075: The line crosses the **administrative frontier** between Chitinskaya and Amurskaya *oblasts*. Also the border between Siberia and the Far Eastern Territories. **Amurskaya** covers 360,000 square kilometres in the middle part of the Amur basin and extends to the Stanovoy Range in the north. The southern region of the *oblast* is a fertile plain where wheat, soya-beans, flax and sun-flowers are grown. Most of the area in the north is under thick forest.

Km 7119: Yerofei Pavlovich (●●●) Named in honour of the Russian fur-trader Yerofei Pavlovich Khabarov who explored the Amur region in the 1650s, and gave his surname to the capital of the Far Eastern Territories. He set out from the military outpost of Yakutsk (1,000km north of Skovorodino) in 1649. He plundered and raped his way through the villages of the Yakut and other local tribes, who appealed to the Manchus for protection. The Chinese sent large armies which put the Russians to flight and the Treaty of Nerchinsk ensured that they stayed out of the region until the mid-nineteenth century.

Km 7211: Urusha (●●) For the next 100kms the train passes through an area of *taiga* interspersed with uncultivated plains, most of it locked in permafrost.

Km 7266: Takhtamigda A small settlement with a view (N) across the river valley. About half a kilometre east of the village, also (N), stands what looks like a prison, surrounded with barbed wire and patrolled by guards in blue uniforms. The good views to the north continue for the next 150kms.

Km 7273: Bam (Bamovskaya) Junction with the line which runs north to join the Baikal-Amur Mainline (see page 111). East of the junction there are good views (S) between km7295 and km7300.

Km 7306: Skovorodino (●●) A ten-minute stop at this station where local women sell berries from the *taiga*. About 20 kilometres east of Skovorodino, the train passes through the town of Great Never (Bolshoi Never). A highway leads from here a thousand miles north over the Stanovoy Range to **Yakutsk**, the capital of the **Yakutsk Autonomous Soviet Socialist Republic**. This must be one of the least pleasant parts of the world to live in, for the region, which is about thirteen times the size of Britain, is entirely covered with permafrost. Even in mid-summer, the soil in Yakutsk is frozen solid to a depth of over a hundred metres. See page 168 for information for visitors to Yakutsk, now an open city.

MAP 15

East of Skovorodino the scenery becomes more interesting. Views at kms7318-25(N) and around km7335(N). After the tunnel (kms7343-5) there is a long view (S) down the valley towards China. More views (S) at km7387 and kms7426-28.

Km7501: Magdagachi (●●) The train continues to descend gently, through Magdagachi, out of the *taiga* and onto a wide plain. There may be a short stop at **Tigda (●)**, about 60kms after Magdagachi.

Km7602: Ushumun The border with China is no more than forty kilometres south-west of here. The train continues south-east across flat lands with small clumps of trees.

Km7723: Shimanovskaya (●) South of here the land becomes more fertile and parts of the wide plain are under cultivation.

The Yakuts
These people, who number about 300,000, form the largest ethnic group in the Far Eastern Territories. They were originally semi-nomadic herders who roamed around the lands beside the Lena River. What seems to have struck nineteenth-century travellers most about the Yakuts is their extreme dirtiness. They never washed or changed their clothes, they shared their huts with their reindeer and preferred their meat and fish once it had begun to rot. They drank a form of *koumiss* (fermented mare's milk) which they froze, sometimes into huge boulders.

To give the Yakuts their due, they were considerably more advanced than many other Siberian tribes. Although they were ignorant of the wheel (hardly much use in such a cold climate), they used iron for weapons and tools. Most Yakut clans possessed a blacksmith who was usually also a shaman, since metal-working was considered a gift from the gods. The Yakuts were unique among Siberian tribes in that they made pottery.

Life was made hard for the Yakuts with the arrival of the Russian colonists who treated them badly and demanded fur tributes for the Tsar. They have now almost completely adopted the Russian culture and although some are still involved in reindeer-herding, most Yakuts work in mining and the timber industry.

Km7815: Svobodny (●)

Founded in 1912, during the building of the Amur railway, this town was originally named Alekseyevsk, in honour of the Tsar's haemophiliac son, Alexis. It stands beside the Zeya River, which is a navigable tributary of the Amur. In 1924 the town's name was changed to Svobodny. It is now an important transportation centre, with railway repair shops, a large river-port and a highway-link north to Fevralsk on the BAM Railway. Leaving the city, the train crosses the Zeya River.

The Amur Railway (kms6532-8531)

The building of this line was proposed in the early 1890s but surveys showed that it would prove expensive, on account of the difficult terrain. More than one hundred bridges would be needed and many kilometres of embankments. Furthermore much of the region was locked in permafrost. In 1894, when the government signed the treaty with China allowing Russian rails to be laid across Manchuria, from Chita to Vladivostok, the Amur project was abandoned in favour of this considerably shorter route. Had the Minister of Ways of Communication known that the East Chinese line would eventually cost more than the whole of the rest of the Trans-Siberian Railway, the Amur project might not have been abandoned.

After Russia's embarrassing defeat by Japan in the 1904-5 War, the government realised the vulnerability of their East Chinese line. Japan was as keen as Russia to gain control of the rich lands of Manchuria and if they did decide to invade, the Russian naval base of Vladivostok would be deprived of a rail link with European Russia. A line within Russian lands was needed. The Amur project was reconsidered and, in 1907, approved.

Construction began in 1908 at Kuenga and for most of the 2,000kms the line would follow a route about 100km north of the Amur River, out of range of Manchuria on the southern bank of the river. Winters are particularly harsh in this region and consequently track-laying could only take place over the four warmer months and even in mid-summer considerable amounts of dynamite were needed to blast through the permafrost. There were the usual problems with insects and disease but now that the rest of the railway was operating it was comparatively easy to transport workers in from west of the Urals. By 1916 the long bridge over the Amur at Khabarovsk had been completed and the railway was opened. The Japanese were now Russia's allies and in 1918 (as allies to the White Russians) took over the running of the Amur Railway during the Civil War.

Km7873: Belogorsk (●●●)

Some of the older folk who make up the 70,000 inhabitants of this agricultural centre must find it difficult to remember the current name of their city, so many times has it changed. It was founded in 1860 with the original name of Aleksandrovka. This stuck until 1935 when the local council decided it should be changed in favour of the rather more impressive Kuybyshevkavostochnaya. Just when everyone had got used to this exotic mouthful, it changed again, to boring old Belogorsk.

MAP 16

Серышево
SERISHEVO

Белогорск
BELOGORSK

Возжаевка
VOZHAEVKA

БЛАГОВЕЩЕНСК
BLAGOVESHCHENSK

Amur R.

Поздеевка
POZDEYEVKA

Екатеринославка
YEKATERINOSLAVKA

Завитая
ZAVITAYA

↑
Ⓜ

Бурея
BUREYA

Домикан
DOMIKAN

Архара
ARKHARA

Рачи
RACHI

AMURSKAYA OBLAST

Кундур-
Хабаровский
KUNDUR-KHABAROVSKIY

Облучье
OBLUCHE

Кимкан
KIMKAN

Известковая
IZVESTKOVAYA

Биракан
BIRAKAN

Теплое Озеро
TEPLOVE OZERO

Лондоко
LONDOKO

Бира
BIRA

Биробиджан
BIROBIDZHAN

Y.A. OBLAST

KHABAROVSKIY KRAY

Belogorsk is the junction for the line to **Blagoveshchensk**, the administrative capital of the Amurskaya *oblast* and a large industrial centre of 190,000 people, on the left bank of the Amur River. The name means 'Good News', for it was here in 1858 that Count Muravyev-Amursky announced the success of the treaty with China that granted Russia the Amur region. The city became a centre of colonisation and grew fast in the second half of the nineteenth century. The locals called it the New York of Siberia, on account of the fact that its streets were laid out on a grid pattern, American-style. It became the major port on the voyage between Sretensk and Khabarovsk in the days before the completion of the Amur Railway.

In July 1900, Blagoveshchensk was the scene of the cold-blooded massacre of the entire Chinese population of the town (several thousand people) by the Cossack forces. This was in retaliation for the murders of Europeans in China during the Boxer Rebellion. Annette Meakin wrote: 'The Cossacks, who were little better than savages, threw themselves on the helpless Chinese.....and drove them down to the water's edge. Those who could not get across on rafts were either brutally massacred on the banks or pushed into the water and drowned. The scene which followed was horrible beyond description, and the river was black with dead bodies for weeks afterwards. I have this from no less than five eye-witnesses.'

Km8037: Bureya (●) On the river of the same name, this town was once the centre of a large gold-mining region. The area was once inhabited by several different tribes most of whom were Shamanists. The **Manegres** were a nomadic people whose sartorial trade-mark was to keep their heads shaven, except for one long pig-tail. The **Birars** lived in hive-shaped huts beside the **Bureya** and grew vegetables and fruit. North of here lived **Tungus** (Evenkis), who were hunters and the **Orochen** who herded reindeer. To the east were the **Goldis**, described thus in the *Guide to the Great Siberian Railway*: 'They are below average stature, and have a broad and flat face with a snub nose, thick lips, eyes shaped after the Mongolian fashion and prominent cheekbones.....The women adorn themselves with earrings and pendants. Some of them, as a mark of particular elegance, introduce one or several small rings into the partition of the nose. The people of this tribe are characterised by great honesty, frankness and good will.....Their costume is very various and of all colours; they may at different times be seen wearing a Russian overcoat, a fish-skin suit or the Chinese dress.'

Km8088: Arkhara (●●●) There are often women selling snacks and fruit on the platform here.

Km8170: This is the **administrative frontier** between Amurskaya *oblast* and Khabarovskiy *kray*. Khabarovskiy is, like much of the USSR east of the Urals, almost entirely composed of swampy *taiga*. In the far south, however, there is an area of deciduous trees. Many of the minerals in which the *kray* is extremely rich, have yet to be extracted. The economy is based on wood-processing, fishing and the petroleum industry.

Km8171-9441: Time zone MT + 7 Local time is now Moscow Time + 7hrs.

East of this frontier you enter an autonomous *oblast* within Khabarovsky *kray*. Between Obluchye and Pryamuskaya, some of the stations have their names written up in Yiddish as well as in Russian, for this is part of the **Yevreyskaya Jewish Autonomous Oblast**, otherwise known as **Birobidzhan**, after its capital. This remote region was thoughtfully set aside for Jewish emigration in 1928 (the *oblast* being formed in 1934) but it never proved very popular. The Jewish population today stands at less than 5% (some say less than 1%!) of the total number of inhabitants of this 36,000 square kilometre territory.

A glossy coffee-table book about Birobidzhan (written in Russian, Yiddish and English) is sold in the bookshops of Khabarovsk. After pages of smiling cement-factory workers, beaming miners and happy-looking milk-maids, the book ends with the following statement: 'The flourishing of the economy and culture of the Jewish Autonomous Region, the happiness of the people of labour of various nationalities inhabiting the Region, their equality, friendship and

MAP 17

co-operation lay bare the hypocricy (sic) of the propaganda campaign launched by the ringleaders of Israel and international Zionism, about the "disastrous situation" of Jews in the Soviet Union, about the "oppression and persecution" they are supposedly being subjected to. The working people of Jewish nationality wrathfully condemn the predatory policy of the ruling circles of Israel and give a resolute rebuff to the Zionist provocateurs.'

Km8242: Izvyestkovaya The name of this town means 'limestone'. There are large quarries in the area.

Km8314: Bira (●●) Near the river of the same name.

Km8358: Birobidzhan (●) The capital of the 'Jewish' region, it was founded in 1928 on the Bira River and was at first known as Tikhonkaya. It is especially famous for its bright red, self-propelled, rice-and-silage chain-track combine-harvesters, made at the Dalselmash factory and exported to Cuba, Mexico and Iraq. Other industries include mining, fish-farming, wood-processing and the manufacture of hosiery, shoes, knitwear and other clothes.

Crossing the 'Jewish' *oblast*, the train passes through **Dezhnevka** (km8493), leaving the *oblast* about 20km after this. Just east of km8511, you reach the **bridge over the Amur**. This 2.5km single-track bridge is the longest on the Trans-Siberian Railway and was completed in 1916. Khabarovsk stretches along the eastern bank of the river and the beaches here are packed with swimmers at weekends in the summer.

Km8531: Khabarovsk (●●●) (Habarovsk) (96m/315ft) (See also page 179). Unless you're travelling to Vladivostok (recently opened), you must **change trains here**.

The Boat Train

A special train, the *Vostok*, is laid on for this most easterly section of the Trans-Siberian Railway, from Khabarovsk to the port of Nakhodka, to connect with the weekly ship to Japan. It leaves Khabarovsk in the late afternoon, arriving in Tikhookeanskaya Port, ten kilometres beyond Nakhodka, the following morning. Since this train is used mainly by foreigners the food in the dining car is of a rather higher standard than usual and beer is often available.

Many travellers in the past, including Eric Newby and Paul Theroux have enthused about the luxurious first class carriages used on this part of the route, fitted out with mahogany and brass fittings, cut glass lamps and red plush seats, like the carriages of the Wagon Lits Company at the turn of the century. Unfortunately there are fewer of them about now and you will probably find yourself in a compartment identical to the one in which you arrived in Khabarovsk.

Km8531: From Khabarovsk the line runs south to Vladivostok following the Ussuri River and the border with China. This region is a mixture of hilly country interspersed with wide flat valleys. Two hundred miles east of the line lies the Sikhote Alin Range of mountains, in which most of the rivers you will cross have their source. In the south the firs and pines give way to a wide range of deciduous trees. As the sun goes down there are good views across the plains into China.

The Ussuri Railway (kms8531-9441)

The first plans for the building of the Ussuri line, as this section between Khabarovsk and Vladivostok was called, were made in 1875 and the foundation stone for the whole of the Trans-Siberian Railway was laid in Vladivostok by the Tsarevich Nicholas in 1891. Priority was given to the Ussuri line as it was seen as vital to ensure that the strategic port of Vladivostok was not cut off by the Chinese.

This was difficult territory for railway building. There was a severe shortage of labour. The local Goldi tribe who at the time were happily existing in the Stone Age were no help. They were unable to grasp the concept of paid labour and couldn't understand the point of the work, never having seen a train. Prisoners recruited from the jails of Sakhalin Island were not as co-operative as convicts used on other sections of the Trans-Siberian, preferring an evening of robbery and murder in Vladivostok to the railway camps. Like their fellow-workers on other sections of the line, the men here were plagued not only by vicious mosquitoes but also by the man-eating tigers which roamed the thick forests beside the line. Siberian anthrax decimated the already small population of pack animals, and rails and equipment had to be shipped from Europe, taking up to two months to reach Vladivostok.

In spite of these difficulties, the line was opened in 1897, 43 million roubles having been spent on its construction. It was double tracked in the 1930s and the branch line to Nakhodka was built after the Second World War.

Km8569: Korfovskaya The town was founded by Cossacks in 1858.

Km8605 The longest bridge on the Ussuri Railway. It crosses the River Khor, one of the largest tributaries of the Ussuri, whose turbulent waters made the construction of the bridge extremely difficult in 1897.

Km8650: Viazemskaya Established as the centre of building operations for this northern part of the Ussuri line. There is often a good selection of things to buy from the old women on the platform - hot potatoes, berries and other fruit in season. From about twenty kilometres south of here the countryside changes dramatically with forests of maple, alder, willow, elm, cork-oak, acacia and walnut as well as the usual cedar, larch and birch. There are also wild vines, roses and jasmine.

Km8764: Bikin A large town on the banks of the Bikin River. According to the *1900 Guide to the Great Siberian Railway*, the line crosses the river here and follows it south for 30kms. It states that 'this is one of the most picturesque parts of the line offering an alpine scenery. The cuttings made in basalt rocks seem to be protected by columns of cyclopean construction. Wide expanses lying amidst the cliffs are covered with a most various vegetation, shading numerous Chinese huts. The river is enlivened by the small boats of the Golds and other natives, moving swiftly on the water's surface.' Unfortunately the line does not follow exactly the same route now, traversing rolling hills and marshy land strewn with telegraph poles keeling over at drunken angles.

Man-eating tiger holds up train

If your train is delayed in the Nakhodka area it might just be because a hungry tiger is blocking the line, awaiting lunch. A report in the *Times* (Tuesday 10 February 1987) states: 'Workers at the main container terminal at Nakhodka on the Sea of Japan, failed to arrive for the morning shift beacause their commuter train was held up by a large Amur tiger - specimens of which can reach more than 10ft in length - sitting on the tracks.' The tigers are being squeezed out of their natural habitat in the north by forest-clearing (each male tiger claims over 150 square miles of hunting territory) and by poachers who have reduced their main food source of deer and wild boar. However, it's not only along the railway that these tigers may be encountered according to the report: 'Last Thursday, Mr Gennady Kiseliev, a Red Army soldier on leave at his suburban home near this modern, bustling Soviet port, drew back the bedroom curtains and found himself face to face with a man-eating Amur tiger.....' In a bid to reassure the understandably distraught townspeople, more permits are being issued to hunters and a special game reserve is planned. The Amur tiger is an endangered species - only 250 are left.

Km9057: Spassk Dalnyi

MAP 18

About thirty kilometres west of here lies Lake
Khanka which is drained by the Ussuri River.
Although a mere drop of water compared to
Lake Baikal, it covers 4,400 square kms.

Km9117: Sibirchevo
A branch line runs
from here through dairy-farming countryside
to Lake Khanka. From Sibirchevo south, the
line winds down to Ussuriysk.

Km9185: Ussuriyisk
Originally called
Nikolskoe, in honour of the Tsar, this was the
largest station on the line. The area has been
inhabited for over one thousand years, first by
the legendary kingdom of Bokhai and then by
the Manchus. In the mid-nineteenth century
European emigrants began to settle on this
fertile land and Nikolskoe increased in importance with the building of the railway. The
town stands at the junction of the Ussuri and
the Chinese Eastern Railways. When the
Tsarevich Nicholas visited the town in 1891,
there were three wooden churches, a half-built
stone cathedral and a population of 8,000
people, many of whom were Chinese. This
has risen to 140,000 and Ussuriysk is a now
an agricultural and engineering centre. The
border with China is about 100km to the west.

Km9208: Baranovsk
About 25km south
of here, the branch line to Nakhodka begins
and the kilometre markers start from zero
again. You should be up by now and if you
didn't notice the change in the scenery last
night you may be surprised to look out now at
landscape that is entirely different from the
Siberian *taiga*. The train winds down out of
the hills through misty forests of deciduous
trees (oak, elm, alder, and maple) and across
European-looking meadows filled with Frie-
sian cows and willow trees.

Ninety kilometres along the main line from
Baranovsk lies Vladivostok. It is the adminis-

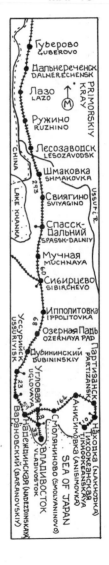

trative centre of the Primorsky Kray and has a population of over half a million. Apart from being the home of the USSR Navy, several large fishing fleets (including two Antarctic whaling fleets) are based in Vladivostok. It was declared a free economic zone in September 1990 and is now open to foreigners (see page 184).

Kms164/9431: Nakhodka

The wide, sheltered bay on which the modern town of Nakhodka stands was discovered by chance in the middle of the last century by Russian ships seeking shelter from a storm in the Sea of Okhotsk. They called the bay Nakhodka, meaning 'the find' and a most important find it was, for unlike the other ports in the area, the sea does not freeze over entirely in the winter. A tiny community grew up on the shore but it was not until the mid-1940s that Nakhodka became important. The main port in the area was (and still is) the naval base of Vladivostok, founded in 1860. Vladivostok was a more convenient port than Nikolayevsk (further north at the mouth of the Amur River), since it was ice-free for more days each year than the old northern harbour.

In the 1950s it was decided that with the growth of the USSR's navy, foreigners should be kept out of the naval base of Vladivostok (re-opened to foreigners in 1990) and foreign vessels were to dock in Nakhodka. The port's growth has been phenomenal but not without problems. In the 1950's the town could barely handle the sudden influx of shipping transferred from the established port of Vladivostok. A rapid building programme brought thousands of workers to Nakhodka and construction continues today. It is hoped that the new Eastern port of Vostochnyy will be open soon; the Japanese have supplied much of the capital and equipment for it. There are very few ports in the Soviet Union that are deep enough for modern bulk carriers and tankers; but it is claimed that Vostochnyy will be able to handle even the largest of them.

Nakhodka is a fast-expanding town with a population of 178,000 people and a severe housing shortage. Apart from handling foreign shipping, Nakhodka is the home of the largest fishing fleet in the region. There are several large fish processing factories and canneries and exports include timber, venison and honey as well as a variety of fresh and tinned fish. There is an Intourist hotel (the **Nakhodka**) but very little to see and on a rainy day the place looks very drab and dismal.

Kms175/9441: Tikhookeanskaya Port The end (or the beginning) of the line and of your journey is at mid-morning when the

train draws into Tikhookeanskaya Station ('a building with the stucco and proportions of a Kabul madhouse', writes Paul Theroux in *The Great Railway Bazaar*).

Transit between station and port Intourist buses are provided for this short trip, supposedly for use by only those who have paid for transfers but nobody checks. The journey takes about the same amount of time by bus as on foot as the bus has to go quite a way up the tracks to cross over. If you wish to walk, cross the tracks, turn left and walk along the road until you see the customs complex on the right. Ask directions if you're not sure as they're unlikely to hold the boat for you.

Customs procedure Collect your luggage from the pile off-loaded into the hall and then wait until customs procedures begin. To help you pass the time there is a Beriozka shop and a cafe/bar (roubles), as well as stacks of propaganda pamphlets. Either spend your remaining roubles or change them for yen at the *bureau de change*. No roubles may be taken out of the country.

Customs procedures are rather less thorough for foreigners than they used to be. You may still be asked to show your currency declaration form as well as your travellers' cheques and foreign currency. There should not be any problems if your form shows that you've not changed much money during your stay (because you've been indulging in a little speculation). It will be presumed that you're either on a tour that includes all meals or that you've been eating in hard-currency restaurants.

After customs there's a duty-free shop charging Beriozka prices that's well stocked with foreign cigarettes (useful as bribes if you're arriving from Japan.)

Then you walk out to the ship beside the building. Cabins and seats in the restaurant are assigned as you board so if you wish to share a cabin or table with someone in particular, you should make sure you board with them. Passports are confiscated, as in any Intourist hotel, 'for safe-keeping'. You are given an embarkation card listing your berth and table numbers.

TRAILBLAZER feedback If you're coming into the USSR from Japan at Nakhodka you may be subjected to intimidating immigration procedures: 'After a short queue you enter the passport control cage where automatic gates lock you in and a tilted, overhead mirror checks out your bald patch, and presumably makes sure you're not standing on a stool.' Steve Oxley (UK)

Ships

Various vessels come in and out of service on this voyage and have included *M/V Felix Dzerjinsky* (carrying 312 passengers and romantically named after Felix Dzerjinsky, head of the Secret Police from 1917 to 1926); *M/V Khabarovsk* (262 passengers); *M/V Konstantin Chernenko* (no swimming-pool) and the relatively new *M/V Russ*.

M/V Russ Built in Poland in 1986, *M/V Russ* can carry 380 passengers in reasonable comfort and all cabins have a shower-room and lavatory attached. There are lockers for valuables and towels are provided. Facilities on the ship include restaurant, bars, 'night-club', souvenir shop, reading-room (with no books in it), sauna, washing-machines (and next-to-useless driers), ironing room and a swimming-pool. There are deck games (including volley-ball), documentary films and a disco in the evenings. A laundry service is available but as this is expensive it's better to use the washing-machines to do it yourself. Intourist hides in Cabin No 121 (no sign) near the Purser's office. Collect your passport, tickets, transfers and hotel vouchers from them on the last morning of the voyage.

Life on board

The ship sails at 12.00 (11.00 from Yokohama) and after lunch there will be a half-hearted emergency drill. On one voyage a few weeks after two Soviet vessels had collided in the Black Sea, the First Officer did not seem worried that very few people had turned up for the emergency drill. 'They are not our people so it is not my problem' he told me. You would be well advised to attend and to make sure you know where your life-jacket is. A little information booklet thoughtfully left beside your bunk advises you that 'Fire on board is a dreadful calamity' and requests that you 'do not develop and dry films in your cabin'.

Meals The meals on board are very good but a trifle over-organised. You are expected to sit at the table assigned to those in your cabin and not wherever you want. Changing your seat is frowned upon though not impossible if you speak to the waitress at your first meal. Although there is a choice of food you must choose whatever you want for dinner while you are eating your lunch, filling in the details on a little questionnaire. The choice includes Japanese as well as Russian cuisine. However, things are further complicated if you happen to sit in the wrong seat for the following meal, in which case you will be brought whatever the last person sitting there ordered. There are four meals a day: breakfast at 08.30; lunch at 12.30; tea at 16.30 and dinner at 19.00. Do not be late!

Nightlife This is a good deal wilder than on the train. On the first evening there are free drinks at the Captain's Cocktail Hour and dancing and singing performed by a professional dance troupe (good) who are joined by members of the crew (not so good). The following night there may be a pre-dinner vodka tasting (Y1000) with a few dances and laboured jokes from the compère. Very popular with the Japanese but over-priced. This is often followed by a 'cultural evening' of dances from around the world. There's also a nightclub (hard-currency only: Y250 for a beer) with a karaoke machine to sing along to.

Daytime Activities People spend the daylight hours lying around the swimming pool on the sun deck. The ship's entertainment committee occasionally organises a special 'Merry Neptune Festival' with fancy dress parade. There are also deck games - table tennis, deck quoits, volley-ball and deck chess. Old Russian movies are shown in the bar (usually at 10.00 and 15.00hrs). A visit to the bridge is popular with travellers - ask at the information desk for times. The sauna and massage (Y1000) is especially recommended but go when it's quiet and the enormous Russian masseuse will give you a long restorative pummelling.

Route The route from Nakhodka takes you across the Sea of Japan, through the narrow Tsugaru Straits between Honshu and Hokkaido and then south along the east coast of Honshu (the largest of the four main islands that make up Japan) to Yokohama. The voyage can be rough owing to the two currents that meet in the Sea of Japan: the warm waters from the south and the cold current from the Sea of Okhotsk to the north. (For information on Japan see page 266).

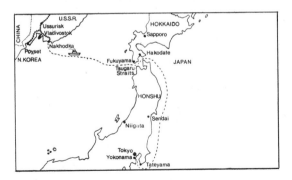

MAP 19 *Pg 226*

ULAN UDE УЛАН-УДЭ
TO MAP 11
Заудинский ZAUDINSKIY
Саянтун SAYANTUN
Ганзурино GANZURINO
Убукун UBUKUN
Сульфат SULFAT
Загустай ZAGUSTAY
Оз Гусиное LAKE GUSINOYE
Гусиное Озеро GUSINOYE OZERO
Селендума SELENDUMA
Джида DZHIDA
Хужир (KHUZHIR)
Наушки NAUSHKI
Сухэ Баатор SUKHE BATOR
Дархаан DARCHAN
Джунчара DZUNCHARA
Улаан Баатор ULAN BATOR
GOBI DESERT
Маанььт MANIT
Чоир CHOYR

247
USSR
MONGOLIA
Selenga R.

Trans-Mongolian Route

The branch line to Mongolia and China leaves the main Trans-Siberian route at Zaudinskiy, 8km east of Ulan Ude. From here it takes five and a half hours to cover the 250km to the Soviet-Mongolian border. Between Ulan Ude and the southern border, the train travels through the heart of Buryatiya, the Buryat Autonomous Soviet Socialist Republic (see page 226).

Note that the line now swings due south from its east-west route. However, in order not to confuse readers I shall continue to use (N) and (S) to show which side of the train points of interest are located, rather than changing to the more correct compass bearings. Thus (N) means left side of the train if you're coming from Moscow.

The suburbs of Ulan Ude extend for several kilometres and there are good views back to the city at km5659(S) as the train climbs high above the east bank of the Selenga. The line follows the valley of the Selenga River all the way to the border with Mongolia. The scenery changes remarkably quickly to rolling green hills which are excellent pastures for the many cows in the area. Passing through the little station of Sayatun (km5677) the line crosses to the west bank of the river at km5689-90 and continues to climb through Ubukun (km5732), stopping briefly at Zagustay.

Km5769: Zagustay In the ugly shadow of a factory belching out thick smoke.

Kms5771-99 Goose Lake Between the stations of Zagustay and Gusinoye Ozero the line passes along the western shore of Lake Gusinoye (Goose Lake). Until the Revolution, the most important lamasery north of Urga (Ulan Bator) was at **Selenginsk**, 20km south east of Gusinoye Ozero and overlooking the lake. In 1887 George Kennan, who was researching his book on Siberian prisons, arrived in Selenginsk and visited the famous *datsan* (lamasery). 'We were tired of prisons and the exile system and had had enough misery,' he wrote. Nevertheless he found Selenginsk 'a wretched little Buriat town'. At the Lamasery of Goose Lake, Kennan and his companions were entertained by the Khamba Lama, the chief lama, who claimed through the interpreter that they were the first foreigners ever to visit his lamasery. They were treated to a dinner and a special dance display. The Khamba Lama had never heard of America, Kennan's native land, and was confused when Kennan explained that 'it lies nearly under our feet; and if we could go directly through the earth, this would be the shortest way to reach it'. The Lama was completely unaware that the earth was anything other than flat.

The Trans-Mongolian Line
This route to China is an ancient one, followed for centuries by the tea-caravans between Peking and Moscow. Travelling non-stop, foreigners and imperial messengers could manage the journey in forty days - forty days of acute discomfort. This was the route of the 1907 Peking to Paris Rally, the great motor race that was won by the Italian Prince Borghese and journalist Luigi Barzini in their 40 h.p. Itala. Until the middle of the present century, the rough track over the steppe-lands of northern Mongolia and the Gobi Desert in the south was the only route across this desolate country.

In 1940, a branch-line was built between Ulan Ude and Naushki on the border with Mongolia. After the Second World War, work started on the line from Naushki south, and in 1949 the track reached the Mongolian capital, Ulan Bator. The line between here and Beijing was begun in 1953 with a mixed work-force of Russians, Mongolians and Chinese. By the beginning of 1956 the work was completed and a regular rail service begun between Ulan Ude and Beijing.

Km5799: Gusinoye Ozero The line leaves the lake after this station and continues to climb from one valley to another, passing though Selenduma (Km5827) and still following the river.

Km5852(S): Azhida There appears to be a small air-base here with hangars dug into hummocks in the ground.

As the line climbs the next 40km to the border you often see border patrols in grey cruisers on the river in this area. The border-post for the railway is at the modern town of Naushki. However the old border for the tea-caravans was near the large town of **Kyakhta**, 20kms east of Naushki. In the eighteenth and nineteenth centuries this town together with **Maimachen** (the Chinese town beside it on the Mongolian side of the border) formed one of the most important trading centres in the world, based almost entirely on the tea trade. Great caravans of camels would transport the precious beverage from Peking across the Gobi Desert to Maimachen and Kyakhta. Kyakhta was a bustling town of wealthy traders and tea-barons but once the Trans-Siberian was built the tea was shipped via Vladivostok to European Russia. On 24 June 1907 Prince Borghese and his team roared into town in their Itala and were entertained royally by local dignitaries. The morale of the tea-merchants that had sunk with the recent decline in trade was greatly boosted by the arrival of the car and they began making plans for their own motor-caravans. An earlier visitor to these border towns was George Kennan who attended a banquet in Maimachen, where he was served dog-meat dumplings, cocks' heads in vinegar and fried lichen from birch trees, washed down by several bottles of French champagne. He was sick for the next two weeks.

Km5897: Naushki (● ● ● + +) At this Soviet border-post the train waits for between 1 and 2 hours. Customs officials collect passports, visas and currency declaration forms returning them (often to the carriage attendant) after about half an hour. Any unspent roubles must be exchanged at the bank here (in the building to the right of the station building) as the export of Soviet currency is illegal. Those arriving from Mongolia are also advised to visit the bank as the Soviet restaurant car accepts only roubles. Note that the loos on the train remain locked until you leave the border. The station lavatories would not win any awards but are located in the building to the left of the station building.

MONGOLIA

(Distances given here follow the Mongolian kilometre markers. For cumulative distances from/to Moscow/Beijing, see timetables at the back of the book.)

Km0: Sukhe Bator/Sukhbaatar (● ● ● + +) Mongolian officials come on board here and seem to have been affected by the Mongolian equivalent of *glasnost*. They are no longer brusque and paranoid about photography. ('The Mongolian border officials were charming and the beautiful passport official looked as if she was straight out of a mid-thirties spy thriller' - Keith Watson (UK).) The process of crossing this border used to be fairly nerve-racking. Whole compartments would be rigorously searched, magazines confiscated and film ripped out of cameras. All rather tame now.

It's possible to get Mongolian visas here (2-day transit: US$11; 5-day tourist: US$15 - though confirmation of accommodation booking may be necessary for a tourist visa.) It's safer to arrange these before departure.

The station building is an excellent example of whimsical Mongolian railway architecture. It's an incredible mélange of architectural styles - mock Gothic, Moghul and modern topped with crenellations and painted what looks like lime green in the artificial light. Strawberry pink is the other popular colour for station buildings in this country.

During immigration and customs procedures a diesel engine is attached. The Mongolian dining-car is not put on until Ulan Bator.

Mongolia

This is one of those countries, like Guyana or Chad, that rarely makes headline news, except when there's a dramatic change of leadership or policy. This was indeed the case with Mongolia in 1989-90 with the pro-democracy movement in the run up to the first free elections in July 1990. These were won by the People's Revolutionary Party (Communist party), who have pledged to introduce a market-style economy.

Mongolia is a sparsely populated place with just over 2 million people (50 per cent of whom are under the age of 25) in an area the size of Western Europe. It contains a surprising variety of terrain - the vast undulating plain in the east, the Gobi desert to the south, and in the west snow-capped mountains and extensive forests. Most of the eastern plain is at an altitude of 1,500m and in this area the sun shines for around 250 days each year.

History For many centuries the deserts and grasslands of Mongolia have been inhabited by nomadic herders living in felt tents (*yurts* or *ghers*). At certain times in the course of world history they have been bound together under a leader, the most famous being Genghis and Kublai Khan in the thirteenth century. Kublai Khan introduced Tibetan Buddhism to the country but it was not until the early seventeenth century that the majority of the population was converted and Buddhism gained a strong grip on the country.

By the end of the seventeenth century, control of Mongolia and its trade routes was in the hands of the Manchus. In 1911 the country became an independent monarchy, in effect a theocratic state since power lay with the 'Living Buddha' (the chief representative of Buddhism in Mongolia) at Urga (now Ulan Bator). In 1921 the communist government that rules today took power and the struggle to modernise the country that was technologically in the Dark Ages began, with considerable help coming from the Soviet Union. Elections were held for the first time in 1990 and the communist government re-elected.

The country is divided into 18 *aimaks* (districts) and the railway-line passes through three of these (Selenga, Tov and Dornogov).

Situated at the confluence of the Selenga and Orhon Rivers, Sukhe Bator was founded in 1940 and named after the Mongolian revolutionary leader Damdiny Sukhe Bator. It grew quickly, superseding the border-town on the caravan route, Maimachen (now named Altan

Bulak). Sukhe Bator is now the third largest industrial centre in the country (although in a country as sparsely populated and industrially primitive as Mongolia this is not a particularly impressive fact). Matches, liquor and flour are produced here by some of the 16,000 inhabitants.

It takes about eight hours to cover the 380km between Sukhe Bator and Ulan Bator. The train passes through the town of **Darhan** (capital of Selenga *aimak*) which was founded in 1961 and has since grown to become the second most important industrial centre in Mongolia, after Ulan Bator. Darhan is a show-town of planned urbanisation and its population increased from 1,500 in 1961 to nearly 60,000 in 1987, 80 per cent of people being under the age of 25. Main sources of employment comprise the thermal power station, the Sharyn Gol open-cast mine, the food combine, the house-building combine and the sheepskin coat factory. You may also be interested to know that the city produces 41.2% of the country's coal and 84.8% of Mongolia's confectionery. The town is an important communications junction with a branch-line running west from here to the big mining complex at **Erdenet**, and the port serves many villages along the Selenga and Orkhon Rivers.

When tourism in Mongolia opens up it will be worth stopping off here in order to get to Ikh-khure, in the foothills of Mt Burenkhan to see **Amarbayasgalant Monastery**. This vast eighteenth century temple complex which once housed 10,000 monks and drew pilgrims from many parts of Asia was desecrated during the anti-religious movement in the 1930s but is now being restored with grants from the Mongolian government and the United Nations Organisation.

If you'd been doing this part of the journey in the not-too-distant time before the railway was built, you would now be swaying back and forth in the saddle of a camel, one of many in the caravan you would have joined in Kyakhta. In the 1865 edition of his *Handbook for Russia, Poland and Finland* , Murray gives the following advice: 'It is customary for caravans to travel sixteen hours a day and they come to a halt for cooking, eating and sleeping.....The Mongols are most trustworthy in their transactions, and the traveller may feel in perfect safety throughout the journey.' He also gives the following useful tips concerning local currency: 'The use of money is as yet almost unknown in this part of the country, brick-tea cut up into slices being the token of value most recognised; but small brass buttons are highly prized.'

Km381: Crossing wide open grass-lands, with only the odd *yurt* to break the monotony, the line begins to descend into the valley where Ulan Bator is situated. Looking south you catch the first sight (at km386) of the ugly factories on the northern outskirts of the city (km396).

Km404: Ulan Bator (● ● ● +) (1350m/4430ft) (See page 185)
The train spends half an hour at the Mongolian capital, a good chance to stretch your legs. There is a whole (open-air) museum collection of old and new steam and diesel engines standing outside the locomotive shed on the east side of the line (N). The display includes a 2-6-2 S-116, T31-011 and T32-508 diesels, a 750mm gauge 0-8-0 469, and a 2-10-0 Ye-0266. They are beside the public road but quite accessible even though there is a fence in front of them. In the station building postcards (and weird Mongolian stamps which leave little room for a message on a card) can be purchased at the bar. Black Marketeers may approach you on the platform to change money but you should remember that Mongolian currency is of no use on the train. US$ only, in the dining-car, for food and souvenirs.

The **Mongolian dining-car** is attached here, complete with smiling waiters and waitresses and vases of blue plastic tulips on the tables. The food is a great improvement on the Russian fare you have either become used to or avoided, but payment is in US$ only. The menu is in Mongolian *tugruks* and approximate US$ prices are: beer $1.50, Coke $0.80, juice $0.40, tea $0.05, beef Stroganov & potatoes $0.80, pancakes $0.20. There is also a souvenir/duty-free corner in the restaurant car with cans of Heineken ($2.00), Bells whisky ($10.50), Mongolian vodka ($3.70), cashmere sweaters ($48.00), postcards & stamps ($1.00) - they say they'll post them for you, and photo-books ($25.00).

Km409: The train begins to leave the city. At around km425 the line starts to climb and for the next 50km, to km470, snakes round giving good opportunities for photos along the train. Good views over the rolling hills both sides of the train.

Km507(S): Airfield with camouflaged bunkers for planes.

Km521: Manit (●) The pink station with its tower and weather-vane looks rather like a church.

Km560: Camels are occasionally to be seen roaming across the wide rolling plain.

Km649: Choyr (●●●) This is a beautiful pink and white wedding-cake of a station.

Km733-4(S): The pond here often attracts groups of camels and antelope.

Km751: Airag The train doesn't usually stop at this small station, in the middle of nowhere.

Smokers roast in hell!
If you're a smoker having difficulty in coping with being allowed to pursue your habit only in the chilly areas at the end of each carriage, be thankful you weren't around at the time of the Third Mongolian Damba Lama Khutukhta, at the end of the 18th century. 'Smoking tobacco', he wrote, 'undermines virtue....The soul of the smoker can't avoid one of these three sad fates: the fires of hell, rebirth into the world as a pret (evil spirit tormented with eternal hunger) or as an animal. Oh you who have gone astray with tobacco! You will eternally wander in hell.' *Mongolia Magazine* 3.89

The Gobi Desert
This vast wilderness extends for 1,000km north to south and 2,400km west to east. Most of the part crossed by the railway is not desert of the sandy, Saharan type but rolling grassy steppes. It is impressive for its emptiness: very few towns and just the occasional collection of *yurts*, herds of stocky Mongolian horses and small groups of camels or gazelles.

Environmental threats
The Gobi is, in fact, rich in wildlife although numbers of some species are rapidly dwindling. This is mainly owing to shooting and destruction of habitat but there are fears that the situation may worsen with the country's move towards a market economy. All political parties, including the ruling communists have pledged to open up the country to the West. Mongolia is desperately short of hard currency and has large reserves of coal, copper, molybdenum, gold, uranium and other valuable exports. It is estimated that up to 10 billion tons of coal exist under the Gobi and Japanese and Western companies are negotiating with Mongolia to extract it, using strip mining techniques, which could seriously affect the delicate environmental balance. An American conservation group, Wildlife Conservation International, is helping the Mongolian Association for Conservation of Nature and Environment (MACNE) to monitor species at risk in the area. Among these are the 500 remaining wild Bactrian camels, the Gobi bear, the *kulan* (Asian wild ass) and Przewalski's wild horse (the last recorded sighting was in 1962).

MAP 20

About 570km south of Ulan Bator the train pulls into **Sayn Shand** (Sajnsand). There's a collection of old steam locos on display at km875(N) as you come into the station.

Km876: Sayn Shand (●●●) (Sajnsand)
This is the largest town between the capital and Dzamin Ude on the southern border and main industries include food-processing and coal-mining.

On the Snowman's trail
'"I've seen him", claims biologist R.Ravjir who logged more than a year searching for the Abominable Snowman in the Mongolian Altai. "I'm positive the Abominable Snowman, commonly known as Almas, really does exist." R.Ravjir saw the Snowman at a distance on three occasions and made 30 snapshots of his tracks. He also taped dozens of oral accounts of people who claim to have seen it....On the night of March 7, 1986, Ravjir and his eight explorers sat in ambush at the Snowman's supposed den in the Khovdo mountains. Someone carelessly struck a match and a piercing cry resounded instantly, followed by the sound of rolling stones. Having switched on their flashlights, the people saw a rather unusual anthropoid, rapidly moving away. Still, they were able to make several pictures of it from behind'. *Mongolia Magazine* 3.86

Km1113: Dzamyn Ude (●●●+)
Mongolian border town with a station building that looks like a supermarket at Christmas with all its festive lights. There's a bank and a restaurant, both usually closed in the evening. Customs declaration forms and immigration forms are collected. Customs officers inspect the luggage of Chinese and Mongolian travellers but don't seem too interested in others.

THE PEOPLE'S REPUBLIC OF CHINA

(Kilometres below show distance to Beijing.)

Km842: Erlyan (Erenhot) (●●●++)
The Chinese station master is obviously trying to outdo the show his Mongolian counterpart

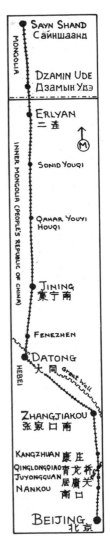

puts on in the evening over the border, with a full-blown son-et-lumière. There's the Vienna Waltz blaring out of the speakers to welcome the train and the building's decked out in red neon and fairy lights. Chinese customs officials come on board here. You will be required to fill in a health declaration form, baggage and currency declaration form and passports are collected.

Bogie-changing The train spends about 20mins at the platform and is then shunted off to the bogie changing shed. It's best to stay on the train until it gets to the shed, get off before they lock the doors (for safety reasons while raising the carriages), and watch some of the bogie changing operations. The Chinese railway system operates on Standard Gauge (as do Europe and North America) and this is 3½ inches narrower than Five Foot Gauge used in the USSR and Mongolia. Giant hydraulic lifts raise the carriages and the bogies are rolled out and replaced. Photography is now permitted but take care not to get in the way or the authorities might restore the ban on photography which was in force for many years. You can walk back to the station building but should take care at night as the path is not well-lit.

Back in the station you can change money at the bank (passport not necessary but you do need to know your passport number), or visit the Friendship Store (beer, tea, Ritz crackers, and other snacks) and bar/restaurant (if open). The Age of the Steam Train has not yet passed in China (more than half of its trains are steam-powered) and it is likely that the train will be shunted out of the bogie-changing shed and back to the platform by a puffing Class 2-10-2 locomotive built in Datong (see below). Passports are returned and you depart shortly thereafter - the whole operation taking between 2 and 3 hours.

Chinese trains ride on the left side of double tracks (unlike the USSR which is right-hand drive). Km markers come in a variety of sizes (usually like little grave-stones down by the track) and there seems to be some disagreement between them and the official kilometre location (on timetables etc) for many places. I've followed the markers where possible but for the last 70km of the journey they are not reliable, altering by 25km at one point!

Passing through towns with weird Mongolian names like Sonid Youqi and Qahar Youyi Houqi, you reach Jining in about five hours.

Km498: Jining (●) The bulky white station building topped by a line of red flags. Beside it is an extensive goods yard full of working steam engines. Travelling due south from Jining the train leaves the province of Inner Mongolia and enters Shanxi Province. This mountainous area was a great cultural and political centre over a thousand years ago and the temples and caves that remain from that era now draw the tourists in large numbers.

There are hills running parallel to the west and wide fields either side of the line. The train follows the course of a river which leads it into a valley and more rugged countryside after Fenezhen.

Km415: Fenezhen Between this drab town and Datong you pass through the line of the **Great Wall** for the first time. Occasional glimpses are all you will get until the spectacular crossing at Km82.

Km371: Datong (●●) Tourists come to the two-thousand year old city of Datong (Tatung) for two reasons - to see the Yungang Grottoes and the steam-locomotive workshop. This large industrial city of more than half a million people stands in the centre of the Datong Basin, a rich coal producing area. The city was founded as a military outpost by the Han armies. The **Yungang Grottoes** (Buddhist cave temples) in the foothills of Wuzhou Mountain (16km west of the city) were hewn during the Northern Wei Dynasty between 460 and 524 AD. They are richly decorated with carved and painted scenes from the life of the Buddha.

If you're stopping off here, a visit to the **Datong Locomotive Works** is an interesting and educational experience. Until recently, this was one of the last places in the world where steam trains were made. In the 1980s they were turning them out at the rate of 240 locos per year. The manufacture of the Class QJ 8WT/12WT 2-10-2 engine (133 tonnes; max speed 80kph) ceased in 1986 and the Class JS 2-8-2 (104 tonnes; max speed 85kph) in 1989. Both classes are used for freight haulage and shunting work. The factory now produces parts for steam and diesel locomotives and has customers in many parts of the world. Tours are conducted twice a week and must be arranged through the tourist bureau (CITS).

At Datong the line turns east and follows the Great Wall, running about 20km south of it as far as Zhangjiakou. One hundred kilometres west of Zhangjiakou you leave Shanxi and enter the province of Hebei (population 55 million).

Km295-272(N): The Great Wall can be seen parallel to the line, on the hillside to the east. Best view is at km284(N).

Km193: Zhangjiakou (●●) Founded two thousand years ago, this city used to be known by its Mongolian name, Kalgan (meaning gate or frontier). It stands at the point where the old caravan route between Peking and Russia crossed the Great Wall. When Luigi

Barzini visited Kalgan during the Peking to Paris Rally he described
it as being like one of those 'cities one sees pictured upon Fu-kien
tapestries: varied and picturesque, spreading over the bank of a wide
snowy river'. He would not recognise it now - it has grown into an
industrial city of one million people. Yet he might recognise the
smell he noticed as he drove into town on 14 June 1907, for tanning
and leather-work are still major industries here. About 15km south
of the city a large factory pollutes the air with orange smoke.

From around km175 the scenery becomes hilly and more interesting
as the line rises over the mountains north of Beijing. There are small
valleys of sunflowers, groves of poplars and even some apple or-
chards. At km93 you cross a wide river above which (N) can be seen
a small isolated section of the Wall.

Km82: Kanzhuang (●) The train stops for a banking engine to
be attached before the steep ascent up through the Great Wall.

Km73: Badaling The first of the stations for the **Great Wall**.
After this there is a 2km tunnel through the Wall. Look up (N) to the
east as you come out for a good view and be ready to get off for the
short stop at Qinglongqiao ½km further on.

Km70: Qinglongqiao (●●) A short stop with good views of the
Great Wall high above this attractive station. The train then reverses
downhill through a spectacular series of tunnels alongside the road.
Progress is very slow because of the tortuous bends and the need for
heavy braking, which gives some people time to jump off the train
and gather the wild marijuana plants which flourish near the tracks in
this area. You pass the Tourist Reception Centre at km68 but will
not have time to take advantage of the camel rides on offer here. An
interesting part of unrestored Wall can be seen at km65(S).

Km63: Juyongguan (●) Continuous application of the brake
blocks makes them very hot necessitating a stop here.

Km53: Nankou (●) A further stop to check the brake blocks
again and detach the rear engine before the train speeds off across
the fertile plain to Beijing. Something strange has happened to the
km markers in this area, with 25km suddenly added around km35.

Km0: Beijing You are now 7865kms from Moscow at the end (or
the beginning) of your journey. Turn to Part 6 for more information.

(Oppos.te) Top: The lii e passes under The Great Wall at Badaling (km73).
Bottom: T'·na· en Gate, Beijing, the main entrance gate to the Forbidden City.

MAP 21

Trans-Manchurian route

Km6293: Karymskaya (●) The branch
line to Beijing via Manchuria leaves the main
Trans-Siberian route at Tarskaya (formerly
Kaidalovo), 12kms east of Karymskaya. Leaving Tarskaya, you cross the Ingoda River and
head through open steppe-land to Zabaikalsk
at the border. Twenty kilometres south of here
you enter the Buryat National Okrug.

Km6444: Olovyanaya Leaving this
picturesque town you cross the Onon River,
which flows north of the main Trans-Siberian
line where it joins the Ingoda to form the
Shilka. Genghis Khan was born on the banks
of the muddy River Onon in 1162. Between
Olovyanaya and Borzya you cross the Adun
Chelon mountain ridge, passing through Yasnaya (km6464) and Birka (km6477).

Km6486: Mirnaya At the western end of
the station there are two small tanks whose
guns appear to be aimed at the train.

Km6509: Khadabulak Small village
below a large telecommunications tower on
the hill. Long views across the plains to the
hills in the north around this area.

Km6543: Borzya (●●) Junction with the
line to Solovyevsk on the border with Mongolia, 85km south-west of here. Black marketeers come aboard here (if you're coming
from Beijing) to tempt you with army uniforms, military watches (from the camp here?)
and rabbit fur hats. Watch your valuables.

(Opposite) Top: Autumnal foliage, Kyoto, Japan.
Bottom: Young temple visitors, Kamakura, correctly
attired in their kimono.

The East Chinese Railway 1897-1901

The original plans for the Great Siberian Railway had not included the laying of tracks across territories that were outside the Russian Empire. However, when surveyors returned from the Shilka and Amur valleys in 1894, with the news that the Sretensk to Khabarovsk section of the line would prove extremely costly, owing to the difficult terrain, the Siberian Railway Committee were obliged to consider an alternative route. Their greedy eyes turned to the rich Chinese territory of Manchuria and they also noted that a line straight across this province to Vladivostok would cut 513 *versts* (544km) off the journey to the port. Since the Chinese would obviously not be happy to have Russian railway lines extending into their territory, the Committee had to think up with a scheme to win Peking over to the idea.

The Manchurian Deal

It did not take the wily Russian diplomats long to work out a deal the Chinese were forced to accept. After the 1894 Sino-Japanese war the victorious Japanese concocted a peace treaty that included the payment of a heavy indemnity by the Chinese. Knowing that China was unable to pay, the Russians offered them a generous loan in exchange for the right to build and operate a railway across Manchuria. They were granted an eighty-year lease on the thin strip of land 1,400km long and the project was to be disguised as a Chinese enterprise financed through the Russo-Chinese Bank. The rest of the world suspected Russia of flagrant imperialism and she proved them right in 1897 by annexing Port Arthur.

Work begins

Construction of the Chinese Eastern Railway began in 1897 but it soon became obvious that the project was facing greater problems than any that had arisen during the building of other sections of the railway. There were difficult conditions (the Greater Khingan Range had to be crossed); there were not enough labourers; interpreters were needed to translate the orders of the Russian foremen to the Chinese coolies and the area through which the route passed was thick with *hunghutzes* (bandits). It was necessary to bring in a force of 5,000 policemen to protect the workers. After the Boxer (anti-foreigner) riots began in the late 1890s it became necessary to protect the rails, too, for when they were not murdering missionaries the Boxers tore up the track and derailed trains.

Set-backs

After the annexation of Port Arthur another Manchurian line was begun - from Harbin south through Mukden (now Shenyang) to Dalni (now Dalian) and Port Arthur (now Lushun). Work was disrupted in 1899 by the outbreak of bubonic plague and a doctor was rushed from St Petersburg to inoculate the labourers. In spite of the Chinese refusing to co-operate with the quarantine procedures, only 1,400 died, out of the total work-force of 200,000. In May 1900 the Boxers destroyed 200km of track and besieged Harbin. The Russians sent in a peace-keeping force of 200,000 men but by the time the rebellion had been put down, one third of the railway had been destroyed.

Despite all these set-backs, the line was completed at the end of 1901 although not opened to regular traffic until 1903. It would have been far more economical to have built the Amur line from Sretensk to Khabarovsk, for in the end the East Chinese Railway had cost the government more than the total spent on the entire Trans-Siberian track on Russian soil.

There are a number of opportunities for photographs along the train as it snakes around the curves between kms6554-70, especially km6564-5(S). The line passes through **Kharanor** (km6583) where there may be a one-minute stop and **Dauriya** (km6609), a small village surrounded by a marsh of red weeds.

Km6661: Zabaikalsk - The Border (● ● ● + +) A small station on the Russian side of the border with China. The bogies are changed, the carriages being raised on hydraulic lifts while passengers go to the station building to have breakfast or lunch and visit the bank. Photography of the bogie-changing operation is now tolerated. It used to be forbidden and I once saw a disobedient tourist having the film ripped out of his camera by an irate border guard. Get off quickly and beat the queue for the **restaurant** (boiled eggs, fish, soup, beefsteak and rice). If you've just arrived in the USSR, don't change too much money in the **bank** as there's little to spend it on on the train and anyway you will soon be approached by black marketeers. If you need smaller denomination US$ bills (for the black market) the bank seems happy to help you out! There is a **Beriozka shop** in the building opposite the station building and across the line. Here you can buy vodka (5.10R), champagne (5.50R), fur hats (46.00R), palekh boxes (38-128R) and 'Gorby' watches (17.00R) with foreign currency only. Next door is a small department store where you can buy small Russian flags (10R), fur hats (147R) and coats (207R) for roubles.

Customs formalities take place on the train and, if you are leaving the USSR, you are required to produce your currency declaration form with your remaining travellers' cheques and foreign currency. Officials don't seem to worry if your form shows that you haven't changed much money in the country (if you've been indulging in a little speculation) since many tours include meals and other expenses and it will be presumed that you're on a tour or have eaten in hard-currency restaurants. Nevertheless several small-denomination currency exchanges look good on the form. Any remaining roubles are confiscated so don't admit to having them if you want some as souvenirs. If you're coming into the country and not going to change money on the black market, declare everything on the form. If you are going to use the black market, only declare what you're not going to be using or as you leave the USSR customs may want to know what happened to this money. In fact this should be less of a problem than it was in the past with all the hard-currency restaurants and bars since you can say you spent it in that way.

MAP 22

THE PEOPLE'S REPUBLIC OF CHINA

(Note that the km markers along this route do not show the distance to Beijing until you reach Harbin. From the border to Harbin they show the distance to Harbin.)

Km935 (Bei:2323): Manzhouli (● ● ● +) (2135ft/651m) At this Chinese border-town (formerly known as Manchuria Station) you are required to fill out a health declaration, baggage and currency declaration form (which you must show to customs officials as you leave the country) and immigration form. The train spends 1½-2½hrs here so you can visit the **bank** and the **Friendship Store** (stock up on food: tins of fruit (4Y) and tins of good quality peanuts (2.20Y) as well as Chinese vodka and beer if you're about to enter the Soviet Union). Postcards (and stamps) are also available here. Puffing steam locomotives shunt carriages around the yard, a particularly impressive sight if you arrive here in the early hours of a freezing winter morning. Loos stink, less so in winter.

Leaving the station you pass **Lake Dalai Nor** and roll across empty steppe-lands. You may see mounted herders from the train as Michael Myres Shoemaker did in 1902 when he was here, on the way to Peking. Of the first Chinese he saw, he wrote (in *The Great Siberian Railway from St Petersburg to Pekin*) 'these northern Celestials appear on the whole friendly, and are flying around in all directions swathed in furs, and mounted on shaggy horses.' European newspapers of the time had been filled with reports of the atrocities committed by the anti-foreigner Boxer sect in Manchuria, hence his surprise at the apparent friendliness of the local population.

Km749 (Bei:2137): Hailar (●●) (2030ft/619m) From here to Haiman the rolling steppes continue. If you'd been travelling here in 1914, you would have the latest edition of the Baedeker's *Russia with Teheran, Port Arthur and Peking* with you and would therefore be looking out for 'the fortified station buildings (sometimes adorned with apes, dragons and other Chinese ornaments), the Chinese carts with their two high wheels and the camels at pasture'. Modern Hailar is an unexotic city of 170,000 people, the economic centre of the region. Local architecture is a blend of Russian and Mongolian: log cabins, some with 'yurt-style' roofs. The average temperature in this area in January is a cool minus 27°C.

Km674 (Bei:2062): Haiman Also known as Yakoshih, this town stands near the foot of the Great Khingan Range which extends from the northern border with the USSR south into Inner Mongolia. The line begins to rise into the foothills of the range.

Km634 (Bei:2022): Mianduhe (●) The train continues to climb the gently rising gradient.

Km574 (Bei:1962): Yilick Ede (●●) Note that the train does not stop here on the journey **from** Beijing.

Km564 (Bei:1952): Xinganling/Khingan (●)
(3140ft/958m) This station stands at the highest point on the line. The long tunnel (3km) that was built here in 1901-2 was a considerable engineering achievement since most of the drilling was done during the winter, with shift workers labouring day and night.

Km539 (Bei:1927): Boketu (●●●) The line winds down through partly-wooded slopes to the town of Balin/Barim (km7135/1866) and continues over the plains leaving Inner Mongolia and crossing into Heilongjiang Province.

Km270 (Bei:1658): Angangxi (●●●) Forty kilometres south of the ancient city of **Qiqihar** (Tsitsikar). By the time he reached this point Michael Myres Shoemaker had become bored with watching 'Celestials' from the windows of the train and was tired and hungry. He writes 'In Tsitsikar, at a wretched little mud hut, we find some hot soup and a chop, also some coffee, all of which, after our days in lunch baskets, taste very pleasant.' Over their lunch, they may well have discussed the nearby **Field of Death** for which the city was notorious. In this open area on the edge of Tsitsikar public executions were regularly performed. Most of the criminals decapitated before the crowds here were *hunghutzes* (bandits). Since the Chinese believed that entry to Heaven was denied to mortals who

MAP 23

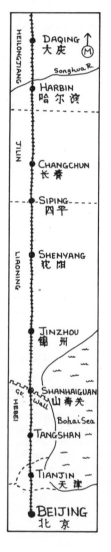

were missing parts of their bodies, their heads had to be sewn back in place before a decent burial could take place. However, so as not to lower the moral tone of Paradise, the government ordered that the heads be sewn on the wrong way round, facing backwards.

Twenty kilometres east of Angangxi you pass through a large area of marshland, part of which has been designated a nature reserve. The marsh attracts a wide variety of waterfowl since it is on the migration route from the Arctic and Siberia down to southern Asia. The **Zhalong Nature Reserve**, twenty kilometres north of here, is best known for its crane centre and several of the cranes found here (the Siberian Crane among them) are now listed as endangered species.

Km159 (Bei:1547): Daqing (●)   At the centre of one of the largest oilfields in China, Daqing is an industrial model town producing plastics and gas as well as oil. Higher wages (300Y rather than the average 100Y per month) attract model workers from all over the country. Apart from the thousands of oil wells in this swampy district there's very little for the tourist to see.

Km96 (Bei:1484): Song   Small station in an island of cultivation amongst the swamps.

Km0 (Bei:1388): Harbin (●●●)
(152m/500ft) Crossing the wide Sungari (Songhua) River (a 1,840km long tributary of the mighty Amur to the north) the line reaches Harbin, the industrial centre of Heilongjiang Province. It was a small fishing village until the mid 1890s when the Russians made it the headquarters of their railway building operations in Manchuria. Michael Myres Shoemaker visited the town in 1902 and wrote in *The Great Siberian Railway from St Petersburg to Pekin*: 'The state of society seems even worse at this military post of Harbin than in Irkutsk.

There were seven throats cut last night, and now, as a member of the Russo-Chinese Bank expressed it, the town hopes for a quiet season.' The *Imperial Japanese Railways Guide to East Asia (1913)* recommended 'the excellent bread and butter, which are indeed the pride of Harbin' and warned travellers away from the numerous opium dens. After the Revolution, White Russians refugees poured into the town and the Russian influence on the place continued.

There are few onion-domes and spires to be seen now in what is otherwise just another Chinese city. The Russian population is now small. The main tourist attraction the city has to offer is the **Ice Lantern Festival**, which takes place from January to early February. Winters here are particularly cold and during the festival the parks are filled with ice-sculptures - life-size elephants, dragons and horses as well as small buildings and bridges. Electric lights are frozen into the inside of these sculptures and when they are illuminated at night, the effect is spectacular.

At the station, good views along the track of the numerous steam locos can be obtained from the bridges between the platforms.

Km1260: The line crosses a wide tributary of the Songhua River. There are numerous small lakes in the area.

Km1146: Changchun (● ●) (230m/760ft) Between Harbin and Changchun you cross an immense cultivated plain, leaving Heilongjiang and entering Jilin Province. Changchun is the provincial capital. The station is quite interesting with white concrete sculptures of 'The Graces' and lots to buy from the snack sellers on the platform. Back in 1913 the *Imperial Japanese Government Railways Guide to East Asia* was reminding its readers (all of whom would have had to have changed at this large junction) about 'the need of adjusting their watches - the Russian railway-time being 23 minutes earlier than the Japanese'. From 1933 to 1945 Changchun was the centre of the Japanese puppet state of Manchukuo and it has now grown into an industrial metropolis of more than one million people. Local industries include the car factory (where Red Flag limousines are assembled - guided tours possible), the rail-carriage factory and the film studios. If you happen to get off here the local delicacies include Antler Broth, Bear Paws cooked in Pine Flowers and Hedgehog Hydnum stewed with Orchid, and the north-eastern speciality, *Qimian*, which is the nose of a moose. However Changchun is probably more popular with rail enthusiasts than with epicureans. RM Pacifics and QJ 2-10-2s are to be seen here and on the Changchun-Jilin line.

Km1030: Siping   Unattractive town but lots of working steam locos in the station. Ten kilometres south of here the train crosses the provincial border into Liaoning Province.

Km841: Shenyang (● ● ●)   (50m/160ft)   An industrial giant founded two thousand years ago during the Western Han dynasty (206BC - 24AD). At different times during the course of its long history the city has been controlled by the Manchus (who named it Mukden), the Russians, the Japanese and the Kuomintang until it was finally taken over by the Chinese Communists in 1948. It is now one of the largest industrial centres in the People's Republic but there are several interesting places to visit between the factories, including a smaller version of the **Imperial Palace** in Beijing. There is also a **railway museum** situated beside Sujiatun shed and containing 14 exhibits under cover. The station has a green dome and the square outside it is dominated by a tank on a high pedestal.

Km599: Jinzhou (● ●)   From here the line runs down almost to the coast which it follows south-west for the next 300km, crossing into Hebei Province. Beijing is just under eight hours from here.

Km415: Shanhaiguan (● ●)   As you approach the town from the north, you pass through the Great Wall - at its most eastern point. This end of the Wanlichangcheng (Ten Thousand Li Long Wall) has been partially done up for the tourists. Although the views here are not as spectacular as at Badaling (70km north of Beijing and the usual tourist spot on the Wall) the restoration at Shanhaiguan has been carried out more sympathetically - it is restoration rather than reconstruction. The large double-roofed tower houses an interesting museum.

Km262: Tangshan   The epicentre of the earthquake which demolished this industrial town on 28 July 1976. The official death toll stands at 150,000 but it is probably as high as 750,000. Many of the factories have been rebuilt and the town is once again producing consumer goods. In 1990 the Tangshan Works was still producing the SY class 2-8-2 steam locomotive although production is said to be ceasing soon.

Km133: Tianjin/Tientsin (● ●)   One of the largest ports in China, with a population of seven million. In the mid-nineteenth century the English and the French marched on Beijing and 'negotiated' the Treaty of Peking which opened Tianjin to foreign trade. Concessions were granted to foreign powers as they were in Shanghai. England, France, Austria, Germany, Italy, Belgium, Russia,

Japan and the United States each controlled different parts of the city, which accounts for the amazing variety of architectural styles to be found here. Chinese resentment of the foreign presence boiled over in 1870 when (during the incident that came to be known as the **Tientsin Massacre**) ten nuns, two priests and a French official were murdered. To save female babies from being killed the nuns had been giving money for them. This had led the more gullible members of the Chinese population to believe that the nuns were either eating the children or grinding up their bones for patent medicines.

Km0: Beijing You are now 9001kms from Moscow. Refer to Part 6 for accommodation list and tourist sights in Beijing, if you've just arrived.

PART 6: DESTINATIONS & DEPARTURES

This section contains basic information for those spending a few days in Tokyo, Beijing, Hong Kong, Helsinki, Berlin or Budapest at the end (or beginning) of a Trans-Siberian trip. Details of how to arrange tickets in these cities for the rail journey across Siberia, are given in Part 1.

JAPAN

General information
● **Visas** Visas are not necessary for passport holders from Britain, other Western European countries, North America and most Commonwealth countries (except Australia).
● **Money/costs** The unit of currency is the yen (Y). Japan has become one of the most expensive countries in the world for foreign visitors. You will need to allow for a minimum of £15-20 per day for the most basic accommodation and the cheapest meals (fast-food).
● **Climate** Japan has four clearly-defined seasons, winter being cold and snowy (though snow rarely settles in Tokyo), summer hot and humid, spring and autumn warm.
● **Language** Since English is taught in schools and the people are very keen to make contact with foreigners, you will always be able to find someone to help you except in the more out-of-the-way places. Station names are posted in English, hotel and youth hostel staff speak English and if you're really stuck dial 3502-1461 (in Tokyo) for the Tourist Information Centre (TIC) and someone will help you. In Yokohama dial 106 and ask for 'Collect call TIC' for the same service.

Tourist information
Before you leave home visit the branch of the Japan National Tourist Organisation in your country. A good selection of useful maps and tourist brochures is provided free of charge. Addresses:
● 167 Regent St, London W1 (071-734-9638)
● 630 Fifth Ave, New York, N.Y.10111 (212-757-5640)
● 165 University Ave, Toronto, Ont. M5H 3B8 (416-366-7140)
● 115 Pitt St, Sydney NSW 2000 (232-4522)
The Tokyo Tourist Information Centre (mentioned above) should be

your first stop in the city, as it is a veritable mine of information on hotels, sights and entertainment. It's at 10-1, Yurakucho 2-chome, Chiyoda-Ku, Tokyo (3502-1461). Nearest stations are Ginza and Yurakucho.

Local transport

If you plan to spend some time touring the country you should purchase a Japan Rail Pass but to qualify for the full discount, it must be purchased before you arrive, from the JNTO branch in your country. For getting around the cities the metro system is your best bet although you will need help buying tickets from the machines.

Arrival

● **Yokohama Port** The boat from Nakhodka docks at the South Pier (Osambashi). The Yokohama Port Authority operates a free courtesy bus to Yokohama Station (Tokyo 30mins), leaving 1½hrs after the boat docks and stopping at the Silk Center (*bureau de change*). There is a tourist information centre in the port building but if this is closed the main branch in Yokohama is in the Silk Center, a five-minute walk from the South Pier. If you need to cash travellers' cheques outside banking hours, some of the shops in the Silk Center may help you out but their rates are rather less than attractive so don't cash too much. The Tourist Info Centre will give you a city plan and an accommodation list (there is a Youth Hostel near Sakuragi-cho station). If you're not taking the free courtesy bus to Yokohama station, the best way to get to Tokyo is to go to Sakuragi-cho station (30min walk from Silk Center; Y160 by bus; Y700 by taxi) which gives you the choice of two lines to Yokohama Main Station and Tokyo. Alternatively you could get a train from the nearer station of Kannai (trains less frequent) which is a 20min walk through a maze of small streets known as 'Chinatown' (good places to eat here).

● **Narita Airport (Tokyo)** Transport to the city centre is expensive since the airport is located forty miles outside the capital. The cheapest way to get in is to take the bus from the airport to Narita railway station for JNR trains to Tokyo. Visit the Tourist Information Centre at the airport for accommodation information and maps.

● **Niigata Airport (Niigata)** During the winter months the boat service between Yokohama and Nakhodka does not operate. There are, however, weekly flights between Niigata (5hr rail journey north of Tokyo) and Khabarovsk to connect with the Trans-Siberian. The Tourist Information Centre in Niigata is opposite the railway station and there are frequent buses from the station to the airport (½hr).

Accommodation

This is expensive - even a bed in a youth hostel will set you back £7.50. Youth hostels are cheapest followed by business hotels. *Ryokans* (Japanese style hotels) are pricey but often include meals and are an interesting experience for the foreigner. The best way to find somewhere to sleep is to visit the TIC and collect an accommodation list and a map. Then phone the hotel/youth hostel (phone-calls are one of the few bargains to be had in Japan). Check prices and places and then get them to give you directions for getting there. Some numbers to try for cheap accommodation in Tokyo are:

- Tokyo International Youth Hostel (Iidabashi) 3235-1107
- Ichigaya Youth Hostel (Ichigaya) 3262-6839
- Okubo House (Shinjuku) 3361-2348
- YMCA Hotel (Kanda) 3293-1911

Food

Ordering food in a restaurant is no problem, even if the waitress speaks no English, for plastic models of the dishes on offer are displayed in the window of the restaurant, prices alongside. Just point to what you want. The cheapest places are in and around railway stations. If you're on a strict budget you'll find yourself living off noodles and hamburgers. Western fast-food chains (McDonald's etc) have branches throughout the country and are cheap places to eat.

Sightseeing

In Tokyo the chief sights are the Emperor's Palace in the heart of the city; Ginza, the fashionable shopping district and the Meiji Shrine (surrounded by beautiful gardens). If you're staying more than a few days you should visit Kyoto, an ancient city of temples that is particularly attractive in November when the maple trees blaze with autumn colours. Full details of tourist sights are available from Tourist Information Centres.

Moving on

Flights are expensive in Japan so try to ensure you have one arranged before you arrive. For details of ferry services to China and the USSR (as well as information about arranging **Trans-Siberian** tickets in Japan) refer to Part 1.

CHINA

General information

● **Visas** These are needed by almost everyone and getting one is now a straight forward procedure. Apply at your local embassy. Hong Kong has always been the easiest and quickest place to get a visa for China. Many travellers use the visa service provided by many HK travel agents (6-24hrs or less). Two photos required.

● **Money/costs** The unit of currency is the yuan (Y) which is divided into 100 fen. Note that there are two types of currency in use: Renminbi (RMB) which is used by the majority of China's one billion people, and Foreign Exchange Certificates (FEC) used by tourists and diplomats. Cash travellers' cheques in hotels or Friendship Stores - the rate is always the same. China is a cheap country to visit: basic accommodation is available for less than £2.00 per night.

● **Climate** Beijing has an unhealthy climate - dry, windy and very cold in winter, hot and dusty in summer.

● **Language** This can be a problem because few people speak English and even if you do know a few words of Mandarin unless your pronunciation is absolutely spot-on you won't be understood. English is spoken in hotels and their restaurants. Get hotel staff to write down addresses on a piece of paper so that you can show this to people while asking directions.

China International Travel Service (CITS)

Otherwise known as Luxingshe, this is the Chinese equivalent of Intourist. There are, however, fewer restraints on travel in China than in the USSR. You are not required to arrange your accommodation in advance and for the majority of tourist destinations you no longer need an Alien Travel Permit. It is also no longer necessary to arrange accommodation with CITS - you can go straight to the hotel. However they will help with booking rail tickets (see Part 1 for information on arranging tickets and visas in Beijing for the **Trans-Siberian** trip). The CITS office in the Chongwenmen Hotel will soon be closing. The new office in the west lobby of the Beijing International Hotel is open now (see page 26 for directions).

BEIJING

Arrival at the railway station

This is a vast building incorporating the largest railway waiting-room in the world (claiming to have space for 14,000 people, but has seats for only 2,000). Once you have found your way out onto the square in front of the station you can join the taxi queue or catch a bus.

Local transport

In Beijing the metro system is good but stations are not always where you need them. The bus service is cheap but very crowded. Most travellers join the rest of the city's population on two wheels - there are many places to rent bikes from. Taxis are easiest to get outside hotels. They are metered and good value when shared.

Accommodation

There's a good range of accommodation - from the **Great Wall Hotel** for more than £70 per night to budget-priced dormitory accommodation at £2. The most popular travellers' cheap place is the large **Qiao Yuan Hotel** - bus No or 20 from outside the railway station. (Turn right outside station, and walk along until you see No.20 bus-stop. Take bus to the end of the line which is to the Yongdingmen terminus (15-20mins) and then it's a short walk along the canal). Other popular 'cheapies' include the **Long Tan** (bus No 41 from Chongwenmen to Long Tan Park) and the **Tiantan Sports Hotel** (bus Nos 39 or 43 from Chongwenmen). The **Beijing Hotel** is expensive to stay in but has a useful coffee-shop, post-office, a left-luggage room and is conveniently located just off Tiananmen Square.

Food

Peking Duck is the local speciality and there are many restaurants (along the road that runs across the southern end of Tiananmen Square) that serve nothing else. There are cheap restaurants catering for budget travellers along the canal by the Qiao Yuan Hotel. The food is generally good in hotel restaurants and menus are in English as well as Chinese.

Sightseeing

The main sights in Beijing are the Forbidden City (the large walled area north of Tiananmen Square); Mao Ze Dong's Mausoleum in the centre of Tiananmen Square; the Lama Temple (Yonghegong) and the Temple of Heaven (south-west of the station). Outside the city are the Summer Palace (beside Kunming Lake); the Ming tombs and, of course, the Great Wall. If you're taking the train via Mongolia, the line passes right through the Wall.

International rail tickets

For information and embassy addresses see Part 1.

HONG KONG

General information

- **Visas** For most visitors planning a stay of less than 30 days a visa is not necessary. British passport-holders get a six-month stay.
- **Money/costs** The unit of currency is the Hong Kong dollar (HK$), divided into 100 cents. As it's tied to the US dollar the rate is a fixed US$1 = HK$7.80. Most things are cheap but budget accommodation is not such good value for money as in other parts of Asia. For changing money, banks offer both the best and the worst rates - it all depends on the commission they're charging. Ask other travellers and check the notice-board in the Travellers' Hostel (see accommodation below) for what's currently the best place. Money-changers are useful when banks are closed but watch their commission charges, some of which are concealed in the rate displayed. Some sell roubles cheaply but check the going rate on the Soviet Black Market from recently-returned travellers. Note that roubles are confiscated if discovered (unlikely) by Soviet customs at the border.
- **Climate** Mild with fairly hot and humid summers, cool winters.
- **Language** Cantonese and English.

Tourist information

The Hong Kong Tourist Association (HKTA) has branches in many countries and can provide you with useful maps and brochures. Branches at the airport and the Star Ferry terminal (Kowloon).

Arrival

- **Kai Tak Airport** Tucked into Kowloon, beside the bay. Landing here is quite an experience as the tips of the wings seem almost to touch the high-rise blocks. Visit the HKTA office and if you have to visit the *bureau de change* do not change more than the price of a bus-fare. There is an airport bus that runs into Tsimshatsui District (where there is budget accommodation available) in Kowloon and also to Hong Kong Island. (Departure tax is HK$120 per person).
- **By rail** There are several alternatives. You can take the direct express train which runs between Canton (Guangzhou) and Kowloon (Hunghom Station). However it is cheaper to take local trains, from Canton to the Chinese border town of Shenzhen (there is also a bus service on this route), where you walk across the border into Hong Kong and then take a local train from Lo Wu station to Hunghom.
- **Ferry/hovercraft from Canton (Guangzhou)** The overnight ferry between Canton and Hong Kong arrives and departs from the Tai Kok Tsui Wharf in Kowloon. There is also a hovercraft service operating between here and Canton (journey time: 3 hours).

● **Boat to/from Shanghai** The *M/V Shanghai* and *M/V Haixing* operate on this 60hr run, prices HK$550-800. The service is popular and heavily booked in the summer. Contact China Travel Service (27 Nathan Rd, tel 721 1331) or China Merchants' Steam Navigation Co (18th floor, 152 Connaught Rd, Central; tel 544 0558 & 815 1008).

Local transport
Most famous is the Star Ferry service which operates across the bay between Kowloon and Hong Kong Island, 60c one-way. There is also a fast and efficient subway system and the old trams still operate on Hong Kong Island. Taxis are cheap but traffic slow-moving.

Accommodation
For a cheap place to sleep, the name is **Chungking Mansions**. In this large block in Kowloon, near the bay and a stone's throw from the famous **Peninsula Hotel**, there are a large number of small hotels with tiny rooms but low prices. Have a look at a few before you settle for the first you see as the rooms vary in size, cleanliness and price. The **Travellers' Hostel** (16f Block A) is a popular meeting place for backpackers and has cheap dormitory accommodation, a restaurant and a travel agency that can organise visas for China. The refurbished **YMCA** (next door to the Peninsula Hotel) should be reopening soon. It provides good value accommodation that is so popular it is often booked up months in advance.

Food
An incredible variety including some of the best Chinese (Cantonese-style) food available anywhere. Try the floating restaurants of Aberdeen in the evening, have *dim sum* for lunch or if it's real junk (!) food you want all the big names are here.

Sightseeing
The main attraction in Hong Kong is really the city itself and its location - thousands of buildings packed around the bay in the shadow of the Peak on Hong Kong Island. Take the Peak tram (rack railway) up to the top of the Peak for a magnificent view over the bay. A trip to the nearby Portuguese colony of Macau and its casinos is recommended (three hours by ferry).

Moving on
For cheap flights or Trans-Siberian tickets see page 28. Visas for China are easy to get in Hong Kong. Either use a travel agent (HK$110-300 in 4-36hrs) or DIY for HK$90 (Counter No 7, Visa Section of PRC, 5th floor, China Resources Building, Harbour Drive. Take the Star Ferry to Wanchai).

FINLAND

General information

- **Visas** Visas are not necessary for most nationalities.
- **Money/costs** The unit of currency is the Finmark (FIM) divided into 100 pennia. As in most Scandinavian countries prices are higher here than in many European countries but not as high as in Japan. Basic youth hostel accommodation is available for under £7.00 per night.
- **Climate** Helsinki is pleasantly warm in summer but winters are long and severe.
- **Language** There are two official languages - Finnish and Swedish (the Swedish name for Helsinki being Helsingfors). Most people also speak English.

Tourist information

There are Finnish Tourist Offices in many capitals of the world. In Helsinki your first stop should be the Helsinki City Tourist Office at Pohjoisesplanadi 19, on the Esplanadia (the park next to the water-side Market Square). They provide good maps, an accommodation list and are particularly helpful and friendly.

Arrival

- **By sea** If you're arriving from Stockholm on a Viking Line ship, or from Travemunde (West Germany) on Finnjet, both companies dock on the east side of the bay. To reach the centre of the city, walk towards the white Cathedral you can see above the harbour. Buses and taxis also available. If you're arriving from Poland (Gdansk) or on the Silja line (from Stockholm), boats dock on the west side of the bay, roughly the same distance from the city centre (15 min walk).
- **By air** The airport is situated 19km north of the city centre, at Vantaa. There is a regular bus service (bus No 615 to Railway Station). The journey takes about half an hour.
- **By rail** The railway station is six blocks west of the harbour and two blocks north. Trains for the USSR and Leningrad usually depart from platform six.

Local transport

The city transport system is efficient and comprises buses, trams and the metro. Tourists can buy a 24-hr unlimited travel ticket.

Accommodation

A full list for all budgets (including Youth Hostels) is available from the Helsinki City Tourist Office. For cheap accommodation try:

- Stadionin maja, Pohjoinen Stadiontie 3B (Tel. 496 071)
- Vataan Retkeilymaja, Tikkurila Sports Ground (Tel. 8393 310)

Food
Most palates are catered for but if you're on a tight budget you can buy several kinds of smoked fish from the stalls by the harbour, as well as a good range of fresh fruit including Arctic cloudberries.

Sightseeing
Helsinki is a pleasant, rather sleepy sort of capital nestling round a picturesque bay but it doesn't have all that much to offer the tourist. Finland is famous for its design and there are some interesting modern buildings. You can visit the monument to Sibelius in Sibelius Park; the Senate Square and Cathedral; the red Uspensky Cathedral; the Temppeliaukio Church (blasted from solid rock) and the Finlandia Concert Hall and Congress Centre. You should not leave without indulging in that most Finnish of occupations: the sauna. Most hotels have one if not several.

Moving on
There are ferries to Germany, Poland and Sweden (which is the usual rail route to the rest of Europe). Discounted flights are available to under 26s or student card holders. A recommended budget travel agent is Travela at Mannerheimintie 5 C, 00100 Helsinki 10.

For information about booking the **Trans-Siberian** see Part 1.

GERMANY: BERLIN

General information
● **Visas** Since the re-unification of the two Germanies on 03 Oct 1990 visa regulations are now as for the western part of the country and are not necessary for most nationalities.
● **Money/costs** The Deutsche mark (DM) is the unit of currency, divided into 100 pfennigs. Living and travelling costs can be high.
● **Language** It's useful to be able to speak a little German. Most Berliners study English at school and many speak it fluently.

Tourist information
The Berlin Tourist Office is in the Europa Center (the building with the Mercedes star on the top of it) along Kurfurstendamm and a ten-minute walk from Zoo Bahnhof. Maps and an accommodation list are available from this office, open daily 07.30-22.30hrs.

Arrival in Berlin
Zoo Bahnhof (Zoo Station) is the station for international trains. There are left-luggage lockers (2DM) and a *bureau de change*. The Berlin Tourist Office is a ten-minute walk away (see above).

Local transport
The underground is the easiest way to get around. There are in fact two systems (as this was formerly two cities) - the U-bahn and the S-Bahn. There is also an efficient bus network.

Accommodation
The cheapest places are the **Youth Hostels** which are luxurious by YH standards but comparatively expensive (around 25DM).
● Ernst Reuter Jugendherberge, Hermsdorfer Damm 48, (Hermsdorf) (tel 404 16 10)
● Berlin Jugendhergastehaus, Kluckstrasse 3 (Tiergarten) (tel 261 10 97)
● Wannsee Jugendhergastehaus, Kronprinzessinnenweg 27, Ecke Badeweg (Wannsee) (tel 8 03 20 34)
● Jugendhotel International, Bernburgerstrasse 27, (tel 262 30 81)
Around Zoo Station, which is where your train will arrive, try:
● Jugendhergastehaus am Zoo, Hardenbergstrasse 9a (tel 312 94 10) Under 27s only; accommodation from 20DM.
● Bahnhofsmission at Zoo Station, office on Jebensstrasse, just outside the station. Dormitory beds 15DM.
The tourist office will give you a list of cheap accommodation including rooms in private houses. They will arrange accommodation for a 3DM commission fee.

Sightseeing

Now that the Wall has come down one of the most interesting things to do is simply to walk around the re-unified city. The contrasts between East and West are still strong. In the western part take a walk down the **Kurfurstendamm**, the main thoroughfare, lined with over a thousand shops. Near the Zoo Bahnhof end of this long street is the **Kaiser Wilhelm Church**, known to the Berliners as the 'Jagged Tooth' and a reminder of the war years. Many of the older buildings were destroyed during the heavy bombing and of those that remain **Charlottenburg Castle** and the **Brandenburg Gate** are the most notable. You can walk past this famous gate into what was East Berlin. The best museums are on Museum Island (a short walk from Friedrichstrasse station). On this island in the middle of the Spree Canal are five **museums** whose world famous exhibits include the altar from Pergamum (Turkey) and the massive blue Ishtar Gate from Babylon. In the western part of the city it's worth seeing the famous bust of Nefertiti in the **Egyptian Museum**.

And then there's Berlin's world famous nightlife, said to be enjoying something of a renaissance now.

Moving on

For cheap flights buy a copy of the weekly magazine *Zitty*, which has several pages of travel deals. Student/discount flights to London start at around 300DM. International trains leave from Zoo Bahnhof. Direct services to London (via Hook of Holland) depart at 00.31 and 12.51 daily. There are two through-trains to Paris daily, leaving at 23.55 and 15.35. There are also coaches to many towns in Germany as well as to several capitals including London. A useful system of car-sharing can be arranged through *mitfahrzentrale* agencies - you pay the agency a 15DM fee to find you a ride in a private car to other European cities. You share petrol costs.

To make a booking on the **Trans-Siberian** in Berlin see Part 1.

HUNGARY: BUDAPEST

General information
- **Visas** North Americans and most European citizens (except those of Greece, Turkey, Portugal, Ireland and the USSR) do not need a visa. If needed, visas can be obtained at Budapest airport and at borders.
- **Money/costs** The unit of currency is the Forint (Ft), divided into 100 fillers (f). You are not required to change a minimum amount of foreign currency for each day you will be in Hungary. Prices for hotels and restaurants are low. Be very careful if changing money on the Black Market (illegal, of course) as several travellers report having been ripped off with bundles of loo paper wrapped in a few 500 forint notes.
- **Language** *Magyar* is one of the world's more difficult languages to learn. Most people connected with tourism speak a little English though knowledge of German is more widespread.

Tourist information
There are a number of tourist organisations that can help both with maps and information as well as with finding accommodation (see also below). The main organisations are **Tourinform**, Suto utca 2, (near Deak ter metro station; tel 117-9800; open 08.00-20.00 daily) and **IBUSZ**, V.Petofi ter 3, (money-changing facilities; tel 118-3925; open 24hrs daily). IBUSZ has several other branches. There's also a useful English-language telephone help-line for tourist information and problems (tel 117-2200, 07.00-20.00hrs).

Arrival
- **By rail** Trains from Vienna come into the East Station (**Keleti Palyaudvar**), and there is a tourist office here, where you can book accommodation. The West Station (**Nyugati Palyaudvar**) is used for trains to and from Prague. Both stations have metro stations nearby.
- **By air** The international airport is 10 miles from the city centre. There is a tourist office and there are shuttle buses to the city.

Local transport
The metro system is a cheap and efficient way to get around. There are also buses and trams. Note that you must buy tickets in advance from tobacconists and stamp them yourself as you board the bus or tram.

Accommodation
Budapest has a good range of accommodation. At the top end there is the **Hilton** which blends well with the ancient walls of the castle

tower it incorporates and stands on the hill above the city. For budget travellers the city's **colleges** offer their rooms during the summer holidays. Many local people let **rooms** in their houses and you can be put in contact with them by visiting one of the tourist offices listed below:

IBUSZ Hotel Service, V Petofi ter 3 (tel 118-3925; open 24hrs). IBUSZ also has branches at Keleti and Nyugati railway stations.
Volantourist, V Belgrad rakpart 6 (tel 118-2133)
Co-optourist, XI Bartok Bela ut 4 (tel 125-1615)
Budapest Tourist, V Roosevelt ter 5 (tel 117-3555)

Sightseeing
Once part of the powerful Austro-Hungarian Empire, Budapest has a wealth of historical buildings including the Royal Palace and National Galleries, the Houses of Parliament, Buda Castle, Matthias Church and St Stephen's Basilica. Hungary's summer playground is Lake Balaton, 70 miles from the capital.

Moving on
Taking the train back to London will cost around £180 and proof that the Forint were exchanged at a bank and not on the Black Market may be required. For details about booking the **Trans-Siberian** in Budapest see Part 1.

APPENDIX A: TIMETABLES

Timetables for the Trans-Siberian, Trans-Mongolian, Trans-Manchurian routes are given below, plus London - Moscow and Beijing - Hong-Kong routes. Unless otherwise indicated **arrival times are shown**; for departure times simply add the number of minutes shown as the stopping time. Since the timetables are subject to changes from year to year, you should consult the table posted on the wall of the carriage corridor to ensure times are correct. Another useful source of information is the Thomas Cook Overseas Timetable.

Table 1   Moscow-Vladivostok & Nakhodka (Train Nos 1 & 2)

Station name		Km from Moscow	Stop (mins)	Eastbound MT*	Eastbound LT*	Westbound MT*	Westbound LT*
Moscow	Москва	dep/arr daily at:		15.05	15.05	15.50	15.50
Aleksandrov	Александров	112	1	16.46	16.46	-	-
				▼ Day 1 ▼		▲	▲
Yaroslavl	Ярославль	284	5	18.45	18.45	11.55	11.55
Danilov	Данилов	357	15	19.50	20.50	10.37	11.37
Buy	Буй	448	2	21.12	22.12	09.24	10.24
				▼ Day 2 ▼		▲	▲
Shariya	Шарья	701	10	00.20	01.20	06.13	07.13
Kirov	Киров	957	15	03.45	04.45	02.44	03.44
Balyezino	Балезино	1191	15	06.55	07.55	23.41	00.41
				▼	▼	▲ Day 7 ▲	
Perm	Пермь	1433	12	10.35	12.35	20.18	22.18
Sverdlovsk	Свердловск	1813	15	16.10	18.10	14.42	16.42
Tyumen	Тюмень	2141	10	20.03	22.03	10.46	12.46
Ishim	Ишим	2433	8	23.22	01.22	07.27	09.27
				▼ Day 3 ▼		▲	▲
Nazevayevskaya	Называевская	2567	15	01.12	04.12	05.35	08.35
Omsk	Омск	2712	12	02.58	05.58	03.38	06.38
Barabinsk	Барабинск	3035	15	06.40	09.40	23.40	02.40
				▼	▼	▲ Day 6 ▲	
Novosibirsk	Новосибирск	3335	15	10.16	13.16	20.06	23.06
Taiga	Тайга	3565	8	13.50	17.50	16.57	20.57
Mariinsk	Мариинск	3717	2	16.16	20.16	14.37	18.37
Bogotol	Боготол	3852	8	18.02	22.02	12.45	16.45
Achinsk	Ачинск	3920	2	19.02	23.02	11.49	15.49
				▼ Day 4 ▼		▲	▲
Krasnoyarsk	Красноярск	4099	15	22.16	02.16	08.13	12.13
Illanskaya	Иланская	4375	8	02.32	06.32	03.49	07.49
Taishet	Тайшет	4516	2	04.48	09.48	01.43	06.43
Nizhneudinsk	Нижнеудинск	4680	8	07.30	12.30	22.43	03.43
				▼	▼	▲ Day 5 ▲	
Zima	Зима	4940	12	11.31	16.31	18.46	23.46
Angarsk	Ангарск	5160	2	15.16	20.16	15.31	20.31
Irkutsk	Иркутск	5185	10	16.13	21.13	14.32	19.32

*(MT=Moscow time; LT=local time)

Station name		Km from Moscow	Stop (mins)	Arrival time			
				Eastbound		Westbound	
				MT*	LT*	MT*	LT*
Slyudyanka		5312	15	18.18	23.18	12.07	17.07
				▼ Day 5 ▼		▲	▲
Ulan Ude	Улан-Удэ	5642	12	23.50	05.50	06.59	12.59
Petrovskiy Zavod	Петровский З.	5782	12	02.10	08.10	04.45	10.45
Mogzon	Могзон	6052	10	06.28	12.28	00.33	06.33
Chita	Чита	6199	13	09.13	15.13	21.46	03.46
Karymskaya	Карымская	6293	12	10.58	16.58	19.45	01.45
				▼	▼	▲ Day 4 ▲	
Shilka Pass.	Шилка-Пасс	6446	12	13.38	19.38	17.02	23.02
Chernishevsk	Чернышевск	6593	8	16.13	22.13	14.24	20.24
Zilovo	Зилово	6670	1	17.49	23.49	12.58	18.58
Mogocha	Могоча	6930	8	21.43	03.43	08.48	14.48
				▼ Day 6 ▼		▲	▲
Amazar	Амазар	7010	12	23.19	05.19	07.05	13.05
Yerofei Pavlovich	Ерофеи П.	7119	8	01.29	07.29	05.08	11.08
Urusha	Уруша	7211	2	03.28	09.28	03.19	09.19
Skovorodino	Сковородино	7306	10	05.10	11.10	01.28	07.28
Magdagachi	Магдагачи	7501	8	08.21	14.21	22.20	04.20
Shimanovskaya	Шимановская	7723	2	11.45	17.45	18.55	00.55
				▼	▼	▲ Day 3 ▲	
Svobodnyy	Свободный	7815	2	12.58	18.58	17.46	23.46
Belogorsk	Белогорск	7873	12	13.50	19.50	16.37	22.37
Bureya	Бурея	8037	2	16.24	22.24	14.12	20.12
Arkhara	Архара	8088	12	17.17	23.17	13.13	19.13
				▼ Day 7 ▼		▲	▲
Bira	Бира	8314	8	21.30	04.30	09.15	16.15
Birobidzhan	Биробиджан	8358	2	22.18	05.18	08.34	15.34
Khabarovsk	Хабаровск	8531	5	01.05	08.05	06.04	13.04
			(Change trains for Nakhodka: see Table 2)				
				▼ Day 8 ▼		▲	▲
Spassk-Dalny	Спасск-Д.	9057	10	09.13	16.13	21.27	04.27
				▼	▼	▲ Day 2 ▲	
Ussuriyisk	Уссурийск	9185	10	11.26	18.26	19.19	02.19
Vladivostok	Владивосток	9297	--	13.30	20.30	17.25	00.25

Table 2 Khabarovsk-Nakhodka (for Japan)

Station name		Km from Moscow	Stop (mins)	Arrival time			
				Eastbound		Westbound	
				MT*	LT*	MT*	LT*
		(dep)		10.20	17.20	05.02	12.02
				▼ Day 8 ▼		▲	▲
Spassk-Dalny	Спасск-Д.	9057	10	18.51	01.51	20.10	03.10
				▼	▼	▲ Day 2 ▲	
Ussuriyisk	Уссурийск	9185	10	21.16	04.16	17.59	00.59
Tikhookeanskaya	Port	9441/175		02.27	09.27	12.50	19.50
(Nakhodka)	Находка					▲ Day 1 ▲	

Table 3 Moscow-Beijing via Mongolia (Train Nos 3 & 4)

Station name		Km from Moscow	Stop (mins)	Arrival time Eastbound MT*	Eastbound LT*	Westbound MT*	Westbound LT*
				▼ Tue/Wed ▼		▲	▲
Moscow	Москва	dep/arr at:		00.20	00.20	12.15	12.15
				▼ Wed ▼		▲	▲
Yaroslavl	Ярославль	284	5	04.10	04.10	07.50	07.50
Danilov	Данилов	357	15	05.34	06.34	06.33	07.33
Buy	Буй	448	2	07.01	08.01	05.13	06.13
Shariya	Шарья	701	10	10.22	11.22	02.08	03.08
				▼		▲ Mon ▲	
Kirov	Киров	957	15	13.45	14.45	22.35	23.35
Balyezino	Балезино	1191	15	17.09	18.09	19.35	20.35
Perm	Пермь	1433	15	20.43	22.43	16.06	18.06
				▼ Thur ▼		▲	▲
Sverdlovsk	Свердловск	1813	15	02.25	04.25	10.23	12.23
Tyumen	Тюмень	2141	10	07.00	09.00	05.50	07.50
Ishim	Ишим	2433	8	10.22	12.22	02.31	04.31
Nazevayevskaya	Называевская	2567	15	12.07	15.07	00.42	03.42
				▼		▲ Sun ▲	
Omsk	Омск	2712	12	14.00	17.00	22.33	01.33
Barabinsk	Барабинск	3035	15	17.46	20.46	18.43	21.43
Novosibirsk	Новосибирск	3335	15	21.30	01.30	15.03	19.03
				▼ Fri ▼		▲	▲
Taiga	Тайга	3565	10	01.17	05.17	11.22	15.22
Mariinsk	Мариинск	3717	2	03.37	07.37	09.04	13.04
Bogotol	Боготол	3852	8	05.33	09.33	07.08	11.08
Achinsk	Ачинск	3920	2	06.36	10.36	06.12	10.12
Krasnoyarsk	Красноярск	4099	15	09.33	13.33	02.57	06.57
				▼		▲ Sat ▲	
Kansk	Канск	4344	1	13.34	17.34	23.07	03.07
Illanskaya	Иланская	4375	12	14.11	18.11	22.23	02.23
Taishet	Тайшет	4516	2	16.26	21.26	20.16	01.16
Nizhneudinsk	Нижнеудинск	4680	12	19.17	00.17	17.13	22.13
Zima	Зима	4940	12	23.14	04.14	13.18	18.18
				▼ Sat ▼		▲	▲
Angarsk	Ангарск	5160	2	02.43	07.43	10.03	15.03
Irkutsk	Иркутск	5185	15	03.36	08.36	08.44	13.44
Slyudyanka	Слюдянка	5312	15	06.03	11.03	06.30	11.30
Mysovaya	Мысовая	5477	2	08.54	13.54	03.56	08.56
Ulan Ude	Улан-Удэ	5642	15	11.26	17.26	01.15	07.15
				▼		▲ Fri ▲	
Gusinoye Ozero	Гусиное Озеро	5799	2	14.40	20.40	22.13	04.13
Naushki	Наушки	5897	1hr§	16.32	22.32	17.53	23.53
				▼ MONGOLIA ▼		▲ USSR ▲	
Sukhe Bator	Сухэ Баатор	5925	1hr§		00.00		20.26
				▼ Sun ▼		▲	▲
Darhan	Дархаан	6023	15		02.56		18.45
Ulan Bator	Улан Баатор	6304	30		09.00		13.20

*(MT=Moscow time; LT=local time)
§(minimum stopping time - often considerably longer)

Station name		Km from Moscow	Stop (mins)	Arrival time			
				Eastbound		Westbound	
				MT*	LT*	MT*	LT*
Choyr	Чойр	6551	15		13.49		08.40
Sayn Shand	Сайн Шаанн	6778	15		17.30		04.33
				▼	▼	▲	*Thur* ▲
Dzamyn Ude	Дзамын-Удэ	7013	1hr§		21.50		23.40
				▼ CHINA ▼		▲MONGOLIA ▲	
Erlyan	二在	7023	2hrs		22.58		20.35
				▼ *Mon* ▼		▲	▲
Jining	棄宁南	7356	4		06.26		16.17
Datong	大同	7483	10		08.24		14.15
Zhangjiakou	张家口南	7661	10		10.50		11.37
Kangzhuang	康庄	7771	8		12.26		09.53
Qinglongqiao	青龙桥	7783	10		13.09		09.28
Nankou	南口	7801	14		14.17		08.40
Beijing	北京	7865			15.33		07.40
							▲ *Wed* ▲

*(MT=Moscow time; LT=local time)
§(minimum stopping time - often considerably longer)

Table 4 Moscow-Beijing via Manchuria (Train Nos 19 & 20)

Station name		Km from Moscow	Stop (mins)	Arrival time			
				Eastbound		Westbound	
				MT*	LT*	MT*	LT*
				▼ *Sat** ▼			
Moscow	Москва	dep/arr at:		01.20	01.20	11.35	11.35
Yaroslavl	Ярославль	284	5	05.10	05.10	07.40	07.40
Danilov	Данилов	357	15	06.20	07.20	06.08	07.08
Buy	Буй	448	2	07.44	08.44	05.09	06.09
Shariya	Шарья	701	10	11.03	12.03	01.57	02.57
				▼	▼	▲ *Fri* ▲	
Kirov	Киров	957	15	14.46	15.46	22.31	23.31
Balyezino	Балезино	1191	15	18.19	19.19	19.25	20.25
Perm	Пермь	1433	15	21.53	23.53	15.56	17.56
				▼ *Sun* ▼		▲	▲
Sverdlovsk	Свердловск	1813	20	03.31	05.31	10.09	12.09
Tyumen	Тюмень	2141	10	07.47	09.47	05.53	07.53
Ishim	Ишим	2433	8	11.21	13.21	02.29	04.29
Nazevayevskaya	Называевская	2567	15	13.21	16.21	00.28	03.28
				▼	▼	▲ *Thur* ▲	
Omsk	Омск	2712	15	15.21	18.21	22.18	01.18
Barabinsk	Барабинск	3035	10	19.10	21.10	18.39	22.39
Novosibirsk	Новосибирск	3335	15	23.03	03.03	14.42	18.42
				▼ *Mon* ▼		▲	▲
Taiga	Тайга	3565	10	02.51	06.51	11.02	15.02

*(MT=Moscow time; LT=local time)

Station name		Km from Moscow	Stop (mins)	Arrival time			
				Eastbound		Westbound	
				MT*	LT*	MT*	LT*
Mariinsk	Мариинск	3717	10	05.13	09.13	08.43	12.43
Bogotol	Боготол	3852	12	07.09	11.09	06.47	10.47
Achinsk	Ачинск	3920	2	08.06	12.06	05.51	09.51
Krasnoyarsk	Красноярск	4099	15	11.09	15.09	02.36	06.36
				▼		▲ Wed ▲	
Illanskaya	Иланская	4375	12	15.45	19.45	22.06	02.06
Taishet	Тайшет	4516	2	17.57	22.57	19.59	00.59
Nizhneudinsk	Нижнеудинск	4680	12	20.48	01.48	16.58	21.58
Tulun	Тулун	4794	2	22.39	03.39	15.17	20.57
				▼ Tue ▼		▲	
Zima	Зима	4940	15	00.56	05.56	12.57	17.57
Angarsk	Ангарск	5160	2	04.51	09.51	09.42	14.42
Irkutsk	Иркутск	5185	15	05.44	10.44	08.41	13.41
Slyudyanka	Слюдянка	5312	15	08.30	13.30	06.12	11.12
Mysovaya	Мысовая	5477	2	11.19	16.19	03.38	08.38
Ulan Ude	Улан-Удэ	5642	12	13.52	19.52	01.00	07.00
Petrovskiy Zavod	Петровский З.	5782	12	16.47	22.47	22.43	04.43
				▼ Wed ▼		▲ Tue ▲	
Chita	Чита	6199	15	00.01	06.01	15.35	21.35
Borzya	Борзя	6543	20	07.24	13.24	07.55	13.55
Zabaikalsk	Забаикальск	6661	1hr§	10.15	16.15	02.26	08.26
				▼ CHINA ▼		▲ USSR ▲	
Manzhouli	满洲里	6678	1hr§		19.30		05.29
				▼ Thur ▼		▲	
Hailar	海拉尔	6864	10		00.13		02.51
Mianduhe	免渡河	6979	6		01.58		01.10
Xinganling	兴安岭	7049	10		03.25		00.02
				▼		▲ Mon ▲	
Boketu	博克图	7074	20		04.05		23.10
Angangxi	昂昂溪	7343	12		08.13		18.44
Daqing	大庆	7454	5		09.54		17.05
Harbin	哈尔滨	7613	15		12.09		14.40
Changchun	长春	7855	12		15.40		11.18
Shenyang	沈阳	8160	15		19.45		07.07
Jinzhou	锦州	8402	12		22.47		04.00
Shanhaiguan	山海关	8586	12		-		01.41
				▼ Fri ▼		▲ Sun ▲	
Tianjin	天津	8868	10		04.50		22.09
Beijing	北京	9001	--		06.32		20.32
						▲ Sat** ▲	

*(MT=Moscow time; LT= local time)

****Between late May and late September a second train runs one day later than the above, leaving Beijing on Sunday at 20.32, and leaving Moscow on Sunday at 01.20 (Saturday night). Note that the 24hr clock is used on timetables so the Saturday/Sunday 01.20 departure time from Moscow means that you should be at the station on Friday/Saturday evening.

Table 5 London-Moscow via Ostend (Ost-West Express)

	arr	dep	arr	dep
London (Victoria Stn)		09.00	19.00	
Dover Western Docks	10.28	11.00	16.45	17.25
Ostend	15.45	18.34	12.09	13.45
Brussels Midi	19.43	19.48	10.55	10.59
Brussels Nord	19.55	19.57	10.44	10.48
Liège	20.56	21.00	09.42	09.46
Aachen	21.43	22.01	08.35	09.03
Köln	22.45	22.50	07.43	07.47
Dusseldorf	23.18	23.22	07.13	07.16
Duisburg	23.37	23.39	06.57	06.59
Essen	23.52	00.03	06.43	06.45
Dortmund	00.28	00.31	06.16	06.19
Hannover	02.39	02.49	03.49	04.04
Magdeburg	04.59	05.02	01.34	01.38
Potsdam Stadt	06.16	06.18	00.18	00.20
Berlin (Zoo)	06.41	07.01	23.40	23.54
Berlin (Hbf)	07.23	08.03	22.50	23.18
Frankfurt (Oder)	08.59	09.44	21.10	21.53
Kunowice	09.52	10.02	20.48	20.58
Rzepin	10.15	10.35	20.20	20.35
Poznan	12.40	12.50	18.00	18.15
Warsaw (Central)	16.50	16.57	13.47	13.55
Warsaw (Wschodnia)	17.04	18.38	12.19	13.40
Terespol	21.10	21.28	09.48	09.55
Brest	23.58	02.05	09.20	11.30
Minsk	05.35	05.45	05.41	05.51
Moscow (Byelorusskaya)	14.59			20.11

Table 6 London Moscow via Hook of Holland (Hoek van Holland)

	arr	dep	arr	dep
London (Liverpool St)		09.25	20.00	
Harwich	10.40	11.30	17.45	18.45
Hook of Holland	19.00	19.57	11.12	12.00
Rotterdam West	20.14	20.16	10.52	10.54
Utrecht	20.56	21.04	09.58	10.07
Amersfoort	21.19	21.22	09.31	09.36
Hengelo	22.28	22.31	08.10	08.12
Bad Bentheim	22.50	23.18	07.22	07.49
Osnabruck	23.57	00.01	06.19	06.35
Hannover	01.14	01.36	04.41	04.46
Potsdam Stadt	04.55	04.57	01.20	01.22
Berlin (Zoo)	05.20	05.29	00.44	00.56
Berlin (Hpf)	06.08	08.03	22.50	00.22
Kunowice	09.52	10.02	20.48	20.58
Warsaw (Wschodnia)	17.04	18.38	12.19	13.40
Brest	23.58	02.05	09.20	11.30
Moscow (Byelorusskaya)	14.59			20.11

Table 7: Beijing - Guangzhou

Station name	Km from Beijing	Departure time		
	Train nos:	47	15	16	48
		▼	▼	▲	▲
Beijing	0	19.04	22.30	06.00	10.32
Baoding	152	21.00	----	----	08.40
Shijiazhuang	283	22.45	01.56	02.45	07.02
Anyang	508	01.28	----	----	04.11
Zhengzhou	695	04.00	06.55	21.36	01.41
Xinyang	997	07.56	10.49	17.39	21.44
Wuhan (Hankou)	1209	11.04	----	----	18.31
Wuhan (Wuchang)	1229	11.37	14.11	14.02	17.35
Yueyang	1447	14.48	----	----	14.24
Changsha	1587	17.00	19.13	08.57	12.16
Zhuzhou	1638	17.56	----	----	11.05
Hengyang	1772	20.17	22.06	05.53	08.52
Shaoguan	2093	03.14	04.46	23.14	01.44
Guangzhou	2313	07.30	09.05	19.00	21.05

(Change trains for Hong Kong)
(frequent departures)

TRAILBLAZER feedback The following information on the rail journey from Beijing to Guangzhou (Canton) and on to Hong Kong was supplied by Colin Baker travelling in late 1990.

'There are two trains a day from Beijing to Guangzhou. Both leave in the evening and arrive in Guangzhou in the morning of the second day.

I was travelling soft class which was in four-berth compartments. Our carriage was air-conditioned and attended by an ever-smiling conductor who supplied us each with a China Railways tea mug for our use on the journey and, of course, the usual thermos of hot water. As I was heading for Hong Kong I thought there would be other westerners doing the same trip. However, apart from the three Poles sharing my compartment, the other passengers were all Chinese, some of them from Hong Kong.

The dining car served Cantonese style cuisine and lots of seafood. There was also an ecologically unsound trolley service offering chicken and rice in white polystyrene boxes. The boxes are thrown out onto the track and in some places along the line there are piles of them.

The line is double tracked from Beijing to Guangzhou and as Chinese trains run on the left, views to the left are not obscured by passing trains. Our train was diesel-hauled throughout the route although parts of the line were being prepared for electrification. Steam locos can be seen at several stations along the route, particularly at Xinyang (km980 from Beijing).The scenery along the route is pleasant rather than dramatic - rolling hills and open fields. There's plenty of opportunity to observe rural Chinese life as you pass by.

Wuhan (km1190-1210 from Beijing)

This is one of the largest cities in China, with a population of three million, and lies on both sides of the massive Yangtse River. As we approached the city from the north we passed many small houses built within inches of the busy railway line. People were sitting outside and had their washing spread over the adjacent (hopefully little-used) track which bordered their front doors. The first of Wuhan's stations is Hankou after which the line crosses the River Hanshui, which is wide but not nearly as wide as the Yangtse which you cross a few minutes later. The bridge is over 1km long, also carries a road and is guarded by sentries at both ends. Before 1957 when it was constructed, the crossing would have been made by ferry. Best views are to the left (when heading south). A stop is made at Wuchang station just over the bridge.

Guangzhou to Hong Kong

This journey takes just under 2½ hours with a brief pause at Shenzen on the Chinese side of the border where the Chinese guards leave the train. Customs formalities take place in the terminii at Guangzhou and Kowloon. FEC's and HK$ can be exchanged in Guangzhou station. Note that in this station the entrance to the platform used by international trains is separate from the main entrance. The gates were opened 45mins before the departure and after customs and immigration we were herded into a large waiting-room with a duty-free shop.

Leaving Guangzhou the train travels through the Pearl River delta (crossing the main river at km69) to the border, past rich agricultural land with hills on the horizon. The train is hauled by a Chinese diesel all the way to the Kowloon terminus.

The city of Shenzhen which borders Hong Kong is reached after about 2 hours. Part of the Special Economic Zone, it seems very westernised with large concrete office and apartment blocks, and advertising hoardings. There is a short stop and railway officials check that no one tries to climb aboard as you leave the station. A few minutes later you cross the river that forms the border and continue through the first Hong Kong station, Lo Wu.

The line between Lo Wu and Kowloon is electrified with overhead cables. The signalling, trackside and station signs all resemble those used in Britain. The journey takes about 20mins through the New Territories to the Kowloon terminus. This used to be on the waterfront at Tsim Sha Tsui where the Star Ferries dock but only the old clocktower remains. The new terminus was built in 1975 further up the line at Hung Hom'.

APPENDIX B: INTOURIST OFFICES

The head office of Intourist (the National Tourist Organisation of the USSR) is at: 16 Marx Prospekt, Moscow 103009 (tel 203 6962; fax 200 0221; telex 871 411211A/B/C).

Information concerning visits to the USSR is also available from the following branches of Intourist:

Australia
Underwood House
34-49 Pitt Street
Sydney NSW 2000
(tel 27 76 52)

Austria
Schwedenplatz 3/4
1010 Wein
(tel 63 95 47)

Belgium
Galerie Ravenstein 2
1000 Bruxelles
(tel 02-513 82 34)

Bulgaria
Bulevard al Stambolijski, 24
Sofia
(tel 87 60 12)

Canada
1801 Mcgill College Avenue
Suite 630
Montreal, Quebec
H3A 2N4
(tel 514-849 6394)

Czechoslovakia
Stepanska, 47
Praha 1
(tel 26 71 62)

Denmark
Vester Farimagsgade, 6
1606 Kobenhavn V
(tel 01-11 25 27)

Egypt
9 Kamel Mohammed Street
Flat 26, Zamalek
Cairo
(tel 3402 549)

Finland
Etela-Esplanaadi, 14
00130 Helsinki 13
(tel 63 18 75)

France
7 Boulevard des Capucines
75002 Paris
(tel 47 42 47 40)

Germany
Kurfurstendamm 63
1000 Berlin
(tel 88 00 70)
also at:
6000 Frankfurt am Main 1
Stephanstrasse 1
(tel 069-28 57 76)

Greece
3 Stadiou Street
Sintagma
Athens
(tel 3233776)

Hungary
Felszabadulas ter 1
Budapest
1053
(tel 180 098)

India
Plot 6 & 7, Block 50-E
Nyaya Marg, Chanakyapuri
New Delhi 110021
(tel 67 63 36)

Italy
Piazza Buenos Aires 6-7
00198 Roma
(tel 06-86 38 92)

Japan
Roppongi Heights
1-16, 4-chome Roppongi
Minato-ku, Tokyo 106
(tel 3584 6617)

Mexico
Insurgentes sur 569 p.B.
Mexico DF
(tel 523 71 39)

Netherlands
Honthorstraat 42
1071 Amsterdam Z
(tel 798964)

Norway
Bygo Alle 62
0265 Oslo 2
(tel 44 17 85)

Poland
Ul. Krucza 47
Warszawa
(tel 29 02 02)

Romania
Strada Biserika Amzei 29
71100 Bucuresti
(tel 50 76 08)

Sweden
Sergelgatan 21
11157 Stockholm
(tel 21 59 34)

Switzerland
Usteristrasse
9/Lowenplatz
8001 Zurich
(tel 01-2113355)

UK (London)
Intourist House
219 Marsh Wall
Isle of Dogs
London E14 9FJ
(tel 071-538 5902)

UK (Manchester)
71 Deansgate
Manchester M3 2BW
(tel 061-834 0230)

UK (Glasgow)
8 Belmont Crescent
S. Clyde
Glasgow G12 8EU
(041-339 9706)

USA
630 Fifth Avenue
Suite 868
New York NY 10111
(tel 212-757 3884/5)

Yugoslavia
Beograd 11000
Molerova 1/5
Stn 7
(tel 45 88 43)

APPENDIX C: LIST OF SIBERIAN FAUNA

There are extensive displays of local animals in the natural history museums of Novosibirsk, Irkutsk and Khabarovsk but the labelling is in Russian and Latin. The following translation is given for non-Russian speaking readers whose Latin is rusty or non-existant.

In the list below the letters given beside the animal's English name indicate its natural habitat. NS = Northern Siberia/Arctic Circle; SP = Siberian Plain; AS = Altai-Sayan Plateau/Mongolia; BI = Lake Baikal/Transbaikal region; FE = Far Eastern Territories. Where a Latin name is similar to the English (e.g. Vipera = Viper) these names have been omitted.

accipiter gentilis	goshawk (AS/SP/NS/BI/FE)
aegoceras montanus	mountain ram (AS)
aegoceras sibiricus	siberian goat (BI)
aegolius funereus	boreal/Tengmalm's owl (BI/FE)
aegypius monachus	black vulture (AS)
aethia cristatella	crested auklet (NS/FE)
alces alces	elk/moose (SP/BI/FE)
allactaga jaculus	five-toed jerboa (SP/BI)
alopex lagopus	arctic fox (NS)
anas acuta	pintail (BI)
anas clypeata	shoveler (SP/BI/FE)
anas crecca	teal (BI/SP/FE)
anas falcata	falcated teal (SP/BI/FE)
anas formosa	baikal teal (BI)
anas platyrhynchos	mallard (AS/SP/BI/FE)
anas poecilorhyncha	spotbill duck (AS/BI)
anser anser	greylag goose (SP/BI)
anser erythropus	white-fronted goose (AS/SP/BI/FE)
antelope gutturosa/crispa	antelope (FE)
arctomis bobac	marmot (AS/SP)
ardea cinerea	grey heron (AS/SP/BI)
aquila clanga	greater spotted eagle (SP)
botaurus stellaris	bittern (SP/BI/FE)
bubo bubo	eagle owl (BI/FE)
buteo lagopus	rough legged buzzard (NS/SP/FE)
butorides striatus	striated/green heron (FE)
canis alpinus	mountain wolf (AS/FE)
canis corsac	korsac/steppe fox (BI/FE)
canis lagopus	arctic fox (NS)
canis lupus	wolf (SP/BI/FE)
canis procyonoides	Amur raccoon (FE)
capra sibirica	Siberian mountain goat/ibex (AS/BI)
capreolus capreolus	roe deer (SP/BI/FE)
castor fiber	beaver (SP/BI/FE)
certhia familiaris	common treecreeper (AS/BI/FE)
cervus alces	elk (AS/BI/FE)
cervus capreolus	roe-buck (BI/FE)
cervus elephas	maral deer (AS/BI/FE)

cervus nippon	sika/Japanese deer (FE)
cervus tarandus	reindeer (NS/FE)
circus aeruginosus	marsh harrier (SP/BI)
citellus undulatus	arctic ground squirrel/ Siberian souslik (NS/BI/FE)
cricetus cricetus	common hamster (AS/SP/BI/FE)
cygnus cygnus	whooper swan (SP/BI)
dicrostonyx torquatus	arctic lemming (NS)
dryocopus martius	black woodpecker (SP/BI/FE)
enhyra lutris	Kamchatka beaver (FE)
equus hemionus	kulan/Asian wild ass (FE)
eumentopias Stelleri	sea-lion (NS/FE)
eutamias sibiricus	Siberian chipmunk (AS/SP/BI/FE)
ealco columbarius	merlin (NS/SP/BI/FE)
falco peregrinus	peregrine (NS/SP/BI/FE)
falco tinnunculus	kestrel (SP)
falco vesperinus	hawk (SP)
felis irbis	irbis/panther (FE)
felis lynx	lynx (SP/BI/FE)
felis manul	wild cat (AS/BI/FE)
felis tigris altaica	Amur tiger (FE)
foetorius altaicus	ermine (SP/BI)
foetorius altaicus sibiricus	polecat (SP/BI)
foetorius vulgaris	weasel (SP/BI)
fulica atra	coot (SP/BI/FE)
gallinago gallinago	common snipe (SP/BI/FE)
gavia arctica	black-throated diver/loon (BI)
gavia stellata	red-throated diver/loon (SP/BI)
gazella subgutturosa	goitered gazelle (AS)
grus cinerea	grey crane (SP)
grus grus	common crane (SP/BI/FE)
grus leucogeranus	Siberian white crane (NS/SP/FE)
gulo gulo	wolverine/glutton (SP/BI/FE)
gypaetus barbatus L.	lammergeyer (AS)
haematopus ostralegus	oystercatcher (SP/BI/FE)
lagomis alpinus	rat hare (FE)
lagopus lagopus	willow grouse/ptarmigan (NS/SP/FE)
larus argentatus	herring gull (BI/FE)
larus canus	common gull (BI/FE)
larus ridibundus	black-headed gull (BI/FE)
lemmus obensis	Siberian lemming (NS/SP)
lepus timidus	arctic hare (NS/BI/FE)
lepus variabilis	polar hare (NS)
lutra vulgaris	otter (BI/FE)
marmota camtschatica	Kamchatka marmot (FE)
marmota sibirica	Siberian marmot (AS/SP/BI)
martes zibellina	sable (SP/BI/FE)
melanitta deglandi	American black scoter (BI)
melanocorypha mongolica	Mongolian lark (AS)
meles meles	Eurasian badger (AS/BI/FE)
microtus hyperboreus	sub-arctic vole (NS/SP/FE)
moschus moschiferus	musk deer (AS/BI/FE)
mustela erminea	ermine (NS/AS/SP/BI/FE)

mustela eversmanni	steppe polecat (AS/SP/BI/FE)
mustela nivalis	common weasel (NS/SP/BI/FE)
mustela sibirica	kolonok (FE)
myodes torquatus/obensis	Ob lemming (NS)
nucifraga caryocatactes	nutcracker (AS/SP/BI/FE)
nyctea scandiaca	snowy owl (NS)
ochotona alpina	Altai pika (AS)
oenanthe isabellina	Isabelline wheatear (AS/SP/BI)_
omul baikalensis	omul (BI)
otaria ursina	sea bear (NS/FE)
otis tarda	bustard (SP/BI)
ovis ammon	argalis (sheep) (AS)
ovis Argali	arkhar (AS)
ovis nivicola	Siberian bighorn/snow sheep (FE)
panthera pardus orientalis	Amur leopard (FE)
panthera tigris altaica	Siberian/Amur tiger (FE)
panthera uncia	snow leopard (AS)
perdix perdix	grey partridge (AS/SP/BI/FE)
perisoreus infaustus	Siberian jay (BI/FE)
phalacrocorax carbo	great cormorant (BI/FE)
phoca barbata groenlandica	seal (NS/FE)
phoca baicalensis	Baikal seal (BI)
phocaena orca	dolphin (NS/FE)
picoides tridactylus	three-toed woodpecker (SP/BI/FE)
plectophenax nivalis	snow bunting (NS)
podiceps auritus	Slavonian/horned grebe (AS/BI)
podiceps cristatus	great crested grebe (AS/SP/BI)
procapra gutturosa	Mongolian gazelle (FE)
pteromys volans	Siberian flying squirrel (SP/BI/FE)
rangifer tarandus	reindeer/caribou (NS/BI/FE)
ranodon sibiricus	five-toed triton (AS/SP)
rufibrenta ruficollis	red-breasted goose (NS)
salpingotus crassicauda	pygmy jerboa (SP/AS)
sciurus vulgaris	red squirrel (SP/BI/AS/FE)
spermophilus eversmanni	Siberian marmot (BI)
spermophilus undulatus	arctic ground squirrel (FE)
sterna hirundo	common tern (BI/FE)
strix nebulosa	great grey owl (SP/BI/FE)
surnia ulula	hawk owl (SP/BI/FE)
sus scrofa	wild boar (AS/BI/FE)
tadorna ferruginea	ruddy shelduck (SP/BI/FE)
tamias striatus	striped squirrel (BI)
tetrao urogallus	capercaillie (SP/BI/FE)
tetrao parvirostris	black-billed capercaillie (BI/FE)
tetraogallus himalayanensis	Himalayan snowcock (AS)
tetraogallus altaicus	Altai snowcock (AS)
tetrastes bonasia	hazel grouse (SP/BI/FE)
turdus sibiricus	Siberian thrush (SP/BI/FE)
uria aalge	guillemot (NS/FE)
ursus arctus	bear (SP/FE)
ursus maritimus	polar bear (NS)
ursus tibetanus	Tibet bear (FE)
vulpes vulpes	red fox (AS/SP/BI/FE)

APPENDIX D: RUSSIAN LANGUAGE

English-speaking travellers are unforgivably lazy when it comes to learning other people's languages. As with virtually every other country in the world, it is possible to 'get by' in the USSR without being able to speak a word of Russian. Intourist guides and some hotel staff speak English but most of the Russians you meet on the train will be eager to communicate with you and unable to speak English. A certain amount can be achieved with sign language but your conversations will (obviously) be rather more satisfying if you know more than a few words of Russian. It is therefore well worth doing a short language course before you go. You might consider evening classes or teaching yourself with books and cassettes from your local library. If you don't have time for a course it is vital to spend the few hours it takes to master the Cyrillic alphabet, otherwise you will have trouble deciphering the names of streets, metro stations and, most important, the names of stations along the Trans-Siberian.

CYRILLIC ALPHABET AND PRONUNCIATION GUIDE

The Cyrillic alphabet is derived from the Greek. It was introduced in Russia in the tenth century, through a translation of the Bible made by two Greek bishops, Cyril (who gave his name to the new alphabet) and Methodius.

Cyrillic letters		Roman letter	Pronunciation*	Cyrillic letters		Roman letter	Pronunciation*
А	а	a	(f<u>a</u>r)	П	п	p	(<u>P</u>eter)
Б	б	b	(<u>b</u>et)	Р	р	r	(<u>R</u>ussia)
В	в	v	(<u>v</u>odka)	С	с	s	(<u>S</u>iberia)
Г	г	g	(<u>g</u>et)	Т	т	t	(<u>t</u>rain)
Д	д	d	(<u>d</u>og)	У	у	u/oo	(r<u>u</u>le)
Е	е	e	(y<u>e</u>t)	Ф	ф	f/ph	(<u>f</u>rost)
Ё	ё	yo	(<u>yo</u>ghurt)	Х	х	kh	(lo<u>ch</u>)
Ж	ж	zh	(trea<u>s</u>ure)	Ц	ц	ts	(lo<u>ts</u>)
З	з	z	(<u>z</u>ebra)	Ч	ч	ch	(<u>ch</u>ill)
И	и	ee	(s<u>ee</u>k)	Ш	ш	sh	(fi<u>sh</u>)
Й	й	y	(read<u>y</u>)	Щ	щ	shch	(fre<u>sh ch</u>icken)
К	к	k	(<u>K</u>iev)	Ы	ы	i	(d<u>i</u>d)
Л	л	l	(<u>L</u>enin)	Э	э	e/ih	(t<u>e</u>nt)
М	м	m	(<u>M</u>oscow)	Ю	ю	yu	(<u>u</u>nion)
Н	н	n	(<u>n</u>ever)	Я	я	ya	(<u>ya</u>k)
О	о	o	(<u>o</u>ver)	Ь	ь		softens preceding letter

* pronunciation shown by underlined letter/s

USEFUL WORDS AND PHRASES

Run the hyphenated syllables together as you speak, roll your 'R's and you should have no difficulty in being understood. If you find the following phrases too tongue-twisting point to the appropriate words in the Cyrillic text below.

General

Hello	*Zdrah-stvoo-iteh*
Good morning	*Dob-royeh-ootro*
Good afternoon/evening	*Dobree den/vecher*
Please	*Po-zhalsta*
Do you speak English?	*Gavar-iteh lee vy pa anglee-skee?*
no/yes	*nyet/da*
thank you	*spasee-ba*
excuse me (sorry)	*izveen-iteh*
good/bad	*haroshaw/plahoy*
cheap/expensive	*deshoveey/daragoy*
Wait a minute!	*Adnoo meenoo-too*
Please call a doctor	*Vi'zaveete, po-zhalsta, vracha*
Goodbye	*Das-vedahneya*

Questions and answers

What's your name?	*Kak vahs zavoot?*
My name is ...	*Menyah zavoot*
I'm from Britain/USA	*Yah preeyeh-khal eez Anglee-ee/S-Sh-Ah*
Canada/Australia	*Kanadah/Avstralee*
New Zealand/Japan	*Novee Zeelandee/Yaponee*
Sweden/Finland	*Shvetsee/Finlandee*
Norway/Denmark	*Norveggee/Danee*
Germany/Austria	*Germanee/Avstree*
France/Netherlands	*Frantsee/Gollandee*
Where are you going?	*Kudah vhee idyotyeh*
I'm going to ...	*Yah idoo ...*
Are you married?	*Vee zhyehnaht/zamoozhyem?**
Have you any children?	*Yest ly oo vas dety?*
boy/girl	*mahl-cheek/de-vooshka*
How old are you?	*Skolka vahm l'et*
What do you do?	*Shto vhee delayetyeh*
student/teacher	*stoo-dent/oochee-tel (-neetsa)**
doctor/nurse	*vrach/myeh-sestra*
actor/artist	*aktor/khoo-dozh-neek*
engineer/lawyer	*een-zheneer/advokaht*
office worker	*sloo-zhash-chey*
Where do you live?	*G'dyeh vhee zhuvyotyeh*
I live in ...	*Yah zhuvoo ve ...*

*(feminine form)

Directions

Where is ...?	*G'dyeh ...?*
hotel	*gastee-neetsoo*
bus-stop	*astan-ofka afto-boosa*
metro/taxi	*metro/taksee*
restaurant/cafe	*restarahn/kafay*
bakery/grocer's	*boolach-naya/gastra-nohm*
box office (theatre)	*teatrahl-naya kassa*
lavatory	*too-alet*
open/closed	*at-krita/za-krita*
left/right	*na-prahva/na-leva*

Numerals/time

1 *adeen*; 2 *dvah*; 3 *tree*; 4 *chetir*; 5 *p'aht*; 6 *shest*; 7 *s'em*; 8 *vosem*; 9 *d'evat*; 10 *d'e'sat*; 11 *adeen-natsat*; 12 *dve-natsat*; 13 *tree-natsat*; 14 *chetir-natsat*; 15 *pyat-natsat*; 16 *shes-natsat*; 17 *sem-natsat*; 18 *va'sem-natsat*; 19 *d'evat-natsat*; 20 *dvatsat*; 30 *tree-tsat*; 40 *so'rok*; 50 *p'ad-desaht*; 60 *shez-desaht*; 70 *sem-desaht*; 80 *vosem-desaht*; 90 *d'even-osta*; 100 *sto*; 200 *dve-stee*; 300 *tree-sta*; 400 *chetir-esta*; 500 *p'at-sot*; 600 *shes-sot*; 700 *sem-sot*; 800 *vosem-sot*; 900 *devet-sot*; 1000 *tees-acha*

How much/many?	*Skolka?*
kopeck/kopecks	*kapeyka/kapeyek/kapeeyek**
rouble/roubles	*rooble/rooblah/roobley**
Please write down the price	*Nap'eesheet'eh, pazhalsta, tse-noo*
What time is it?	*Kato'riy chahs?*
hours/minutes	*chasof/meenoot*
today	*sevodna*
yesterday/tomorrow	*fcherah/zahftra*

*1st word is for 1 unit, 2nd word for 2-4 units, 3rd word for 5 or more

Food and drink

menu	*menoo*
mineral water	*meenerahl-noi vady*
fruit juice	*sokee*
vodka/whisky	*vodka/veeskee*
beer	*peeva*
wine/cognac	*veenah/kanya-koo*
champagne	*sham-pahn-skoya*
Cheers!	*Zah vasheh zdaro-vyeh!*
caviare	*eek-ry*
salmon	*lasa-seeny*
sturgeon	*aset-reeny*
chicken	*tsy-plonka*
duck	*oot-koo*
steak/roast beef	*beef-shteks/rost-beef*

pork	*svee-nooyoo*
veal	*atbeef-nooyoo telyah-choo*
ham	*vechina*
sausage	*kalba-soo*
potatoes	*kar-toshka*
bread	*khlee-ep*
butter	*mah-sla*
cheese	*sir*
eggs/omelet	*yait-sa*
omelet	*amlet*
salt/pepper	*sol/perets*
tea	*chai*
coffee	*koh-fee*
milk	*mala-ko*
sugar	*sahk-har*
bill	*shchot*

APPENDIX E: BIBLIOGRAPHY

Baedeker, Karl *Russia with Teheran, Port Arthur and Peking* (Leipzig 1914)
Barzini, Luigi *Peking to Paris. A Journey across Two Continents* (London 1907)
Byron, Robert *First Russia Then Tibet* (London 1933)
Collins, Perry McDonough *A Voyage down the Amoor* (New York 1860)
De Windt, Harry *Siberia as it is* (London 1892)
Des Cars J. and Caracalla, J.P. *Le Transsiberien* (1986)
Dmitriev-Mamonov, A.I. and Zdziarski, A.F. *Guide to the Great Siberian Railway 1900* (St Petersburg 1900)
Fleming, H.M. and Price J.H. *Russian Steam Locomotives* (London 1960)
Gowing, L.F. *Five Thousand Miles in a Sledge* (London 1889)
Hill, S.S. *Travels in Siberia* (London 1854)
Hollingsworth, J.B. *The Atlas of Train Travel* (London 1980)
Imperial Japanese Government Railways *An Official Guide to Eastern Asia Vol 1: Manchuria & Chosen* (Tokyo 1913)
Jefferson, R.L. *Awheel to Moscow and Back* (London 1895)
Jefferson, R.L. *Roughing it in Siberia* (London 1897)
Jefferson, R.L. *A New Ride to Khiva* (London 1899)
Johnson, Henry *The Life of Kate Marsden* (London 1895)
Kennan, George *Siberia and the Exile System* (London 1891)
Lansdell, Henry *Through Siberia* (London 1883)
Levin, M.G. and Potapov, L.P. *The Peoples of Siberia* (Chicago 1964)
Manley, Deborah *The Trans-Siberian Railway* (London 1988)
Marsden, Kate *On Sledge and Horseback to Outcast Siberian Lepers* (London 1895)
Meakin, Annette *A Ribbon of Iron* (London 1901)
Massie, R.K. *Nicholas and Alexandra* (London 1967)
Murray *Handbook for Russia, Poland and Finland* (London 1865)
Newby, Eric *The Big Red Train Ride* (London 1978)
Pifferi, Enzo *Le Transsiberien*
Poulsen, J. and Kuranow, W. *Die Transsibirische Eisenbahn* (Malmo 1986)
St George, George *Siberia: the New Frontier* (London 1969)
Shoemaker, Michael Myres *The Great Siberian Railway from St Petersburg to Pekin* (London 1903)
Theroux, Paul *The Great Railway Bazaar* (London 1975)
Tupper, Harmon *To the Great Ocean. Siberia and the Trans-Siberian Railway* (London 1965)
Westwood, J.M. *Soviet Railways Today* (London 1963)

INDEX